The OTHER Blue Sky

ABOUT THE AUTHOR

Shari J. Ryan is an International Bestselling Author of more than twenty novels. Shari was once told she tends to exaggerate often and sometimes talks too much, which would make a great foundation for fictional books. Six years after beginning her publishing journey, Shari's main objective is to make her readers feel the realism within her books through descriptive detail, lively characters, and raw emotions.

While Shari devotes much of her time to writing, she always puts her family first. Shari is a devoted wife to a wonderful and supportive man, and a mother to two little boys who remind her daily why she was put on this earth.

For weekly love notes, subscribe to her newsletter:
http://geni.us/ShariJRyanNewsletter

f facebook.com/authorsharijryan

𝕏 twitter.com/sharijryan

◉ instagram.com/sharijryan_author

BB bookbub.com/authors/6090

a amazon.com/author/shari-j.-ryan

g goodreads.com/shari_j_ryan

ALSO BY SHARI J. RYAN

Literary Fiction:

Last Words

The Other Blue Sky

Romantic Comedy:

Manservant

Man Flu

Man Handler

Man Buns

Spiked Lemonade

Queen of the Throne

Contemporary Romance:

A Heart of Time

A Missing Heart

A Change of Heart

Raine's Haven

Ravel

Romantic Suspense:

Darkest Perception

Red Nights

TAG

You're It

No Way Out

The Schasm Series

Schasm

Fissure Free

When Fully Fused

To those who have broken hearts and are afraid of never healing...

Everything will be okay again someday.

ACKNOWLEDGMENTS

I have my tribe—they stick with me through thick and thin, and I never wake up, wondering if one of them will walk away. When I meet friends who will offer help without being asked, or still listen when I'm silent, it's easy to feel the love. It's easy to know who will be there in the end.

Julie and Linda, Linda and Julie — you both are the reason I push myself as hard as I do. You motivate me, you share my passion, pain, happiness, and I hope I do the same for you. When a team becomes a partnership, it's an incredible thing. I love you both for everything we have accomplished together. Thank you for being by my side.

My beta ladies—This time, my request for beta readers was hidden on Facebook, so a few of my constants were left out of the loop, so please know, I love you all, and no matter what book I'm working on, I never question whether you will be there for me. Erin, Heather, Lin, and Julie — Thank you for loving me enough to be honest and share your true feedback to help make my story greater. I'm lucky to have you all! Kelly and Samantha—thank you for offering to jump in and help when I needed it. Someday, I will get to squeeze you in real life!

My family - Dad, Mom, Mark, Ev - Your support, as always, is what gets me through some days. Feeling your pride makes me feel accomplished, and I'm grateful. Love you all!

Lori—still my #1 even though you're being crawled all over by two tiny loves. I know when you have a free moment (which may be in five years haha), you'll be reading chapter by chapter again. Love you, sis.

My friends—I believe in quality over quantity, so I'm confident, you know who you are. I know I'm quiet about my writing life, and somehow, you still understand that part of my life even when I tend to fall off the face of the earth for a couple months at a time. Being my mom besties has gotten me through these grueling years of raising two little boys, and I'm forever grateful for our friendship.

Josh—I'm going to keep this serious this time since I usually poke fun at you … I know I put you through a lot of ups and downs when I'm emotionally drowning myself in words, and you still sit there with a smile and open arms. You are my world, my forever, and my lifelong happy story. I love you!

Boys—Bryce and Brayden - My heart warms whenever we go to the bookstore together, and I know you get the same feeling inside that I do. You both love to read, and even want to read my books, which is the most amazing feeling in the world. While, I can't let you do that just yet, someday, I'll share these words with you, and I hope you'll be proud of me. You two are my heart and soul, and I don't know what I would do without you. I love you more than words could ever describe. Never forget that.

DISCLAIMER

If you have not read *Last Words*, *The Other Blue Sky* can be read first, and on its own.

At the beginning of *Last Words*, I mentioned this note, and in case you are new to my books, I would like you to know a little bit about my background and where these two particular stories came from:

The Other Blue Sky and *Last Words* are both fictitious novels made up of many non-fictitious details of the Holocaust, but based on true facts.

I am a descendant of two Holocaust survivors, from whom I have had the privilege of learning facts of my history and heritage. In addition, hours of research have been conducted to keep historical facts accurately laced in with this story that brings forbidden love to another level.

I have wanted to write these books for many years, but it has been challenging to relive a life experience my grandmother and great-grandmother survived, while knowing the rest of my family did not make it.

DISCLAIMER

With the taboo nature of this story, please know I do not condone or support the typical enemy's behavior portrayed in my story. On the contrary, I have lived in fear of hatred, hiding my religion and beliefs for many years. Therefore, I hope this story is as enlightening to you as it has been for me.

PREFACE

I didn't know one could be missing when a visible reflection states otherwise. I also didn't realize how many of us, former prisoners, are still considered missing people, especially since we were once missing children. There's a bond between the strangers we are, and though many of us haven't met, we think of ourselves as a family, in a sense because our stories are the same.

There is a book cover with a simple image, one that could tell any story. There's a spine—strong and built to hold everything inside, and though there isn't much of a description written on the back, inside ... on the yellowed pages ... is where our stories line up perfectly. For the thousands of us who have not been accounted for, there are no words to trail in our footsteps.

During the time of the Holocaust, people were taken, murdered, and tortured. All different types of people—mothers, fathers, sisters, and brothers. Books were burned, money stolen, and heirlooms were left to rot. Those who survived curated the information we have in our history books, passing forward the stories we read about and could never imagine, but many stories remain untold, hidden within memories too painful to revisit.

My mother lived through this horrible time, and she is one of the survivors who has chosen to remain silent about her time in the prisoner camp. I didn't earn a right to comment on her choice because unlike me, she has memories that linger inside her mind, memories that likely haunt her every night.

As for me, I have spent my entire life trying to figure out who I really am. I've been a humble person, appreciative and grateful for the life I have, but there is one thing I need—the truth. I desperately need to know who I am and where I came from, but it must come from the person who is responsible for making me one of the *lucky* missing prisoners of the Holocaust.

CURRENT DAY

I'VE DECIDED without knowing the effects it may cause. However, life moves too quickly, and the idea of forever is variable. Nobody really knows how much time they have. I should certainly know the importance of living in the moment. I understand what a moment's decision can influence. All these years, I've been sure about keeping certain thoughts to myself, but I can't hold them inside any longer.

I pull out the heavy, black iron chair from the garden table and slowly ease down into the seat, resting in front of a steaming cup of tea and two sets of eyes, both full of wonderment.

"Annie, you're scaring me," Mom says, her voice frail and meek, as it has been since she had the stroke last year. "You look ill or upset. What's bothering you, dear?"

I inhale slowly, taking in the late spring air infused with a mixture of lilacs and hydrangea. The mist from last night's rain still lingers, leaving the morning damp but warm enough for comfort. The trees around us fold us in their embrace, offering us a feeling of protection from the outside world. It's lovely here, and

I'm often jealous of the assisted living community that Mom finally agreed to move into. It would be a little bit like heaven, if I were to imagine such a place.

I've lost my train of thought as I subconsciously avoid the task at hand. I'm about to place a heavy burden onto their shoulders. As my attention snaps back to the anxious looks on Mom and Charlie's faces, a knot of uncertainty tightens in my stomach, but I need to get it out. They need to hear this. I clear my throat and take a quick sip of the steaming tea, hoping the sweet, chamomile-infused water will alleviate some of the tension in my chest. "I don't want scare you, either of you. I've—" the words aren't forming as I had hoped they might. "I have something I want to give to you."

Mom clutches her hand over her heart with what appears to be relief. Maybe she thought I would say I'm sick, or something else along that line, though I'm not sure this gift will be any easier for her to receive.

I place a brown, paper-wrapped package down onto the woven metal slats, settling it gently between the plate of pastries, the vase of fresh lilacs and their two teacups. Mom gazes at it for a moment as if she's trying to see what's inside without removing the paper wrapping. She runs her puckered fingertips across the top, and the sound of her soft skin gliding against the coarse paper causes my shoulders to tighten. "What is this, Annie?" Mom asks. Her question is filled with curiosity, but no concern. I hope she feels the same way once she looks inside.

I stare into Mom's eyes, noticing the faded grayish-blue hues filling her once vibrant, sapphire-coated irises. Old age has taken its toll on her body throughout the last year, and the evidence is overwhelmingly obvious.

"Annie, may I have a word with you for a moment?" Charlie interrupts. He lifts his forefinger from the table top, and the slight gesture from his hand matches the rise in his left brow. I've learned that this particular look of his is full of contemplation and worry. He protects Mom from the air she breathes, and I've found his love for her to be quite endearing, especially considering how late in life they found one another.

A small smile flutters through my lips as I attempt to appear happy and unafraid of what thoughts he has, but speaking to Charlie, as he wishes, is the very least I can do for him after everything he has done for me.

"Of course." I lift my purse from the stone slabs beneath the table and place it down on the chair in my place. "We'll just be a moment, Mom."

"Take your time," she sings, waving us off as if we were pesky bugs.

Charlie grumbles a bit as he stands from his chair, so I offer a hand, which he denies as usual. "Don't treat me like I'm an old man, young lady," he always says. His replay of words eases my tension and allows a soft laugh to break up the clusters of fog in my head.

Charlie places his hand on my back and guides me down the dirt path toward their condominium. No more than a hundred feet from where Mom is seated, we stop in front of a group of trees and take a seat on a stone bench left behind as a tribute to the owner of this community.

I feel restless, waiting to hear what Charlie would like to say, and I find myself brushing away a small pile of sandy dirt from the space between us.

"Annie, I only have one question to ask you before your mother opens that package."

"Of course. What's the question?" I ask, sounding short of breath, which I am.

He places his hand down on top of mine before speaking. "Are you sure you want to do this?"

"Do what?" I ask, wondering what he knows, or how he knows the solemnity of what it is I have to share.

Charlie turns and leans in, staring at me with his freckled brown and green eyes. "Are you sure you want to reopen the past?"

"How—"

"I know the look on your face. I've seen the way you've studied me. You, Annie, are a wonderful woman who has gifted your mother exactly what she tried to gift you."

I'm not sure if Charlie knows precisely what I am giving Mom, but it seems as though he has more insight than I might have assumed. "With your blessing, Charlie, I'm sure I want to say what's in my heart," I tell him.

Charlie's lips tighten and curve into a slight bend. "Very well, sweet girl. My only request is that you unravel your story slowly. She's weak, but I agree, she should know. Secrets don't truly help anyone, do they?"

I lose my words as he throws an unexpected curveball. *Secrets.* My life has been built upon secrets. "No, secrets don't help at all. Thank you for understanding," I tell him in a mere whisper, a tightening in my throat leaving me momentarily unable to speak. When a breeze settles over us, I relax enough to say one last thing to Charlie. "Thank you ... for more than I will ever have words for."

Without thought or a need for further explanation, Charlie places his hand on my cheek and smiles, grimly. A tear percolates in the corner of my eye, then slowly spills down the side of my cheek, leaving a cool chill in its trail. *It's been such a long time with these secrets.* "Sweet girl, you don't have to thank me for doing what I wanted to do. It was the best decision I have made throughout my entire life." He knows. There isn't a doubt in my mind about what he knows.

In silence, we stand from the stone bench and make our way back to Mom. She's gazing off into the distance where the trees are grouped together. With the leaves starting to fall, the woods we couldn't see through just a month ago are now showing their cavernous depth. I wonder what she's thinking. I always wonder what she's thinking when I notice that look in her eyes. It's as if she's not present in her body, but lives in another world that exists only in her mind.

There is another world …

We take our seats at the table, and I move my purse back down by my feet. "I may be old, but I'm not stupid," Mom says.

"What do you mean?" I ask, placing my elbows down as I lean toward her.

"I already know what's in the package, Annie. When you've lived as long as I have, there is little surprise left in the world."

Charlie's recent reappearance in her life surprised her. I know that much.

"Oh really?" I ask. "Well, then, I suppose you don't need to open it."

Her focus switches to my face, and she stares intently into my eyes. The grounds here are so peaceful and quiet that I can hear my breaths, even in the open space. I also hear the orchestra of crickets and birds emanating from within the barricading woods.

Mom finally lifts the package and plucks the adhesive tape from the paper's edges, freeing what's inside.

"Just as I thought," she says without surprise.

"You knew?"

"That you had a journal? Yes, of course, I watched you write in it many nights when you were a child. I watched you write in it until you were eighteen and moved out. I assumed you kept up with it, but as journals should be private, I never asked what was inside."

"I did keep it private," I assure her.

She lifts the lavender, velvet-covered notebook and holds it against her chest. "Then why are you handing it to me as a gift right now? These are your personal thoughts, Annie. Plus, I'm not dying right now, if that is what's going through your head."

My chest tightens at the mention of Mom dying, especially after the strokes she suffered. "This isn't about you dying, Mom. This is about freeing something from my soul—my heart."

"Annie, I'm not sure I want to know the secrets of your adolescence. I do feel that a healthy dose of mystery in your child is necessary for the longevity of a parent's heart. You were such a good girl. I didn't, and still don't, feel the need to consider the thoughts that are contained within this binding."

"My birth name is not Annie, Mom," I say, sharply.

Charlie takes Mom's hand and compresses it between his. "Annie—"

"You don't have to explain anything."

"I didn't want you to experience the pain of knowing what that would bring," she says. "How long have you known?"

A tight-lipped smile presses into my cheeks with a sense of guilt—the guilt I knew was coming. "Most of my life—from the time I was old enough to understand, I suppose."

"But—" Mom tries to speak, though what is there to say?

"It's all inside—everything. I need you to know," I tell her. "I don't want there to be any more secrets. I can't live with them anymore."

"I am so sorry, Annie," she says with disdain. I knew this was going to be painful for her, which is why I have put it off for so long, but I can't wait any longer.

"Mom, you have nothing to be sorry about. That's the reason I want you to read what's inside the book."

Mom places the journal back down on top of the brown paper. "I want to hear it all—I'm sure Charlie does too—but we need to hear it through your voice."

"My search for answers started on my twelfth birthday," I told Mom.

"What? What happened that particular day?" she asks.

It was the beginning of a new world filled with questions and no answers.

2

IT WAS MY TWELFTH BIRTHDAY. Each birthday prior to that day, I would receive a teddy bear or charm bracelet, but I told Mom I didn't need anything extraordinary since I was becoming older. I knew money was a burdening factor in our lives since we didn't have much of it. The last thing I wanted to do was ask for something I didn't need. Still, Mom wouldn't let a birthday pass without some type of gift.

To my surprise, I received a beautiful, purple velvet book, filled with blank pages just waiting for me to write down my thoughts in. I was even more pleased with the texture of the cover than the thought-provoking pages inside. "I'm not sure what to write in here," I told Mom. "The pages are all so clean and crisp. It would be a shame to ruin them with ink. Don't you think?" For some reason, I couldn't fathom tarnishing the insides of the book, although at that time, there weren't words in my head that felt adequate to leave a mark anyway.

"Annie," Mom said sweetly. Her smile lit up the room, and she took the book from my hands, opening it against the crinkling scream from the inner binding. The pages fanned from one side to the other. "It is healthy to write down the way we feel because it cures us of our fears, aches, and pains."

I didn't understand what she meant because I hadn't experienced those types of emotions yet. "I don't have those kinds of feelings, though, so how can I write about them?"

She closed the book and handed it back to me before continuing with her reason. "It doesn't have to be today, Annie. It can be whenever you feel the need to write down how you feel." I remember her eyes lit up like the sky as she stared up toward our discolored ceiling like it was a beautiful piece of art instead of a hideous slab of plaster. "Journals are like treasure chests ... places that can keep all our feelings secure and safe from everyone else. I strongly believe every girl should have one."

"What about me, Mom?" Clara piped in, as she always had when the topic was about me rather than her.

"Next year, when you turn twelve, I will buy you a journal to write in, as well." She cupped her long, narrow fingers around Clara's chin and pinched gently. "It is time for bed, girls. Go get washed up, and I'll be there to tuck you in shortly."

Clara, being dramatic, scuffled her feet against the wooden floor and ran to the bathroom. It was our nightly routine. She would slam the flimsy wooden door in my face and laugh because she got there first, and I would have to wait. It bothered me for a while, but eventually, I preferred to take those few extra moments and sit by our bedroom window, staring out at the millions of glittering lights throughout the New York City skyline. I tried to count the lights, but my eyes would eventually tire, and the glowing flickers would blur into one. By that time, the bathroom would be free, and Clara would be on to her next nightly routine of singing at the top of her lungs while changing into her nightgown.

I placed my new journal down on top of my bureau and claimed my time slot in the bathroom. I was quick as usual, knowing the one small bathroom we had was shared by all four of us, and it seemed someone was always waiting their turn. Clara was the only one who didn't seem to notice, but she was a bit younger, so I figured she would grow out of her ignorance eventually.

Meanwhile, I was so busy thinking of Clara's rude behavior that I didn't consider a consequence of quietly sneaking back to the kitchen to thank Mom for making Weinersnitchel—my favorite meal—as well as for the cake and the gift. In hindsight, I should have listened when she said she would be in shortly to say goodnight.

The moment I rounded the corner toward the kitchen, I stopped short when I heard Mom and Dad having a quiet argument on the other side of the wall. I shouldn't have been listening, but I heard my name mentioned, and curiosity got the best of me. I remained hidden behind the corner and pressed my ear up against the wall to listen.

Mom continued speaking in a harsh voice to Dad, "What are we going to do, Maxwell? They have no records of Annie, and they're going to find out sooner or later that she doesn't belong to us. She'll be taken away."

The words "taken away" were all I heard, or they were all I retained. Suddenly, my world was collapsing in on me. Everything I knew was questionable. I was sure I was misunderstanding what I heard, but I couldn't erase the thoughts plunging through my head. My chest felt tight, and my throat was closing in on itself.

"Let me see the letter, Amelia," Dad said. He sounded nervous, not as nervous as Mom, but not like his usual self.

I heard paper rustling as it was exchanged between them. That noise was deafening compared to the silence that followed. "The state is demanding proof of her birth records. I don't understand why they suddenly need this proof, though?"

A hard, tired sigh spilled from Mom's throat, making her sound strangled. "Maxwell, do not be ridiculous. I just emigrated here a few years ago. You know how this state has been with their records lately. Annie is in public school. Her name is in public records. We knew it was only a matter of time before speculation broke out."

I felt like I couldn't breathe as I continued to listen, frozen in place.

Dad sighed, "Oy, Amelia. I don't know what we're going to do, honey. We must keep her safe, and we will do whatever that means. You know that. I will not let anything happen to that beautiful girl. I promise you, Amelia."

Safe. The word suddenly sounded like a haunting note. I had no clue why I wasn't safe, or why they made it seem as though I wasn't their daughter. My only question was—did they take me? Did they kidnap me? Were *they* the monsters they had warned me about so often? Weekly, I was reminded not to speak to strangers, and especially never to give anyone personal information, including our religion, address, or even my name. At that moment, I think I finally realized why I had to be so careful.

I knew Mom and Dad loved me. They showed it in so many ways. I couldn't recall a day when I didn't feel loved. Mom wasn't fond of saying the words "I love you" out loud, but I hadn't thought much of it. I suddenly began to assume she had an actual reason for avoiding the expression. My thoughts raced. I didn't belong there, and I didn't know what to do.

Deep in thought, through automatic movements, I made my way back to the bedroom, where Clara had managed to settle herself down into bed.

I glanced at her with confusion, studying her blonde hair and light blue eyes that blended seamlessly into her frosty pale complexion. I had never given it any thought before then, but her looks were entirely different from my dark hair and eyes, especially my light olive skin. There had never been much of a reason to consider the difference in our looks because Mom often said, "Every person looks like themselves."

Suddenly, I realized that Clara and I didn't have any similarities. I wondered if that was possible between siblings. It felt as though my thoughts were spiraling out of control, and I wanted to believe that none of what I was assuming could be right. I told myself I must have misheard Mom and Dad because, surely, they would tell me if I wasn't their real daughter. Surely, they would have told me if they had taken me from my birth parents.

Surely.

3

CURRENT DAY

I DID my best to rehash my experience to Mom, and it seems I explained enough to make her realize how much I knew, and at such a young age.

"Annie, I can explain some of that," Mom says. I'm not sure she has considered the amount of information I potentially know or don't know, but it's easy to see she wants to clarify whatever I have assumed. I thought the journal would be an excellent way to share the truth of what I know with Mom, but at first sight of the words I have written throughout the years, my words seem to be flowing on their own.

"Mom, there's honestly no need to explain anything. I figured you would need to digest this revelation slowly." I reach across the table and place my hand over hers. "All you need to know is, my love for you has remained consistent—never faltered—upon comprehension."

"That night of your birthday," Mom says, her voice quivering and hoarse. "I hadn't felt so scared since we arrived in the United States. Annie, the nightmares I endured—they were horrendous."

"I don't know what happened with the letter you received from the state. It was the last time I heard you or dad mention my missing records."

Mom looks relieved to hear this, but it doesn't seem to take her long to glance down at my journal, then back up at me. She's smart enough to assume why there are so many more pages in my journal, filled from front to back.

"I will tell you whatever you would like to know, Annie. I will. I was determined to rest peacefully beneath the earth with my secrets, but I won't let you wonder any longer than you already have."

With the number of questions I want to ask, I know I have to pace myself. "Did anyone come after me for not having a birth record?" The way my question comes out makes it sound as if I'm interviewing her.

Charlie leans back into his chair and crosses one leg over the other, appearing uncomfortable. I wonder how much of this story he knows? I can't help but wonder if I'm the only one who has been left in the dark about my own history.

Mom stares beyond my face, toward the gardens outside the window. Her eyes focus and unfocus for a minute until words begin to form. "It was about two weeks after we received the official letter questioning your identity. Your father—Maxwell," she says, clearing her throat, "he had just gotten home from the press house, and we were sitting down for Shabbat dinner at our worn, oak table. I placed our candles in the center of the table and returned to the kitchen to retrieve the Challah and wine. The moment I placed the bread and wine down by the candles, a ferocious knock on our front door startled all of us."

The reminder rings a bell, but the memory is foggy. I've learned that my memories have become quite sporadic the older I get, so if I didn't write it down in my journal as a major event, I don't remember all the details like I once could. "I vaguely remember that night," I tell Mom. "You were worried about people outside seeing our candles and bread because they would know we were

Jewish. We hid everything as fast as we could, right?" Hiding the fact that we are Jewish is something I *do* remember because that revolving thought was present from the time I can remember anything until I moved out, and even then, Mom would remind me to keep personal details as such, to myself.

"Yes, I was very scared back then. Enough time hadn't passed between the end of the war and the time we were living in. It seemed safer to keep our religious views to ourselves."

"I suppose I can understand that," I tell Mom.

"In any case, our religion was not what was going to get us in trouble that night. It was your sister, if I recall correctly. Clara was shouting at whoever was at the door, telling them to go away."

I don't remember that happening, but it sounds typical for Clara.

"That doesn't seem to surprise me about Clara," Charlie adds in. "That type of behavior reminds me of someone else I know." Charlie raises an eyebrow at Mom and snickers.

Charlie has a valid point. Mom has never been shy or quiet about much. I took that role in our family—being the most silent of the four of us, but to others who didn't know the rest of this family, I was considered a bit mouthy and easily excitable.

"Hush," she tells Charlie. "I'm telling Annie what happened that night." I wonder how she remembers these details so clearly. For a woman who hasn't given anyone much insight into her past, it's interesting to find out how much she keeps in her head.

"I apologize," Charlie says. "Carry on."

"Anyway, Maxwell had rage in his eyes that night. Interrupting Shabbat dinner wasn't something he could tolerate. It was all we had for ourselves as far as religion went. He stood from his chair with wrath, tossed his napkin onto the table, and stomped over to the door. I'm sure you can remember that your dad didn't exactly agree with my fear of hiding our religion, so the act of hiding our evidence was making him angrier by the second."

"I remember how important Friday nights were to Dad," I tell her.

"As your dad opened the front door, we were all clearly in sight of the visitor since our apartment was quite small, and the dining room took up most of our living quarters." Mom closes her eyes for a second and her forehead crinkles, telling me she's trying to recall the scene. She sighs before continuing. "There were two men, dressed in police uniforms. One of the men said, 'We're looking for Annie Baylin. We'd like to have a word with her, please.' I was terrified, Annie. I recall squeezing your knee beneath the table, so you knew not to speak up. I wasn't sure if you understood the meaning behind my gesture, but I prayed you did."

I only remember bits and pieces of that night, but with her story, I'm beginning to recall a little more of what was happening.

"The men were very rude, but your father didn't care who they were or what they were there for. He wasn't going to tolerate it. I could tell that much before anything more was said. He placed his hands on his hips, shifting his weight from foot to foot like he did when he was upset. 'What is this about?' Maxwell asked them. The officer who hadn't yet spoken seemed to be staring past your father and right at you, as if you were a target. You didn't seem to notice, thankfully."

Right. I remember now. I thought those police were there for an entirely different reason. I didn't even consider the thought of them being there concerning the letter I overheard them speaking about. "I thought I had gotten in trouble at school that day," I tell Mom, interrupting her story. "I couldn't figure out what I had done that warranted two police officers at our door, but I was sure I had made some mistake."

"Well, that wasn't the case. All I know is … your dad took the police officers out into the hallway outside of our front door, and when he returned, I never heard another word about what was said. I asked, but he told me not to worry about it, and I listened."

I'm not sure I would have wanted to know what happened either, though I am curious now. Not that it matters, since Dad passed away years ago. He was buried along with the secrets he and Mom shared.

"Annie," Mom chortles. "You know, I don't believe you ever got into trouble in school, but if that's what was crossing your mind at that moment, I'm glad that's all you were capable of thinking."

"I'm sure the police were searching for my birth certificate," I tell Mom.

"Yes," she responds, simply. "That was a complicated situation, but we made it work."

Not exactly.

By the way our conversation is going, I don't think Mom plans to tell me any more than what I already know, and she isn't exactly aware of how much I do know.

"Why didn't I have a birth certificate, though?" I continue. I need to hear this from her. I have to.

"Oh, sweetie, it was right after the war. Documentation went missing. Things were so terrible that immigrants changed their names once they arrived in New York. You know that." I only know the stories I've been told. She must understand that. I'm not a child now, and I'm capable of comprehending more than she gives me credit for.

I have accepted Mom's stories—the parts she wants to explain —but I know that the truth remains, and much of it is hidden. However, despite my need to know the truth, I have done my best to appreciate Mom's vow of silence because I know her reason for it was to protect me. This one fact has been the anchor that kept my words and questions mute over the years.

"Amelia ..." Charlie prompts with abruptness, then lifts his hands to question her. He knows there's more she isn't saying, but he must not know she won't say any more.

Mom places her hand on Charlie's, pushing it back down to the table. "Hush," she tells him.

In the short time since Charlie has become a permanent fixture in Mom's life, I've become very aware of how little he argues with her decisions. Though I can see a fire inside his eyes sometimes, he is very good at controlling whatever it is he wants to say.

"I think we should go inside now. It's almost time for lunch," Charlie says. "I don't want to be late today. They ran out of the ham and cheese croissants last week."

"Dear heavens, we couldn't let that happen," Mom says. "You were cranky for an entire hour after lunch that day." Mom snickers at Charlie, teasing him like she often does.

"I'm serious, Amelia. I want my sandwich today."

"Okay, okay, don't get all worked up," Mom says, waving her hand around at him.

Mom hands me back my journal as if I didn't gift it to her. "What are you doing? I gave this to you."

"Now, I'm giving it back," she says.

"Okay, but why?"

Mom slowly stands from her chair, using the table to balance her weight across her unsteady knees. "Because, Annie, I don't plan to read it on my own, and you know how I can be forgetful sometimes. Plus, I told you, I don't want to be read to. You can fill in the gaps you want to tell me, okay?" I don't understand why she doesn't want the book. Maybe she's afraid to know my truths since she's aware of how much she kept from me over the years.

Charlie winks at me and nods his head with agreement. "You should hang onto the journal," he says to me.

"Is this your way of suggesting I leave?" I ask, as they both begin their departure from our garden table. I'm still seated, watching the two of them, wondering about so much, but it seems like they don't have a care in the world, and I'm envious.

"Yes. Go, enjoy your life. You have no reason to be sitting around an old folks' home when you're a capable woman. Go be with your husband or something," Mom says.

"Well, then," I say with a huff, glancing around to see if anyone overheard this elderly woman scolding her grown daughter. *It doesn't look like anyone heard, thankfully.*

"I will see you tomorrow, Annie," Mom says.

"Have a good day, sweet girl," Charlie says to me.

That's that, for today. I should have figured our discussion would go something like this.

Knowing I've been dismissed, I stand from the chair and reach for my journal, but a beautiful monarch butterfly lands on the cover. I pause and place my hand on my heart.

A day doesn't go by without a sign from above.

The butterfly flies off as one of the courtyard doors closes, and I take a deep breath as I grab my journal and hold it against my chest.

My thoughts stir, and more long-forgotten memories jolt my mind as I head for the car.

4

1954 - NEW YORK CITY, NY - 12 YEARS OLD

A WEEK after my twelfth birthday, I made it home from school before Mom had come back from her weekly trip to the market. If it were any other day but a Tuesday, she would have been home. Dad was never home before six, and Clara stayed after school for cheerleading practice, which meant I was in the clear.

Even though I knew no one was home, I remember tiptoeing around in fear of being caught. The thought of possibly being a kidnapped person was snowballing in my head, and I hadn't slept much since I heard the conversation between Mom and Dad. I wanted to ask them about it, but I was terrified of what they would say, or wouldn't say, for that matter. Despite my fear, I felt it was best if I found out for myself, some way or another.

I made my way through our apartment with an echo of creaks from the floor following in my footsteps. I knew if there were pieces of information to be found, they would most likely be tucked away inside of Dad's desk. All our family's important papers were kept in his bottom drawer, and we each had our own file folder, labeled with our name.

I continued to tiptoe, making my way through the galley kitchen and into the small family room where our sofa and television were, as well as Dad's desk, which was tucked into the far corner behind a small folding wall that supposedly offered him quiet and privacy for when he was editing work papers. He had trouble focusing with even the littlest distractions, so when he had extra work to do at night, Clara and I would spend that time reading quietly in our bedroom.

Dad's wooden desk was flimsy, and it wobbled when I touched it. I didn't want anything to appear out of place when he got home, so I was extra careful while opening his bottom drawer. A neatly bunched collection of papers rested neatly within my labeled file folder.

My heart fluttered in my chest as I pulled the stack out and placed it down neatly on top of the desk. I gently thumbed through the pages, looking for one that might appear official, from the state. Less than a dozen pages in, I found what I was fearful of seeing. I separated the pile of papers, so I could replace them back in the proper order once I was done.

My hands shook as I read the state's letter. It was precisely what I heard Mom and Dad recite the previous week, but I was hoping there would be something more on there to help me understand why I didn't have a birth certificate—or why Mom and Dad didn't have my birth certificate.

The last part of the letter mentioned that a follow-up would occur within two weeks after the stamped date. Then, I read a line that made my stomach morph into a giant knot.

"In case of failure to comply with this request, a state official will contact you to handle the matter appropriately. Proof of citizenship or legal residence is a requirement in the United States of America, and we appreciate your willingness to adhere to the governed laws."

I didn't understand why they were suddenly searching for my identity. I had already been in the public-school system for years, though that year we had a new headmaster, and I couldn't help but wonder if he had something to do with the search. I wanted to think it was all just a simple misunderstanding or a misplacement of my records, but Mom and Dad's private conversation made it sound clear that it wasn't a matter of confusion.

"Annie?" I heard my name called from the front door. It was Mom. "Annie, are you here?"

I quickly rejoined the stack of papers and neatly placed them back into Dad's drawer, closing it ever so quietly.

I scurried across the floor, desperately trying not to make a sound until I made it into the kitchen. "I'm in here, Mom."

"Annie, why on earth didn't you walk home with your sister today?"

"She had cheerleading practice, I thought," I stumbled over my words, trying to recall if I had mistaken the schedule.

"No, that's on Wednesdays," she says, as if I should have remembered, but my mind had been so preoccupied, I forgot.

"I guess I wasn't thinking. I wasn't feeling too well, so I wanted to get home quickly and had in my head that her practice was today. I'm sorry. I won't let it happen again."

"Oh dear," Mom sighed, making her way toward me with her hand outstretched. She placed her cool palm gently on my forehead, then the back of her hand on each of my cheeks. "You don't seem to have a fever. Maybe you ate something bad?"

"I'm not sure," I said with a shrug. "I'm sure I'll be fine after I lay down for a bit."

"Good idea," she agreed.

She stared at me for a moment longer, with a lingering look in her eye as if she were trying to figure out what was going through my head. I didn't want her to know what I was thinking, so I jolted from my spot and made my way around the corner toward my bedroom.

I didn't have my second foot under the covers of my bed before Mom opened the door. "Annie, I want you to tell me the truth … now."

I couldn't figure out how she was so sure I was keeping something from her, but maybe it was written across my face in a way only a mother knows. I struggled with the thought of keeping my feelings to myself because I wasn't sure how long I could go without knowing the truth.

"Why do you talk differently than I do?" I asked her. It was a simple question, one that could bloom into some of the deeper ones I was pondering.

"Why, Annie, you already know we moved to America when you were just about two years old. We moved from Switzerland."

I felt as though I had cornered myself in the center of a maze and had nowhere else to turn after that question, not without sounding suspicious.

My lips pursed to the right as I thought of my next question. "How did you and Dad meet?" I was sure that question might lead to more. I'm not sure why the question hadn't come up before then, but it hadn't crossed my mind. I must have assumed they met at some dance, fell in love, and lived happily ever after. Most love stories I had heard of at that age seemed to fall along those lines. At that moment, though, I was questioning everything I had comfortably assumed to be true.

"Well," she said, elongating her response by filling up space between the sounds of letters with a lungful of air. "I met your dad in Switzerland."

My next analysis formed on its own, as if we were in a trivia game, and I knew the answer before the question had been completed. "Dad sounds like me, though. He was born in America, wasn't he? Dad isn't from Switzerland." I was confused about everything, but holding on tightly to the few facts I did know.

"Yes, you are correct. Your father is an American. He was visiting Switzerland for work. That's when we met." For a person who has always been long-winded with responses, her answers seemed very short and concise.

I pulled myself up against the wall my bed rested against—my curiosity was piqued. "Did you get married in Switzerland?"

She gasped for air, but then calmed herself just as fast. "Oh—oh no. We got married here, in New York."

The world began to crumble, both within my chest and within Mom's eyes. She knew I had caught her in a lie. "You said I was born in Switzerland. So was Clara, right?"

Two things were going through my mind at that moment; neither were very pleasant thoughts. At twelve, I wasn't well versed on the progression of marriage and childbearing, but I knew it took a mom and dad to make a baby, and a mom and dad were supposed to be married first—especially in those years. Not to mention, with as strict as Mom had been with rules, I couldn't fathom her doing anything out of turn.

My forehead wrinkled with concern and lack of understanding. "Were we born before you and Dad got married?" I asked, my question formed slowly and came out sounding hesitant, just as I was feeling about prospective answers.

"Darling, it's complicated. It's nothing you should worry about. Immigration laws were a bit of a mess when you were born, but it was handled appropriately, and all that matters is that you're here, I'm here, and we're all together. Right?"

I forced a smile, scared to react in any other way. I was lost and had no further questions to ask. "Of course," I mumbled.

Mom placed her hand under my chin and squeezed before pinching her lips into a tight-lipped smile. "It is time to rest now. You do not want to be sick for school tomorrow."

I slouched back down beneath the covers and pulled the sheet up to my neck, holding it over me as if it offered security, truth, and answers.

5

CURRENT DAY

WITHOUT HAVING to look through the pages of my journal, memories of writing the words are enough to bore into my mind and reopen old wounds. It's all I've been able to think about since yesterday when I left Mom and Charlie. I'm not sure I slept a wink last night.

"Annie, sweet pea, were you awake all night again? You look like you haven't slept a wink," Fisher says through a loud yawn. Ever since he retired from the fire department a couple years ago, he does his due diligence to ensure himself nine hours of sleep every night. In truth, I believe he's bored out of his mind and just trying to fill the hours in his day, since he won't listen to me and find a hobby.

"Not all night, no," I tell him while fluffing the pillows behind my back.

"Are you having those nightmares again?"

"No, no, I'm not having nightmares. I just have a lot on my mind."

Fisher tends to wake up fairly quickly and in a good mood, due to his forty-year career of round-the-clock alarms, so he's attentive and sitting up beside me. "What's on your mind, Annie? You've been quiet since yesterday morning. I know you don't like me to bug you when you get like this, but I can't go about my day acting like everything is fine with you, either."

I didn't tell Fisher my plan to give Mom the journal. Fisher isn't the type to hit a bees' nest with a stick; however, I suppose I might fall under that category. I take in a deep breath and pivot to face him. "It's getting harder and harder for me to pretend like I don't know certain things. Every day Mom wakes up is a blessing, Fisher. So, what if today is the last day I have the chance to ask her to fill in the blank spots in my story?"

"Your story doesn't have blank parts, Annie. Plus, some things are better left unsaid, and I've told you that time and time again. I wish I knew what has suddenly sparked your desire to obtain puzzle pieces that won't fit with your current life."

I place my hands on Fisher's. "I have to know. It has been bothering me most of my life, and when I thought Mom was going to pass away last year, it was one of my deepest regrets."

"Why have you waited so long since she was discharged from the hospital, then?" Fisher asks.

"She seems so smitten by Charlie, and the last thing I want to do is tarnish any of her happiness, but since they moved into assisted living a few weeks ago, things have settled down, and it seems like the right time, I suppose."

Fisher runs his hands through his messy salt and pepper hair, and wraps his arms around the back of his neck. "Then ask. Get it all out there."

"I tried. I think it's just going to take a bit. There are a lot of missing pieces—whether they are important in my life today, or not. Something inside of me won't let go of the unknown."

"Listen, sweet pea. I've been with you for longer than I can remember not being with you. You know your story. You know where you came from and why you're here. I think you just need some reassurance that everything happened for a reason, and then you can move on with acceptance, as you have before."

I tilt my head to the side, giving him a pointed look. "I have never accepted anything, Fisher. Plus, you should be glad I haven't given up because if I didn't care enough to find my answers, I wouldn't have found you."

"You remember the day we met?" he asks with a sly grin, his eyes sparkling.

Even all these years later, a blush still rushes through my cheeks and I smirk at my husband. "Yes, Fisher, I remember the day we met, and all the following days, as well."

Fisher stares through me toward the bay window of our bedroom. "God, I remember that first day too," he says. "You were dressed for perfection, walking in heels down a dirt road. Your hair was pinned up in some fancy do, and your hat covered just one of your beautiful cappuccino-colored eyes. Your other eye was like dazzling dark gold mixed with the reflection of your red lipstick. I thought I was dreaming when I first saw you. I thought for sure you would walk away when I greeted you because women like you didn't typically give the time of day to a man dressed in ten-year-old work pants and a dirty plaid shirt."

I didn't seem to notice much more aside from Fisher's sultry dark eyes, the smooth tones of his Czech accent, and the charm emanating from each and every one of his gestures. His clothing and profession at the time were inconsequential. They had no effect on how I felt about him as a person. However, I did enjoy teasing him after we got to know each other a bit more, and I still have my moments of poking fun.

"You did smell a bit like a cow," I jest. "One that possibly just sat in manure, but you sure were handsome."

"Charming too," he adds in.

"Yes, you were certainly charming too."

"I took you all over town to help you look for what you were searching for."

"That, you did," I confirm.

"Do you remember that night?"

I swat at him, blushing at our youthful memories. "Fisher, do not start reminiscing about your boyhood dreams, now."

"Boyhood dreams, eh? I was a man, Annie. I was twenty-something years old. Don't go calling that version of me a boy."

"Fine, you were a man," I validate.

Fisher leans over and places a soft kiss on my cheek. "You are brave, Annie Benson. You always have been. Go ahead and keep talking to your mom until you feel fulfilled, sweet pea. Okay?"

I smile at Fisher because I don't know what I would do without this most understanding man, who has stood beside me for so much of my life. I'm truly blessed to have him. I curl into his chest, finding my spot beneath his collarbone, knowing he will wrap his arm around me as he always has. Time has passed, aged us, and strengthened us, but this is the one place I have continuously wanted to be—in his arms, within his embrace, feeling the warmth he continues to share with me. I gaze up at the man I still adore admiring, and smile with contentment. "I love you, Fisher Benson."

Mornings are routine, even with Fisher out of routine. I tend to keep things orderly for the sake of sanity. I like my coffee at eight every morning, my two-mile walk at eight-thirty, a shower at nine-thirty, and the rest of my day to begin at ten-thirty. Keeping a schedule gives me balance, predictability, and meaning. I'm the only one in my family who schedules everything in life. Clara thinks with her imagination, and Emma, my sweet niece, is an artist. Then, there's Mom. She likes to live moment to moment without a plan, calendar, or notepad. She wasn't always like that, but as she got older, she threw away her routine and started dancing to the beat of her own drum in her head.

Dare I show up at the wrong moment to visit her? Mom may very well tell me to leave and come back later because she has suddenly become busy. Her doctor said some of her controlling behavior stems from the mild memory loss she experienced during her stroke, but besides the off-tempered times she has, even before the stroke Mom never had a hard time utilizing her power of control, even without a plan set forth.

I tap my knuckles lightly on her wooden door, nicely decorated with a wreath, like the way a front door of a house looks. I like the homey touch it offers. It has a feeling of home, rather than a nursing facility for the elderly.

Par for the course of my daily visitation, it takes several minutes for either Mom or Charlie to answer the door, but patience is something I've mastered over the years, especially with my life's mysteries unfolding one day at a time. Part of me believes I won't have every answer I'm looking for until my dying day. I hope that's not the case, however.

Mom answers the door today, fully dressed, and with a smile. "Good morning, sweetheart," she says, opening the door a bit wider. "Why didn't you sleep last night?" She pinches my cheeks, one at a time. "Goodness, you are pale. You need some color."

"Ow! Mom, please," I tell her.

"There, you look better now. Still, I'd like to know why you didn't sleep?"

Her question comes at me like a curveball. "What are you talking about?" I wonder if she spoke to Fisher before I arrived; although, Fisher doesn't typically contact Mom. He'll visit her when he's free, or when I go in the mornings sometimes, but I don't remember the last time he's called her. Her hearing isn't that good, so I hardly ever call her, either.

"You have bags under your eyes," she says, pointing to my face, with a look of assurance painted across hers. "Your eyelids are puffy too. It's obvious you didn't sleep."

It's only obvious to my mother—the woman who has studied my face for longer than anyone else in this world. "Oh, I'm fine. I just had a hard time falling asleep."

"Nonsense," she grumbles while moving slowly over to her tufted, lavender-colored sofa and matching ottoman. She's had this furniture set for what must be thirty years, and she refuses to part with it. The silly old thing is falling apart. Cotton is poking out of the sides, and threads have come loose from the decorated buttons. Clara and I tried to buy her a new one years ago, but she put up such a stink, she made us promise never to bring up the subject again. So, we haven't.

"How do you figure, Mom? I'm just fine. I promise." I'm lying, though. Mom takes ahold of the armrest of the sofa and eases down into the nearest cushion. "Where's Charlie?"

"Oh, he has a doctor's appointment this morning. It's just a checkup."

"I see," I tell her.

"So, you didn't sleep because you were worked up all night about rehashing old memories. Am I right?" Mom starts in again.

My eyelids close on their own because I can't lie more than I have. Plus, she knows me so well, there's no point in trying to influence her thoughts. "Okay, maybe that was why I had trouble falling asleep," I concede.

"Annie, birth certificates were lost very easily back then. I assure you, it wasn't a big deal. For God's sake, by the looks of you, your mind must be spinning out of control—"

"Mom, stop," I tell her, feeling exhausted by the drilling questions.

Surprisingly, she does as I request, or more like, demand. "What is it?" Her eyebrow rises along with her question. The look forces the same pinch of fear into me that it has many times before.

"I don't have a birth certificate because I wasn't born in Switzerland, or by the name of Annie Baylin."

"How so?" Her question is vague, but it feels like I've just won a game of chess, and I've checkmated her.

"I know you were trying to protect me," I begin.

"Protect you from what, Annie?" My accusation clearly angers her, but I'm not saying anything other than the truth. I know this for sure.

"You were trying to protect me from knowing anything about the Holocaust," I tell her, keeping my voice quiet and gentle. I don't want to work her up, but I do want to talk about this.

Mom clutches at the hemline of her shirt, squeezing so tightly, her knuckles whiten. "The Holocaust," she repeats. It's as if the word itself is a ghost that shouldn't be spoken of, nor has it been spoken of much throughout my life. She mentioned it from time to time with brief minute-long stories that she would not elaborate on, no matter how many questions Clara and I followed with. "I talked to you and your sister about the Holocaust plenty of times, Annie."

"You talked about the history of the Holocaust and told us it was a very sad and sickening time, but you lived through it, you're stronger, and that there wasn't much else to say. You also said there was nothing worth mentioning because that time in history doesn't deserve any attention."

"Precisely," she affirms.

"Except, you and I both know the Holocaust deserves a certain kind of attention, a kind that allows future generations to understand what hatred can cause, in order to prevent it from happening again, correct?"

Mom settles into the cushions, appearing mildly uncomfortable, which I don't want, but this part is like ripping off a bandage. I know I can't go any further without removing the top layer. "What is it you want to know, Annie?"

"I want to know about your time in Theresienstadt," I say.

"That isn't a question," she replies, nearly snapping in response.

"Please, tell me about it ..."

"Annie ..." she says with a pause. It's because she has nothing to follow my question with, unless she would like to be honest.

"Mom, I don't think you understand the questions and thoughts that were going through my mind when I was just fourteen years old."

"What do you mean, Annie? What was going through your mind at such a young age?" Mom asks.

"Do you remember when I took that job at the local library?" I ask her.

6

1956 - NEW YORK CITY, NY - 14 YEARS OLD

I WAS FOURTEEN. Mom and Dad were struggling for money. There was a recession in the city due to the aftereffects of the Korean War. Dad's paycheck was cut in half, and we were living beyond our means. I heard Mom and Dad in the kitchen each night, sometimes arguing, sometimes planning what they would do to supplement their income. There was one night Mom said she couldn't afford enough groceries to make dinner for the week, and I remember feeling utterly helpless. I had my studies at school under control, and my scores for each class were above average. I felt like it was my turn to contribute to our family's welfare. At fourteen, it seemed as though I was teetering on the edge of adulthood and what remained of my childhood, but I needed to step up and do what I could.

"Annie, it is Saturday morning. Why are you dressed and made up so early in the day? Do you have plans?" Mom asked in the morning. I was going out to seek a way to help with the family's income. I knew if I told Mom what I was doing, she would argue and put her foot down, so I was forced to fib.

"I'm just meeting a girlfriend at the library. We have an exam next week, and she needs a little help. I won't be gone long. I'll be home before lunch, if that's okay?"

Mom smiled at me as if I were a picture of perfection, which filled me with guilt. Even though I was only trying to help, I was nearly foaming at the mouth, ready to confess my lie to the woman I have looked up to for so long, but at that moment, I realized I was finally the same height as Mom. She was fairly young to be a mother of two grown girls, and the difference between the three of us was so slight, we could have passed for sisters more than mother and daughters. Even though we didn't have much money, Mom was frugal and found ways to make dresses for the three of us, so we looked as though we had more than we did. She also found ways to create makeup products from household items, and the three of us girls put on a good front to hide the financial suffering we were experiencing.

Mom spent her days caring for the family, cooking, cleaning, and running errands. She tutored at night and taught piano lessons on the weekends. She couldn't possibly take on any more work, even if she tried. Though she was young looking, she also looked very tired, and watching that transition became a motivation for me to help her and Dad however possible. "You're such a good girl, Annie," she said.

I couldn't look at her and continue to lie any longer, so I turned for the door and thanked her before leaving.

The thoughts of where I would find work hadn't even crossed my mind at that point. I hadn't planned that far ahead, but it wasn't hard to spot help-wanted signs downtown. Of course, there wouldn't be help-wanted signs for high-paying jobs, but surely, there had to be something I could do to earn a little money.

Before entering the busier part of downtown, I spotted the small public library on the corner. The building was run-down, and before today I never considered walking inside, since there was a much better library just a few blocks away. It was so disheveled outside that I had often wondered if they were even open. Of course, I studied the building a little harder that day as I was in search of employment, and sure enough, I noticed a faded "help wanted" sign hanging crookedly on the window. I knew my chances were slight, but it couldn't hurt to poke my head inside.

I scuffled up to the wooden door and tugged on the bronze handle. It felt stuck at first but then budged enough so I could open it against the blustery wind. The door was so heavy, it ushered me in.

The building was as dark and dismal inside as it was on the outside. It smelled of dust, and there surely must have been cobwebs, but I didn't take the time to look around that carefully at that moment.

To my surprise, I saw an older woman with gray, springy hair loosely tied with a piece of yarn, which dangled behind the nape of her neck. In typical librarian fashion, she also had small spectacles that were so low beneath the bridge of her nose, I wasn't sure how she could see out of them.

In any case, she didn't seem startled to have a visitor, which surprised me, considering how run-down the interior looked. I can't imagine anyone choosing this library when there were nicer ones so close by.

The woman placed a stack of books down to her side on the counter she was standing behind. She folded her hands curtly, then rested them on the countertop. "How may I help you, young lady?" the librarian asked, sounding prim and proper, despite her somewhat-unkempt appearance. The closer I moved toward the counter, the more details I noticed—her bony facial structure and the pressed white blouse she wore buttoned to the top and accessorized with a brooch that was adorned with a crystal blue-and-yellow butterfly.

The librarian's hands were wrinkled and covered with different-colored spots of pigmentation. Mom called those dots liver spots, but I wasn't sure why. The old woman looked as though her personality had gone missing at some point in the prior century, leaving her in a cold, emotionless state of life—probably not the ideal person to spend my days with after school, but I was there to help my family, and I didn't want to back away just yet.

"I noticed you have a hiring sign out front. I wanted to inquire about the job, if it is still available?"

The woman tilted her head to the side and narrowed her eyes. "How old are you?" she asked.

"I'm fourteen, ma'am."

"That's a bit young to be looking for work, isn't it?"

"I want to help my family as best I can, and fourteen is old enough to work in New York." I couldn't tell if she was coming around to the idea or trying to find a way to get rid of me. Either way, I stood complacently, hiding my nerves as she looked me up and down very carefully.

"What experience do you have with books and document archives?" she asked, sounding as if the questions she was asking were exhausting her. I was sure the conversation was about to end, considering what my answer was going to be. What experience could I have had at fourteen? She must have assumed I wouldn't have any at that age.

"I enjoy reading and writing, ma'am. I have perfect scores in school, and I enjoy learning." It was all I had to offer.

To my surprise, the slightest of smiles touched her lips, and she released her clenched fists, placing her palms down on the stack of books. "How about we start tomorrow after school? I'll need a form of identification—a birth certificate to prove you're legally allowed to work, and we'll take it from there. What is your name, young lady?"

My words fell short, and my tongue felt like it was stuck to the roof of my mouth. I had almost completely forgotten about the search for my birth certificate when the scare arose two years prior. I was pacified with Mom's reason, so I had dropped the subject and never brought it back up again. Once again, I needed to convince myself that Mom was telling me the truth. With that truth, however, I would also have to come clean about where I was that day since I would need to obtain my birth certificate from Mom and Dad. I couldn't help feeling like the opportunity to financially help the family was moving farther out of reach. "I'm sorry," I said to the librarian, taking a few steps back toward the door.

"Dear, what is your name?" she asked once more, sternly that time.

"Annie Baylin," I replied, before turning around and pushing through the heavy, wooden door, back into the cool temperatures outside, although by then, I knew that Annie Baylin may not be my real name.

The walk home felt colder than it did when I left my house earlier. The clouds had settled in, and winter was beginning to show its fury. I wasn't sure why, but when the clouds took over the sky and hid all hints of blue, I tended to feel the same way—as if the bright light inside of me was being covered by a dense matter. I wasn't at the age where I would be thinking so symbolically about life, but as I recall that time, it seems appropriate that the blue sky had gone away.

I ran up the stone steps leading to our apartment building and rushed down the first-floor hallway toward our door. All the residents in that building were close, and trust wasn't an issue, so our doors weren't typically locked during the day. It was easy to come and go without much fuss. That day, I recall wishing there was, in fact, a mild interference that could separate myself from the question I would have to ask Mom and Dad.

When I barged in, both were resting comfortably on the sofa just on the other side of the front door. Dad was reading the newspaper, and Mom was working on her needlepoint. It was a typical Saturday routine for them both. They tried to unwind from the week and do what made them happy, though I don't think needlepoint ever made Mom happy. She complained that she wasn't very good at it, and something must have been wrong with her because all women are supposed to be good with fine motor skills in crafting. I didn't necessarily agree with that particular point because I had no desire to learn those type of crafts, nor did Clara. Maybe it ran in our blood—if our blood was the same, of course.

"Why do you look like you just ran away from a ghost, Annie?" Mom asked.

I wanted to say it wasn't the ghost I was running away from, that I was running toward my fears, instead. "I need a copy of my birth certificate, and I don't want you to ask why, but if you must ask why, I don't want you to argue with my reason for needing it. Okay?"

Both Mom and Dad chuckled at me as if I were a comedian on a stage. "What could you possibly need a birth certificate for?" Dad asked.

"I'm going to be working at the library down the street, after school, just a few hours a week. I thought it might be a good chance to earn some money and help out a little."

"Annie, no, I do not want you rushing home to go to work after school. You should be participating in school affairs and enjoying the company of your friends." I didn't have many friends, and attending after-school events was not high on my priority list. Though I enjoyed sharing jokes and spending time with the couple of friends I did have, I was mostly devoted to reading and writing in my spare time. Clara was the exact opposite, however. She was the most popular girl in school, the most beautiful girl in school, the girl all the boys wanted to ask out on dates, and basically, the socialite of the community. I didn't compare much in that respect.

"I asked you not to argue with me," I replied. "It's something I want to do, very much so. Please let me do what I want, Mom."

"There's nothing wrong with learning to have a work ethic at a young age," Dad said, which surprised me. He was very overprotective and didn't like Clara or me doing anything out of the ordinary for children our age.

"Maxwell," Mom snapped at him as soon as he got the last

word out. "I think we should discuss this privately before agreeing to anything."

I clasped my hands together in front of my waist and peered down, looking away from them. "I'll just be in my room if you need me," I said, quietly.

Neither of them spoke a word as I left the room and closed myself inside the bedroom, where Clara was layering on her makeup. Dad only let her "play" with makeup on the weekends and wouldn't allow her to wear it to school at thirteen years old. I agreed with him. We were both too young to wear makeup on a regular basis. It should have been for fancy dinners or parties, which we rarely attended. It became more and more obvious that Clara got her desire to live and look bold from Mom. I was much demurer.

I plopped down on my bed and pulled my journal out from beneath my pillow, ready to enter my day's woes, even at such an early hour.

"What's the matter with you?" Clara asked.

"I don't want to talk about it," I replied.

"Are you sick?" she continued, staring at me in the reflection of her vanity mirror, while pressing an applicator brush to her cheek.

"No, Clara, I'm not sick. Nothing is wrong," I responded, pointedly.

She rolled her eyes as she usually would and refocused her attention on the reflection in the mirror.

"Do you think Mom and Dad kidnapped me?" The words came spilling out on their own, and it was the first time they had. I had thought about it so many times but kept my mouth shut, in fear of her repeating my words. I regretted letting it slip that time. Right away, I knew her response wouldn't be a good one.

She slapped her brush down onto the vanity and swiveled around to face me. "How in the world could you even think such a thing?"

"We don't look anything alike, for one," I told her.

"So what? Lots of siblings don't look anything alike," she responded.

"Mom and Dad don't have a birth certificate for me. I once heard them say some things that made it sound as though I could be taken away if the state found out."

I sat up straight, keeping my focus solid to assert my seriousness, and for a moment, Clara's face contorted with understanding, as if a light bulb lit up inside her head. Whatever thoughts were scattered in her mind, lingered but never came to fruition. "It's impossible. You're overreacting, Annie. I wouldn't give it another thought."

It was too late for that. I laid back down with my journal in hand and reached into my nightstand drawer for a pencil. My heart was beating as fast as my thoughts were rushing in, and once again, nothing in my life was making any sense.

A knock on the door interrupted the line I began to write on the clean page of my journal. "May I come in?" Dad asked.

"Of course, Daddy!" Clara sang.

Dad opened the door and walked directly up to my bed. He pulled a paper out from behind his back and handed it to me. "Your birth certificate. I'm proud of you for stepping up like a grown woman to help our family. It shows great maturity. Thank you, sweetheart."

"You have my birth certificate?" I asked in amazement, taking the paper from his hand.

"Of course, I do. Why wouldn't I?"

"Well, two years ago ..." He looked wide-eyed and confused, as if I was making this story up in my head. Then I remembered, I overheard them talking in the kitchen, and I never admitted to hearing what they said about not having a birth certificate for me. "Never mind."

"Good job, Annie. I think this will be a great experience for you."

Clara rolled her eyes and turned back to the mirror. She called me Miss Perfect, and I called her Miss New York. We loved each other the way sisters were meant to love each other through their teen years. There are days when we still talk to each other in that same way. *Sisters.*

"Is Mom okay with the idea of me working?" I asked Dad.

"No, but she'll come around to it."

"Thank you, Dad."

"Thank *you*, Annie."

7

CURRENT DAY

"Gosh, I do remember you taking that job," Mom says. "I don't know how you worked with that witch of a woman, but I didn't want to kill your spirit, so I refrained from making mention of her."

As I respond to her, I feel like I'm about to poke a hole in an overfilled water balloon that has been resting on my chest since I walked in here. I choose my words carefully, not sure how this conversation will go.

"Actually, she was a very nice woman. She was sour because her daughter moved out when she turned eighteen and never came back. She never wrote to her or even called. She was her only child, and her husband had passed away years before then. She was just lonely," I explained.

Mrs. Hegler and I spent so many afternoons together, from the time I was fourteen until I was seventeen. The job didn't pay much, but it was income, and I had access to all the books I wanted. Plus, the library's document archives became an asset I hadn't considered when taking the job.

SHARI J. RYAN

"That's too bad—I didn't realize she was going through such heartache," Mom says, without much concern in her voice. I realize we're talking about something that happened a long time ago, but Mom doesn't do well when it comes to showing emotion for others and their life stories. It's hard to be sure what's going through her mind because she's able to mask it like no one else I know.

"During the time I worked with Mrs. Hegler, I learned quite a bit," I tell Mom, leaning forward to straighten the set of coasters on her coffee table.

"Well, with all those books, I'm sure you did," Mom says. She looks down at her watch and over to the door, which strikes me as a bit odd until I hear a key click against the lock. "He is so predictable ... that Charlie. Whenever he goes to the doctor, he's gone for precisely ninety minutes."

When Charlie walks in, he greets us with a big Charlie-like smile and makes his way across the space to give me a hug, before giving Mom a kiss on the forehead. "Good morning, sweet girl. How are you doing today?"

"I'm well, thank you," I tell him.

"Can I make you ladies some tea?"

"Oh, Charlie," Mom says. "You're such a charmer."

That, he is. How does a couple their age find love so late in life and make it look as though they've been doing this forever? "Thank you, Charlie. I would love some tea."

"Anyway," Mom says, slapping her knee. "What is it you were saying about Mrs. Hegler?"

I glance over my shoulder toward Charlie, then back at Mom, buying a bit of time to procrastinate on the topic I was about to bring up. I was moving seamlessly toward the revelation I experienced back then, but the mood is offset now, with Charlie being home. "I was just saying, she was a nicer woman than many people gave her credit for," I say.

"Well, to each their own, I suppose," Mom says, while scooping her thin, white bangs off her forehead with her pinky finger.

46

"She had access to archived documents," I spit out. My words sound so abrupt that I startle myself. I haven't said what I plan to say, but now I feel like I just dove in face first.

"A lot of libraries do, or did, I should say. Ever since the Google came out, there hasn't been much of a need for physical archives, I suppose," Mom replied.

I don't understand why nothing I'm saying is alarming to her. Has she forgotten everything, or has she gotten so good at hiding facts that it feels normal to lie?

"She couldn't find an Annie Baylin when confirming my identity for employment purposes," I manage to mutter.

Mom sits up a bit straighter and lifts the decorative pillow from beside her, placing it down on her lap. "You wonder why no one liked her, Annie? She had a pea-sized brain, obviously."

"Mom," I scold her. "Just stop."

Charlie clears his throat from the kitchen, pulling my attention toward him. When I peer over, he's waving his hand up and down slowly, silently shushing me, or maybe telling me to slow down. He's right. I can't be abrasive with Mom. *This is exactly what I was afraid of.*

"Annie, what is the problem you're having, exactly?" Mom asks. Her fingernails are pillaging threads from the worn pillow.

"Confirm my real name, please. Confirm the name given to me at birth, the one you didn't give to me." A heavy feeling fills my chest, forcing me to clench my fists tightly to push away the emotion building from within the steel walls I have in place around my heart. I know Mom well enough that I sense she's feeling the same way, due to the look on her face and the tiny hole she's making in the poor pillow.

Charlie places a cup of tea down on the coaster in front of Mom and returns to the kitchen to retrieve the second cup for me, then takes a seat to join us.

Mom hasn't taken her eyes off me, but it doesn't seem as though she's looking at me, either. I could be a glass statue at this moment, the way she's looking right through me.

"Amelia," Charlie says, placing his hand on Mom's shoulder. "Are you okay, darling?"

"Lucie," she says.

"Lucie?" I repeat, wanting the rest of my name.

"That's all I know," Mom says.

"How?" How is it that is all she knows of my given name? That can't be true.

"Because you are Annie to me," she says.

"Mom, I have a right to know who I am." My words are clear, crisp, and direct, making my point firm on all parts. I am not questioning who my mother is—I am questioning who I am. "I'm not your daughter by birth, am I?"

Mom closes her eyes, and her lips wrinkle as her jaw visibly tightens around her chin. "Sigel," she mutters through a breath. "Lucie Sigel is your real name."

"Lucie Sigel," I repeat, through gasps of air, shocked to finally learn my real name after all these years. "My name is Lucie Sigel?" Tears well in my eyes, and droplets form in the corners near my nose, falling one by one, trickling down my cheek. *Lucie Sigel.* The name feels foreign on my tongue, but the more I pronounce the syllables, the less odd it feels. Part of me hoped that when I learned my real name, my life would make sense, but it still doesn't. Maybe I had pinned too many hopes on learning my name.

Charlie stands up and sits down beside me, taking my hand within his. He's gripping tightly, but I can't feel it. I can't feel anything right now. The pain of waiting so many years to learn a name that was once mine, only to realize it is simply just a combination of syllables and sounds, rather than a useful link to my unknown past, hurts so badly. I don't know what to say or how I should feel. A name does not, in fact, define me like I thought it would. There must be more to this. I know there's more, and I just need her to say what she isn't saying.

"Shh, sweet girl," Charlie hushes me as if I were a child. "Now, now—"

"No," I tell him.

"Are you my birth mother?" I ask Mom. Though I know the answer to my question, I need to hear the truth out loud. "Or did you take me from my birth parents?"

Mom's face is stale, frozen. She's lost in her mind—probably going back in time to when this all happened. There's a reason, and I know it's a good one because a mother protects her child from evil. A mother isn't evil ... right? Especially a mother who has treated her child with love for so many years.

"Your mother did not take you from your family. I did," Charlie says.

"That's entirely impossible," I argue. "We just met you less than a year ago," I say with a raised brow. "Right?"

"I'm afraid that's not true, dear. I was there when you were born," he says.

"Please, continue," I mutter while reaching toward the ground for my shoulder bag. I slip my journal out from the open zipper and begin flipping through the pages, looking for something that wouldn't be in here—something I didn't write. In truth, I need a minute to busy myself, so I can digest Charlie's words because they don't make sense.

Even though I wasn't looking for anything particular, an excerpt within my pages catches my eye—or a word, I should say.

Wait ... that can't be right.

He can't be right.

8

1958 - NEW YORK CITY, NY - 16 YEARS OLD

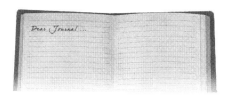

A HOT SPELL IN MARCH. I couldn't remember a time when it was over eighty degrees in the city so early in the year, but I recall that particular week because there were no fans or any air circulation in our schools, and for some reason there was an influx of new students that year too. We were crammed into classrooms and practically elbow to elbow with one another.

Each year, the tenth-grade class had a week-long, World War II history practicum, which included guest speakers. It wasn't like that week was different from other weeks in the school year, but instead of going to all our classes, we just focused on history ... history that was almost too recent to be called history back then. That year's practicum happened to be scheduled during that unseasonably hot week, and we were all on edge. Maybe that's why things turned out that way they did.

There wasn't much I thought I was missing about World War II. We had been studying the events that took place as if we were the golden generation, learning it to ensure that history would not be forgotten or repeated. As it turned out, we weren't the golden generation. We were in the tail end of the generation that did the horrible things that happened in World War II. The atrocities that occurred during the Holocaust happened in *my* lifetime.

On that first day of the practicum, we were scheduled to have a guest speaker, but I didn't bother to check the syllabus to see what the talk would be about. I enjoyed history, but at that point, I wasn't enamored by the past—more like focused on the future, I suppose.

Right after the morning announcements, we were led to the cafeteria, where the guest speaker was waiting for us. I believe the tenth grade was most likely made up of about two hundred students, which meant the cafeteria would be packed to capacity, just like all the classrooms. It was going to be hell, and I considered playing hooky for the rest of the day.

"Annie," Gracie whispered as she grabbed ahold of my elbow and tugged me in the opposite direction from we were supposed to be heading.

"What are you doing?" I responded just as quietly. Gracie was my closest girlfriend. We had been in classes together since sixth grade and spent most of our free time together. I was sure Gracie and I would be best friends forever, just as most young girls do, but that wasn't the case. She never spoke to me again after that day.

"Want to get out of here? A few of the guys are heading down to Hoppers for fries and shakes. It'll be a fab time. Come on!"

I considered the thought of ditching the speech, but my reputation hadn't been tarnished, and I didn't see a purpose in causing trouble during my last two years of high school. Most importantly, the last thing I wanted to do was anger Dad. He was already miserable while dealing with a long streak of unemployment. The New York Times had laid him off a month earlier due to cutbacks. Since then, he had been struggling to sell articles to magazines and other newspapers, but I don't think he sold more than a few, which wasn't enough to keep us fed.

Of course, I wasn't supposed to know about that, but I heard things I wasn't intended to hear, far too often. Living day by day while wondering about my identity—whether I was, in fact, Annie Baylin—may have given me enough reason to be a snoop, but I still hadn't heard anything on the topic since the night of my tenth birthday. "I can't today, Gracie. I have a meeting with Mrs. Betsy during lunch, to talk about internships for this summer."

"You're gonna bail so you can sit with the guidance counselor during lunch? Bummer, dolly." There was nothing "cool" I was going to say to make her understand my reasons for staying out of trouble.

"No one's stoppin' *you*, Gracie," I told her.

"You're such a drag, but I'm not just going to leave you behind. Come on, let's go be goodie goodies with the nerds," she groaned and threw her arms around my shoulders, barreling us forward toward the line of students.

We entered the cafeteria, finding very few seats still available at the lunch tables. After a moment of digesting what I was looking at—what was on display behind the speaking podium—I didn't care where I was seated. Maybe I did. I wanted to be closer, so I could hear what the speaker had to say. There were signs about the Holocaust, old flyers, and maps. At that time, I only knew Mom lived through part of the Holocaust, but no matter how many questions I had asked her, I got very little in return. There wasn't a whole lot of information to learn about that piece of "history" either, so my curiosity was piqued.

I blindly walked forward, moving closer to the podium. I found two seats up front and sat down in one of them. Gracie plopped down beside me. "I can't believe one of them is here," I said to her.

"One of what?" she asked, while popping her chewing gum near my ear.

I cupped my hand over my mouth and whispered, "A Nazi," to her.

"Oh," she snickered. "He's one of them Jew killers. So what?"

As soon as she uttered those words, I recall a stabbing sensation plunging into the center of my chest. I felt as if Gracie had literally taken a knife to me. I wondered how she could say something like that, and I looked around the cafeteria, wondering what the other kids thought about the man standing before us. We didn't live in a predominately Jewish area like most of the other Jewish population in that part of New York, so I was a minority— secretly, anyway. Staying away from the Jewish-populated areas was a decision Mom and Dad purposely made, but for a reason I didn't yet understand.

Mom also begged me to promise that I would never tell anyone I was Jewish. She didn't want anyone to find out. I hardly understood her reasoning since the war of religious hatred was long over, right? We should have been proud to represent our heritage, rather than scared to discuss our religious beliefs. In any regard, I didn't argue.

I knew Mom had been held prisoner in a concentration camp for a few years while living in Prague. It was the only information she gave us about her experience. Therefore, I respected her beliefs on the matter. Even though I didn't know much about her personal experience, I knew the Nazis helped Hitler kill millions of Jewish people. Yet, there I was, sitting right in front of a Nazi—or at least, I assumed he was a Nazi.

The display forming the backdrop of his presentation was not ironic. It was terrifying.

Although I was caught up in fear of the Nazi speaker's presence, I also had an overwhelming sense of curiosity. Questions were silently building in my head as I wondered if anyone in my family was hurt during the war. I didn't even know if Mom had gotten hurt, or if maybe … she had seen so many horrible sights, she was avoiding the subject for that very reason.

I guess I hadn't thought of it much before then because my mind was probably too immature to process the reality of war, but it was hitting me like a ton of bricks at that moment. I wasn't sure why I hadn't considered what Mom truly may have endured, since the Holocaust was such a major part of World War II, and she spent time as a Jewish prisoner in a concentration camp. What struck me as even more odd, was acknowledging the fact that we hadn't learned any facts about the Holocaust in school. We only studied the other parts of the war.

Mrs. Bloch, our school's principal, held her hand up to silence everyone. "Boys and girls, please settle down so we can graciously allow our volunteer speaker to take the stand. I ask that you please hold all questions until the end, and please practice your manners. Let's give Mr. Crane a warm welcome."

I was fuming with rotten thoughts, wondering how a man who once supported Hitler would be allowed in the United States, let alone a high school. I wanted to stand up and curse at him, but I was frozen, stuck to my chair as if I had been tied down. My body felt as though it doubled in weight, and I couldn't do anything but listen to the man.

"I know what some of you may be thinking," he began, as I stared at him with what I wish were daggers shooting from my eyes. The nerve he had! Everyone around me was silent, waiting for his next words. Maybe they were scared or felt the way I did. In any case, no one moved an inch. I would have heard a pin drop in that large room. "I should be dead, or locked in prison." It took everything I had not to scream my thoughts in agreement with his statement. "Well, I wasn't killed, but I was punished for several years, post-war."

"Why only a few years?" I asked out loud. I shouldn't have asked anything. I should have remained quiet. I brought attention to myself, and that was stupid. The heat radiating within the cafeteria felt as though it had increased dramatically within the last few seconds. I was sweating for multiple reasons.

"I was put in prison, but not for assisting Hitler, as my job dictated me to do." All I could think was how ludicrous it was that the school had not only brought in a Nazi, but one who was a former prisoner too. I can't imagine what they must have been thinking.

The man removed his hat and placed it on the table beside him.

Then, he tore off the red band, exhibiting a swastika, from around his arm. He set that on the table beside him too. His cross-body belt and waist belt were next, followed by him plucking the buttons free from his grayish-green jacket. He placed each item on the table. I was confused, but curious as to where he was taking his speech. I could only figure he was hot from the heat like everyone else and was working the uniform removal into his speech as a way to cool off.

Once the Nazi's gear had been completely removed, he appeared simple, like an average businessman in a white, button-down shirt and green trousers.

"This is who I really am," Mr. Crane said. "A man."

"You're a Nazi," I shouted back. Immediately recognizing my mistake, I cupped my hand over my mouth again, wishing I could take back my outburst.

Gracie elbowed me in the side. "Are you crazy?" she asked.

"Well, he is," I whispered to her.

"Do ya want him to kill you?" Gracie replied, suddenly affected by the man's presence.

I chose not to answer her, instead I turned my attention back to Mr. Crane as I fanned myself with a piece of paper I tore out of my notebook. "I was referred to as a Nazi. Yes," Mr. Crane responded to me. "You see, there are good and bad people in this world. You don't know many of the people you cross on the street daily. Some of them could have done terrible things in their life-time. Others may have never hurt a fly. We only judge each other from assumptions, or possibly, appearances, which is exactly what Hitler did."

"Hitler was protecting his country, though, right?" asked a girl in the back of the room. The question made sense, but the Holo-caust would never make sense. There is no way defending a country could justify the brutalities the Nazi's committed during World War II.

Mr. Crane leaned back against the table he had placed his wardrobe on top of and crossed his arms over his chest. He looked too relaxed and comfortable with his words. Nazis killed innocent people. Killed. How could he stand there with a look of ease?

"To answer your question, back there, the answer is yes, and no. World War II was congested with hatred and unnecessary ideology. Adolf Hitler believed that the German people should not intermix with Jewish men and women. His beliefs snowballed into what became a genocide, the deliberate killing of all Jewish people —the repercussions of adhering to the Nuremberg Laws, which more or less stated that Jewish people should be banned from Germany, as well as Germany's allied countries. As a result, the Jewish men and women had nowhere to go. The laws were Hitler's way of making Anti-Semitism, or discrimination against Jews, acceptable. However, law or no law, it led to the largest mass murder in history."

"Did you kill anyone?" A boy from the next row over asked while chuckling with his friends. I didn't understand how anyone could find murder funny. "And what happened to your arm? Did you lose that in the war?"

Mr. Crane stood up straight and pulled his shoulders back as if he were standing at attention. He unbuttoned his collar, loosening his shirt from his red, overheated neck. "I did not, nor will I ever, kill another man, but yes, I did lose my arm in combat," he said, his words spoken without inflection. They were loud, pointed, and clear as day. "You know ... there were Nazis innocent of commit-ting crimes. There were Nazis following orders in fear of their death. There were Nazis who were brainwashed to think the way Adolf Hitler thought. Three of us who served under the Nazi regime could be standing side by side right here in front of you, but no one would know who, among the three, may have killed because he believed in the doctrine of the Nazi party, or who killed out of fear for their own safety or that of their family. Assuming such a thing is also an act of being prejudiced, just like those who discriminate against Jews."

The speaker was becoming robotic. It was clear he had given the speech many times before, but when the questions began, his confidence seemed to waver. I started to wonder what he had been through.

"Why were you in prison, then?" Another voice—another question.

"He disobeyed Hitler," I answered for him. It was obvious. By process of elimination, if he did not murder anyone, and it seemed as though he didn't share the same beliefs as Hitler, then either he was lucky enough to avoid having to murder someone, or he disobeyed orders. At least, that was what I assumed to be the case. It was clicking in my head, making sense, but then again, killing innocent people, being brainwashed to do so, or threatened to do so—there wasn't a real reason why. If there was, I didn't understand.

"Correct," Mr. Crane answered, looking directly at me with a pinch to his right eye. "I saved a Jewish woman and her child—helped her escape one of the concentration camps."

"That's why you were put in prison?" I asked, confirming my thoughts.

"Yes, miss."

"So, you're a hero?" *A Nazi—a hero.* I had never heard such a thing.

"No, miss. No, I would never accept that title. It was the least I could do for the woman and her child."

He was good, but no one would ever see him that way as long as he wore that Nazi uniform.

"Thank you," I said to him.

His eyes narrowed in on me again. "Are you Jewish, miss?"

Suddenly I couldn't feel the hot temperature in the room. Instead, I felt ice cold—as if death were hanging over my head. *Mom told me not to tell a soul.* I closed my eyes, swallowed hard, and fought against the agreeing nod I couldn't control. When my eyes opened, Mr. Crane had his lips pressed together, and his jaw swiveled from side to side. He pulled in a deep breath and ran his palm down the side of his face.

58

It took him a long moment to recompose himself, but he did. Then he asked for three volunteers.

While he was choosing the three students, Gracie's hand clamped around my shoulder, pinching my skin under her fingernails. "Annie," she scolded.

Without hurry, I panned to look at her wide, startled eyes. "Hmmm?" I responded.

"Why in the world did you tell that Nazi you're a Jew. What were you thinking, Annie?" She was shouting in a whisper. The word Jew rolled off her tongue as if it were a curse word.

Rather than responding to Gracie, I focused my attention back on Mr. Crane and the three students who were then standing in front of the room. Gracie was shaking my arm, trying her best to regain my attention. I didn't want to respond to her.

"Do you see these three students?" Mr. Crane asked everyone. I looked at them carefully, noticing one had dark hair and eyes, one had dark-colored skin with matching features, and one had blonde hair and blue eyes. "Which one of these students do you think could be German? With a raise of your hands, please vote when I hold my hand above each of their heads."

He saved the blond boy for last … and everyone saved their vote for last.

"If you were Nazis during the Holocaust, you would have just punished the wrong people. It was that easy. Now, I don't know the religions or family origins of these three students, but I do know that people of all races and religions look different. I believe … everyone just looks like themselves." That's what Mom always told Clara and me. "Everyone looks like themselves." It was nice to hear someone else think the same way, but a little odd to hear it said by someone else too. "By remembering this fact, you can look at a girl with blonde hair and know she could be a Buddhist, just as well as a man with dark skin and coarse hair may be Jewish. It is life's path as well, as our choices, that dictate who we are."

The room erupted with a round of applause, except Gracie. She was still staring at me, waiting for an answer I hadn't given her.

"It was a pleasure sharing this hour with you," Mr. Crane says. "I hope I lent you some insight into a part of history that I personally hope never reoccurs. I also hope you will not judge people by how they look, and I also hope this heat breaks soon. It is quite hot in here." He ended his speech with a quiet chuckle, but his face was as red as my body felt. I was melting inside and out.

Mrs. Bloch made her way to Mr. Crane's side and shook his hand with a smile. I continued to watch as they spoke for a moment.

"Charlie, I can't thank you enough for your presentation. It was simply remarkable and inspiring. Oh, and again, I do apologize for the heat in the school. I can't believe how warm it is outside," Mrs. Bloch told him.

"New York is full of surprises, Mrs. Bloch," he said. "You never know what the next day will bring, right?"

"Right you are, Charlie. Right, you are."

Charlie, the good Nazi.

Before then, I didn't know there was such a thing as a good Nazi. I was glad I didn't miss that session.

"Are you, or are you not, a Jew?" Gracie asked me again. That time, her face was covered with a look of disappointment, and anger laced her words with what felt like poison.

"I am," I told her, disobeying Mom's wish.

The futile look in her eyes burned as she looked me up and down. It felt as if my body had suddenly become disfigured, or that she thought I was some dangerous animal. Disgust filled Gracie's pale, freckled face, deforming her features into a look I wished I could immediately forget. "Oh my God, Annie. We can't be friends. Never again. Do you realize what you just did? I can't believe you didn't tell me. If I had any idea—we would never have been friends. You are—you are simply disgusting."

After just listening to the incredible words from Mr. Crane, it seemed as though Gracie didn't hear, or want to hear, anything he said ... because she stood up from her chair, walked away, and *never* looked at me again.

9

CURRENT DAY

I PLACE the journal down as I finish reading the excerpt I hadn't intended to read. I didn't think it had much relevance to the conversation we're having, but now I'm thinking otherwise.

"Mr. Crane," I repeat from the excerpt, unable to look at Charlie.

"Charlie Crane," he confirms. "I had no clue who you were, or that you were a student in that cafeteria. That was Midwood High School, right?"

"What is this nonsense you two are talking about?" Mom asks.

I remember that day so clearly, but his name didn't stick with me. What are the odds that Nazi soldier would have been Charlie? "I told you I spoke at schools for a while," Charlie tells Mom.

It seems Mom has figured out the answer to her question without further explanation, though she still looks confused. "I knew you were speaking at schools, but you failed to mention they were schools in the New York City area," Mom says to him, her eyebrows bowed upward.

"I started in New York," Charlie replies curtly.

"In the town I happened to be living in?" Mom snaps back. "What are the odds of that, Charlie?"

My mind is spinning in so many different directions, I can't seem to wrap my head around any of it. I'm listening to their sudden spat, and replaying Charlie's words, telling me he was present for my birth. How can Mom not understand the mixture of confusion I have been living with? It is as if there was a bread-crumb trail that just faded into dust. It's not fair.

"Amelia, please, let's focus on Annie right now," he says.

Yes, for the love of God, please give me some insight.

"How were you there when I was born?" I ask sternly, centering my focus on Charlie.

Both Mom and Charlie fall quiet as they share a look that could mean any one of a thousand things.

"I was on guard in Theresienstadt when—"

"Charlie," Mom interrupts him. "Please."

"Look, I know you aren't my birth mother," I admit to Mom, giving her a break from having to make up another story, or worse. "Tell me the truth, please."

"I—Annie. I—" She sighs, sounding like she's in pain. I've been so worried about hurting her all these years, but she doesn't understand how much this has been hurting me. "I did not carry you in the womb, nor did I birth you, but ..." Her voice cracks and trails off as her face falls into a look of distress.

Having already known the truth, it's easier to hear it from her mouth. It's all I've wanted to hear for a very long time. If she had told me sooner, I would have relieved her of the guilt I assume she may be feeling because I've had a response to offer from the time I found out the truth on my own. "Mom, you are *still* my mother," I say clearly. "I would never say or feel otherwise."

Mom stops talking and inhales sharply through her nose as she rests her unsteady hands on her lap. "I raised you as my own," she says. "I adore you as my own. I would give up my life for you, then or now."

There was a time I questioned her motives, but when I could

piece my story together with the particles of information I could find, I was able to see the motivation behind her actions.

"I never questioned your devotion to me," I assure her. "I never questioned your reason for keeping the truth from me, either." That isn't exactly true, but from the time I was old enough to understand the true meaning of love, I understood as much as I could.

"It was wrong," she continues. "How did you know—how did you find out?"

"It doesn't matter, Mom. I know, and I was hoping you could fill in some of the blanks, that's all."

"It matters very much to me, Annie. I don't know how to help you, though."

Without offering her a direct response, I begin spilling the facts I do know—the ones I've been holding onto for years. "I know I was born in Theresienstadt."

Mom closes her eyes for a moment and takes in a long inhale. I wish there were another way to go through this with her. I feel like a monster for subjecting her to this.

"Yes," Mom says, simply. She stands up from her chair with a struggle. Usually, I would rush to her side and help her, but she is not the type who likes assistance, and right now, I think it's best I let her do things on her own, unless she asks for help.

It takes a minute for Mom to make her way around the coffee table, but she sits down on the coffee table and leans forward to place her hands on my cheeks. I look into her eyes—the sweet, soft gray eyes of the woman who has always been there for me, who has always been my mother.

"Your mother's name was Leah." I notice the tension in Mom's head as the slight wrinkles above her eyes tighten. I swallow hard, feeling apprehensive about what she will say next. "We were as good of friends as two people could possibly be while living as prisoners. She was there for me the day my mother died, and I was there for her the day you were born. We shared a bond I could never properly describe. Just after you were born, I helped her with as much as I could. I would steal food and any materials I could from the medical block to help her keep you hidden and safe."

These are the holes in my story. I didn't know how long I spent with my birth mother. Throughout all these years that have passed, I've wondered if she possibly abandoned me, left me to die, or gave me up. "Did she ask you to take me?" I question. There's an acidic feeling in my stomach and a pain similar to a hunger pang snarling through me. I couldn't eat this morning, knowing I was going to be brave and ask the questions I've wanted answers to for such a long time.

Mom breaks her focus between our eyes and looks down between our feet. "Each night before I left her block, she would take me by the hand, squeeze with all her might, and look at me with raw heartache. It would take a moment for the words to find her tongue each time. It never got easier for her to ask what she needed to ask me," Mom begins.

I look past Mom for the moment, noticing Charlie's expression and the sadness in his eyes. He's shaking his head and glancing up at the ceiling. "God bless her," he mumbles. "God bless her."

Mom is seemingly blocking Charlie out as she continues with her thoughts. "She would say, 'Amelia, please promise me that when they find me, you will try and protect Lucie, and keep her as your own if you are lucky enough to survive. Please promise me you'll try your best.' All she wanted was my promise, even knowing I could have died just as easily as she was assuming she would."

"She loved me?" I ask, though it's clear by what Mom just said.

"She loved you, Annie. God almighty, she loved you with every ounce of her soul."

"They took her away?" I continue, trying my best to keep a brave front, despite the feeling of everything inside of me turning to ash.

Charlie stands from his chair and leaves the room. The sound of his footsteps end when a door down the short hallway closes quietly. The gesture of him leaving the room tells me more than I thought I would figure out so quickly.

"She was executed, sweetheart," Mom says impassively. The internal wall she has built up inside is obviously unbreakable, and I don't understand how she can be so strong this many years later. "I watched. She was so brave, Annie. She was brave for you."

Digesting each word and allowing it all to sink into my brain and my heart, a horrid thought takes over, and I can't stop the words from coming out. "Did Charlie kill her?"

Mom's hands flop against her chest. "God, no! Charlie was a good one. He helped me keep you safe." *That's right.* I remember his speech at the school. He was a *good* Nazi. A good Nazi. How do those words work together? "Charlie helped us escape, Annie. Charlie is the reason we are alive." This is the first time she has admitted to me that Charlie didn't just step into her life out of the blue last year. We were supposed to believe he did, and I did believe it for a while until I began remembering details from some of the research I collected.

"Why did you keep this from me?" It's all I can think to ask. The other questions seem unimportant now. "Why?"

"Your mother was gone, Annie. There was no bringing her back. I could raise you, give you a good life, then destroy your innocence with facts no child should have to bear, or I could let you live happily without the truth. I chose the latter option. Whether it was right or wrong, I still don't know, but I was trying to protect your heart. I never kept secrets for the sake of lying. I promise you that."

"My dad? I mean … my birth dad?" I ask her. "What about him?"

"I don't even know his first name. There were so many men with the last name of Sigel, and I didn't know what camp he was transported to, if he was transported. I just know he and Leah were separated upon arriving at the camp."

"So, he could be alive?" I spit out with haste. My heart fills with ridiculous hope, but I'm no stranger to the happenings of the war. The chances of my birth father being alive are slim, especially considering how few survivors are still alive today. In fact, I may be one of the youngest survivors.

"It's quite doubtful. I tried my hardest to find that information, but I didn't get far," Mom says. "Technology wasn't available to us back then, as you know."

"I understand. I took the hard way, seeking my answers, as well."

"So, tell me then. How did you find out you were born in Theresienstadt?"

1960 - NEW YORK CITY, NY - 18 YEARS OLD

THE THOUGHT of college had crossed my mind far too many times throughout the previous two years. For each application I sent out, I had to skip the part where they needed proof of citizenship, and, or birth records. Of course, I had the ones Dad had given me to use, but I knew they weren't real records. I vaguely mentioned the notion of my birth records being inaccurate, but Mom and Dad laughed as if I were telling them a joke. It wasn't a joke. My birth certificate—the one Dad handed to me, was not real.

When Mrs. Hegler went to verify that my birth certificate matched up my birth records in the library's archive, it became clear what I was dealing with. After that revelation, Mrs. Hegler seemed to pity me and allowed me to work, despite being unable to prove my age. She paid me weekly with cash that was collected on late book returns.

There wasn't always a lot of work to be done there, especially since I had the card catalog in perfect condition. When a book was returned, I immediately placed it back in its spot on the shelf and resumed whatever task I was tending to. I spent most of my free time at the library, even when I wasn't working. I became infatuated with the archives, researching abstract topics about the Holocaust. I didn't think there was research in the library or the archives that would bring me answers I desired, but it filled in other informational gaps I was curious about.

As the years seemed to fly by at a rate faster than a speeding freight train, immigration laws became stricter to protect the United States due to the rising fears brought about by the Cold War. To most eighteen-year-old Americans, the tightening of security didn't mean much, but me the impact was significant as I was beginning to understand the potential consequence of using a fake birth certificate.

College was a dream, but it was one that was slipping by. I tried to focus on my writing after graduating from high school. Dad told me it would be my best asset until I could secure a spot at a university. Since he had acquired a new job at a small press magazine around the time I graduated, I had an in—so he was able to sell some of my articles to his editor in chief. It wasn't what I had planned for my future, but I was doing what I could with what I had.

The day Clara left for Wellesley College in Massachusetts, I felt myself breaking down. It was *my* dream to go to college. She had no real plans of continuing her education but luckily ended up with a foreign language scholarship. It wasn't as common for women to be bilingual then, but since Mom was fluent in Czech and used it around the house a lot, we picked up on the language too. Evidently, Clara was interested in translating and transcribing, and she was a shoe in.

I just wanted a liberal arts degree, and I thought I might find a passion throughout my studies, but it was beginning to look like I would have to find my passion some other way.

Dad assured me the morning Clara left that everything would be okay. He told me I should write about the emotions of being a woman in my generation, and how it felt to not receive an acceptance to a college.

What else was there to do? Writing usually came easy to me, but that day, I needed better inspiration than my anger and jealousy of Clara living my dream. No one was around that day, so my feelings led me to Mom and Dad's closet in their apartment.

I should have known the dangers of going through their personal belongings, but my life was being affected by withheld information. At least, I was quite sure of it by that point. Nothing felt like it was going right, and I was done waiting for life to sort itself out.

I took down the boxes from the top shelf of their small closet and placed them down neatly on their perfectly made bed. I was careful not to move the quilt. Mom had a knack for noticing every little thing that was out of place, even if it happened to be a loose thread.

The boxes contained photographs of Clara and me throughout the years. There was nothing in the boxes that had any secretive meaning. I had already gone through those before, but I thought maybe I'd see something different this time around. I was wrong, though. Actually, I wanted to throw the boxes across the room and scream through the anger that was reeling inside of me, but as I learned to do, I took a breath and calmed myself down. I picked the boxes back up and replaced them precisely where I found them. I closed the accordion door and turned away to leave without a trace of my intrusion.

Except … I spotted a paper lying on the floor, nearly staring up at me. I only saw it for a half a second before accidentally stepping down on top of it. I was aggravated that I had to take the boxes back down and figure out where the paper had come from. However, I didn't see any other papers, so I wasn't sure where it belonged.

My conscience was weighing me down. I wanted to look at the paper, just as much as I wanted to find something in those boxes, but something was telling me there was information on the paper, while at the same time there was guilt firing through my blood.

I had to know, though. If there was something about me, I needed to know the truth.

The paper wasn't a typewritten sheet of paper. It was notepaper from what looked like a journal of sorts. I turned it over and found Mom's neat writing filling each line.

At first, my eyes didn't want to focus or cooperate. Everything seemed blurry, and dizziness took over my body. I should have taken that as a sign to put the paper away, but my nerves were electrified, and nothing was going to stop me from seeing what was written, even if it was nothing of importance. At least, I would know that I had tried.

I swallowed the lump in my throat and took the note next door to my bedroom. I closed the door and sat beneath my windowsill, feeling the slight September breeze ruffle the loose strands of hair on the top of my head.

I blinked, holding my eyes closed for an extra-long second and then reopened them to focus again. The words became clear.

Dear Journal,

I didn't think it was possible to feel anything other than pain after what I've gone through in the past few years. I wasn't sure I'd be able to feel much of anything, in fact.

Though, the one thing bothering me more than the memories and heartache, is guilt.

The moment I stepped foot onto U.S. soil, I was greeted by a man in customs who needed our information. I had nothing but my word. I told the man my baby's name was Annie. Her mother didn't give me the right to change her name, but I did so to protect her. I did try to find Annie's father, to confirm whether or not he was alive, but if he is still alive, there is no one by his surname back

home in Prague—not according to the letter exchanges I had with a
city clerk there.

If he did go elsewhere, and he's alive, I must live with the fact
that I have taken his only child from him because I have run out of
ideas about how to find him. I don't even know his first name.

In any case, it's too late to do much of anything. I certainly
don't intend to return to Prague, or worse, Theresienstadt. Finding
my way here was by no other means than luck. Now that the
prisoners have, thankfully, all been liberated, I'll most likely always
wonder if there are paperwork trails containing the prisoners' family
bloodlines, but if there are such records, I'm sure they are buried
somewhere along those prison grounds. From the day we escaped,
my one and only instinct was to protect Annie from the soldiers
who might try and take her back to Theresienstadt. Despite the war
coming to an end, I will, as I promised her mother, protect this little
girl with everything I have.

    -Amelia

THE JOURNAL ENTRY fell from my shaking hands and slid beneath
my bed. The proof, the answers, the comprehension I needed for
the previous few years had come to fruition. I was not Annie, and
my parents were not my birth parents. I was taken during the
Holocaust, and no one in my real family knew where I was.

Coming to terms with my unknown identity took a toll on me.
To say I felt sick would be an understatement. After the words
from Mom's journal entry saturated my mind over the course of
several minutes, an acidic burn ran through my stomach, and I
vomited my breakfast and lunch all over my bedroom floor. I was
curled into a ball, lying beside my own bile, and I couldn't figure
out how to blink my eyes, or even move. All I could do was tell
myself that my entire life had been a lie.

Tears never found my eyes, even when they burned from going

without blinking for so long. It must have been due to a state of shock. Each moment that passed was another opportunity for clarity to set in, but my mind felt blank.

Clara wasn't my sister.

I didn't know if I had biological siblings.

I wondered if my situation was common among the Jews that either escaped or were liberated.

I had no clue how many displaced people there were.

However, I had facts, and they were swimming through my head along with all other realizations.

I was born in Theresienstadt, and my parents were from Prague. I thought for sure there had to be someone who could help me find out more.

Mrs. Hegler, the librarian, seemed to have so much information that I figured it would be best to try my luck with her first. She had postal addresses for important locations across the world and, though I wasn't sure there was any specific place to write to, I wanted to ask.

It took me an hour to bring myself up to my feet. I felt weak and stressed. I had tunnel vision too because I forgot to clean up the mess I had left, and I didn't remove the journal entry from beneath my bed before running out of the apartment. By the time I reached the library, those thoughts began to hit me. If Mom came home and found that mess, she'd be terribly worried. She would likely clean it, and it would be difficult to miss the paper lying all on its own, beneath my bed. We didn't keep items under our beds because we had water leaks from the old windows, and anything on the ground could easily get destroyed. I only knew Mom was out running her daily errands. I didn't know what time she would be back home.

When Mrs. Hegler spotted me walking into the library, a look of concern marked her face almost immediately. It could have been the bile stain on my dress or the look of despair painted across my face.

"For the love of all things holy, what in the world is wrong with you?" she gasped.

"I need your help. I don't have time to explain everything, but I'm hoping you have the resources to find me a postal address." I was breathing heavily from walking tiredly at a pace that could match a runner's jog, but I was not athletic by any means. Once I took a moment to catch my breath, I leaned onto Mrs. Hegler's countertop. "I need to know if there is a location in Terezín, Czechoslovakia, that stores information on the missing people from World War II."

Mrs. Hegler didn't seem surprised by my question. In fact, it looked as though she was waiting for it. "You've learned more about your incorrect name, haven't you?" she asked softly.

When Mrs. Hegler was trying to confirm my identity between my fake birth certificate and her records, she was straightforward and honest with me when she didn't find anyone by the name of Annie Baylin registered in the state of New York. However, without any other information, there was nothing more to research before that day. "My birth parents are from Prague and I think they were prisoners in the Theresienstadt concentration camp. I've heard there are still missing people. Therefore, I'd like to think there is someone tracking them. Don't you think so too?"

Mrs. Hegler pressed on the center of her white glasses, pushing them up the length of her nose. "Follow me," she said with confidence.

I ducked under the counter and followed her toward the back of the library, where I had spent a lot of time organizing, sorting, and filing for Mrs. Hegler during the last two years of high school.

When money became tight at the library the previous year, she had to let me go, but I knew it wasn't a personal situation. Therefore, I would still stop by often and offer my help without pay. She had stories of her time in Russia, and I was fascinated to hear about her life. I had no idea how profound my life had already been, especially since I was only eighteen.

Mrs. Hegler had catalogs of paperwork, bound and organized.

I was never sure where she acquired the paperwork from, but I think anyplace that had certified archives received worldwide information on a regular basis. She never confirmed that fact with me, but I assumed.

Just as Mrs. Hegler knew where each book's home was within the library, she knew exactly where to look for the information I was requesting. With the massive catalog of papers opened like a book, she ran her finger down the page of some typed information and stopped halfway down the paper. Her red painted fingernail was pressed firmly against a line of words—so firmly her fingertip turned white from the pressure.

She took the pencil from behind her ear and placed it between her teeth, then reached for an old catalog card that she had left in a bin for scrap paper. Quickly, she wrote down an address. "This is it. This is the location that keeps the missing people records for Terezín. You should start with them. Prague is less likely to have the information you need since you were never marked as a resident, I assume."

"My parents were, though," I told her. I wasn't sure why I argued. She had basically given me gold.

"It will be easier to track your family down once you know your given name," she said, closing the catalog with a loud clap from the clashing papers.

Mrs. Hegler grabbed my chin and lowered her head down to my eye level. "This is your answer, Annie. If you'd like to me to look over your letter before you send it, I will be happy to do so. Also, make sure you fill out the postal address exactly how I have it written here on this card. Lastly, ask the post office to help you send a letter to Czechoslovakia. The postage will cost extra."

I wrapped my arms around Mrs. Hegler's neck and kissed her soft, wrinkled cheek. "Thank you for helping me. Thank you," I breathed through a mere whisper.

I took the card and ran all the way back to the apartment, silently praying that Mom had not gotten home from her errands yet.

My world may have shattered into a million pieces that day, but I considered myself lucky to come home to an empty apartment. I was able to clean up my mess and place Mom's journal entry back in the closet before she returned.

Once I knew I was in the clear, I took a seat at my writing desk and pulled out a piece of note paper and a pen.

I didn't know where to start with my inquiry. With my thoughts scattered, I peered down at the card Mrs. Hegler gave me and noticed the location I would be sending the letter to. It was a memorial building for the former prisoners of Terezín.

I pressed the tip of my pen to the paper, closed my eyes, and after a long minute, the words came to me as if the letter had been prewritten in my head.

September 3, 1960

Annie Baylin
 4051 Turner Road, Apartment 204
 Midwood, New York 11201

To Whom This May Concern,

My name is Annie Baylin, but that is not the name I was given at birth. I am well taken care of here in the United States and loved dearly by the people who rescued me during the Holocaust, when I was a small child. My birth date is April 18th, 1942. I was born in the concentration camp, Theresienstadt, and my birth parents were taken from their home in Prague. I would like to find information about my birth parents, and whether my birth father is still alive. I don't know if there is any kind of information you can help me with, but if so, anything would be kindly appreciated.

Sincerely,

Annie Baylin

I FOLDED the letter up neatly and slid it into an envelope, then addressed the front. It was helpful that Mom still hadn't come back yet because I had a minute to look for a postage stamp in Dad's desk drawer. The process of mailing the very letter that could determine my past and future went smoothly, considering how dark the paths to my answers had become over the years.

Looking back on that time, I realize how valuable the ability to be patient can be. Even with patience, though, I knew there was a chance I would not receive a response to my letter.

WEEKS DID PASS, in fact, before an envelope addressed to me was dropped into our mailbox. I had been checking the mail daily to make sure I would see the letter before Mom or Dad was tipped off.

The envelope was covered with neat penmanship, and I knew immediately it was from the memorial office in Terezín. The same sick feeling I encountered the day I found Mom's journal entry, was reforming. My stomach felt heavy, and there was a tightness in my throat that I thought might lead to another bout of sickness.

Once upstairs, inside our apartment, I ran to the bathroom and slid the metal lock into place, so no one could walk in and find me looking so ill.

I slid down the salmon-colored tiles that lined the bathroom wall and pulled my knees into my chest as I rested the letter and my hands on the cold linoleum flooring.

I felt as though there was a pinball rolling around inside of me, causing pain throughout all my organs. However, it was the nerves firing up inside of me that was worse than feeling sick. There was a possible answer within the envelope, and I was too scared to look inside.

I had to remind myself that I had gone years without knowing who I truly was. I didn't intend for the letter to change my life. I just needed to know more. I was certain that Mom and Dad would not volunteer the information up to me, and wondering why they wouldn't, was what upset me the most. I knew there had to be a reason they kept that information secret.

I pressed my lips together and swallowed hard, forcing away the lump in my throat. My fingers folded over the envelope and I squeezed my hand around it as I carefully pulled the glued flap away from the opening.

The white piece of paper inside was folded with a sharp crease. The paper was thicker than the paper I used to write the initial letter. It looked like official paperwork, even before I removed it from its containment.

I wanted to move faster, but my body was not keeping up with the speed of my thoughts. Seconds were in slow motion, and I felt like it took me an eternity to remove the letter and unfold it.

September 30, 1960
Terezín Memorial

Dear Ms. Baylin,

Thank you for utilizing our resources at the Terezín Memorial. I am grateful you were fortunate enough to be rescued from such a treacherous location during the time of the war.

I have conducted the research on your behalf in accordance with the information provided within your letter.

It appears there were three babies born on April 18th, 1942, within the prison barriers of Theresienstadt. It was uncommon for babies to survive their time in the prison camp, but it appears all three of you are listed as either missing, or were never found after death.

A large majority of Theresienstadt was made up of former residents of Prague. It appears that each baby born on that day was connected to parents who originated from Prague. Therefore, I'm afraid the residence of your birth parents does not help with the information I was able to find.

We would love to help you continue researching your family's history, so we can mark you as found.

At our location, we have a list containing missing children of the Holocaust who were kept in Theresienstadt, as well as those who have been marked as found, or have been confirmed as deceased. Some of the survivors who were located have graciously given us their mailing addresses, so we can offer other displaced children of the Holocaust a way to connect with one another, for the sake of emotional support.

On the bottom of this letter, you will find several names and mailing addresses of the survivors who have offered to help. In addition, I have listed the three names of the babies born on April 18th, 1942, in the prison camp of Theresienstadt.

I'm sorry I don't have more information at this time, but please check back in with us frequently so that we may continue to help you with your search.

Best Wishes,

Ina Goldstein

ANNIKA, Lucie, and Zaila were the names listed as possible matches, but I had no clue how to narrow those names down to one.

11

CURRENT DAY

I've kept my eyes locked on the floating words within my journal. I haven't been reading the entries to Mom. I've been reliving them out loud. That letter I sent to Terezín was the beginning of a new world for me. It was like a hidden door in an attic—one I didn't know existed—but when I came across it, I found my reason for existence.

Mom shudders through a deep inhale. "I had no idea," she says.

"I asked you so many questions, Mom, but you always seemed to have an answer that would steer away from the direction I was heading."

"I know," she responds quietly.

I place my hot, clammy hands on my cheeks, trying to piece myself back together from that time of confusion. "You're a Jewish Holocaust survivor living with a former Nazi," I say out loud. I don't mean anything by it, but I needed to say it out loud to define the reality behind my statement. "Did Dad know Charlie?"

"He knew of him, but I never saw Charlie between the time he helped us escape and last year."

"I can't wrap my head around this. How—"

"I am a woman, and he is a man. Nothing else matters to us," Mom states.

"Did you have a relationship with him ... back then?" I ask, curious about how a situation like a Nazi helping a Jewish prisoner would happen.

"Annie, do you remember when I told you that a journal was a place for a woman's personal thoughts?"

"Yes," I tell her, remembering that day clearly.

"Well, I don't wish to discuss my past with Charlie. Do you understand?"

"Yes, I do." Of course, now I want to know more about their past. I have about a million questions, but I will respect her wishes for now, since this is their relationship.

I had hoped Mom would continue her life with a friend or companion after Dad passed away because she seemed so lonely. I just need to focus on the fact that Charlie is filling that role and be grateful they found each other again after so many years.

Dad's death was very hard on all of us, but he had been sick for a while, and his passing seemed more like a blessing at the time. Of course, that meant Mom no longer had anyone to take care of, and the loss was the hardest on her.

I didn't see Mom's relationship with Charlie panning out the way it did, though. Mom always told me that people come into our lives when we need them the most, so I suppose that's why Charlie came back into her life when he did.

"All you need to know, Annie, is that love is something found within our hearts and soul. It doesn't define our bond."

"You are right about that," I agree.

Mom clears her throat, which she often does when she wants to change the subject. It's obvious I've made her uncomfortable, but she can't blame me for wanting to understand why my life ended up the way it did. "Sweetie, it seems as though our lives have been sprawled out on a map, and you've been crossing off routes along your way, while in search for the right path. I feel as though you're not understanding that I blocked off certain roads on that map because I wanted better for you."

I can understand her explanation, but for a child, not a grown woman who is desperate to find information about her history. "What about what I want?" I would never typically speak to Mom like this. It's disrespectful and sounds ungrateful, but I don't want to feel resentment someday when it's too late.

"What is it you want, Annie?"

"I want the truth, all of the truths—the whole story," I say, as if it wasn't obvious. There is more to my history than what I know, but I'm not sure I will ever peel enough layers away from Mom's barrier to obtain it all.

"You have the truth now, but it seems I'm the one who has been lost in the dark all these years," she tells me.

"What do you mean?" I squeeze my journal against my chest, feeling like a child being cornered after lying about something terrible.

"You have left me in the dark too, Annie, but I'm not as oblivious as you may think." Mom crosses one leg over the other, holding onto her knee for what looks like support. "For example, you told me you met Fisher while working at the art gallery in Manhattan. You said he was visiting from Europe, but you didn't meet Fisher in the states, did you?"

A long, lingering gaze freezes on Mom's face, and I'm wondering what she knows about my relationship with Fisher and how she found out.

Even though I'm not a child by any means, Mom still makes me nervous when I face her pointed stare. She has had this look down pat for as long as I can recall.

The door from down the hall opens and closes, but Mom doesn't remove her focus from my face. "Sorry about that," Charlie says from around the corner.

"I know you took a trip to Czechoslovakia without telling me," she says.

Her words steal the wind from my lungs. "Okay, and I am going back to the bedroom," Charlie says, pivoting mid-step.

"Charlie, don't be so foolish. You can stay. You should hear what sweet Annie did at twenty years old," Mom says, with an eyebrow arched. "She gave her father and me, God rest his soul, quite a moment of anger—one we chose not to address with her. I'm still not sure how we managed to let that go without saying anything, but it was our way of making peace with the fact that you were held back from so many things in life, I suppose."

"Mom, I don't think it is necessary to rehash things that happened so many years ago." I attempt to stop the conversation before it goes any further. After all, she doesn't want to explain her earlier relationship with Charlie, so I should be able to keep my relationship with Fisher private too.

"True, but I want to know how you managed to accomplish something so incredibly stupid," she says bluntly.

It was more than stupid. It was by far the dumbest thing I have done in my entire life, but at the same time, it was the best thing I've ever done.

"How did you know?" I ask her, feeling my fingers become numb from gripping my journal so tightly.

"A mother knows everything," she answers. "You should know that." *She didn't mean to say that to me.* Those words slipped from her mouth, and I can see by the look on her face how much she is regretting her words. One of her hands covers her mouth, and she closes her eyes while gently shaking her head. "I am so sorry, Annie. I'm sorry." Mom leans forward and cups her hands around my face, squeezing tightly to move me from my unblinking emotional state. "I'm sorry."

She doesn't believe me when I tell her I'm all ice inside. She never has.

"My life," I say, through sharp words, "happened the way it has because of history. My life has been a lesson in a book. My life

82

has greater meaning because of what happened. If my life's lessons give just one person an ounce of appreciation for their life, then every chapter that has evolved from my existence has had a purpose. Just like your legacy."

"I just wanted you to live a happy life," Mom says, still holding onto me tightly. "I don't understand why bad things have happened to us. I don't, but even though we don't share the same blood inside, our experiences—the ones we remember or don't— have created a bond between us that is stronger than anything biologically bound."

She couldn't be more right. Even throughout my determination to find my roots, I have not considered my family life to be less than what a normal family might have. "I've always needed you to be my rock, Mom. Always. I would never look at you as anything other than my mother, and I will keep saying that to you until I can't say it any longer."

"I know that," she says.

Mom releases her hands from my face but slaps one palm against my cheek before resting her hands on her lap. "Now, fill in the cracks about your journey to Eastern Europe."

"Should I still stay here?" Charlie asks. "I am feeling quite uncomfortable, and this seems like it's probably a mother/daughter conversation, right?"

"Yes, stay here," Mom and I echo each other.

"Charlie, sit down and grab yourself a cup of tea. I have a feeling this story is going to be a doozy," Mom says.

The word "doozy" doesn't even come close to describing my young and dumb decision to take an undocumented trip to Czechoslovakia.

12

1962 - NEW YORK CITY, NY - 20 YEARS OLD

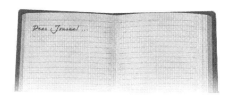

THERE WERE WORSE things I could be doing ... maybe. Mom and Dad wouldn't have let me go. The world was still a dangerous place, and I had no business leaving the country without telling someone.

Thank goodness for sisters, though. Over the years, Clara and I had different opinions on just about everything, but regardless, we were still close.

When Clara left for college, I felt the separation between us become smaller. It was as if we realized how much we needed each other when we weren't together. We would write letters and occasionally call each other, but most often, I went to visit her on the weekends. It was a way for me to experience college life since I still hadn't been accepted anywhere.

I considered sitting Mom and Dad down to explain the real reason why I hadn't been accepted to a college, but I knew they had no more control over the situation than I did. Mom saved me from probably dying in that prison camp, and I'm sure the last thing going through her mind then was obtaining my birth records, if it were even possible. After all she had done for me, placing the blame on them wouldn't help anyone. It would have just hurt them.

I came to terms with forgoing a college education and focused on writing and trying my hand at different mediums of art.

Anyway, I had made my decision on where life was taking me next. It felt like a "now or never" choice, so I had to go with it. The weekend before my planned adventure, I took the train to Boston to visit Clara at school.

As she normally did, she met me at the train station with her big bright eyes, a smile larger than the sun, and her bright red lipstick accenting her beautiful features. That day, she was dressed in a long, navy blue pea coat that fell just above her knees. With her black leather gloves and polished pumps, she looked like she fell out of a women's clothing magazine. Fashion was her passion, and she showcased that with every outfit she had on. I was envious of Clara's looks and style because I didn't have the same stylistic sense that she did, but she never spared me a lecture on how to apply makeup better to suit my features, or which colors and patterns would complement each other more. I listened and took it all in, but I was more of a plain-Jane type of woman. I liked to wear black and white, and natural tones on my face. It made me feel like myself, I suppose.

With vibrancy pouring out of her like rays from the sun, Clara flung her arms around my neck and squeezed the air out of me as if it had been a year, rather than two weeks, since we had seen each other last. "I missed you so much," she spoke loudly into my ear, "my big sister." *Sister.* That word had taken on a different meaning to me in the prior two years, but at the same time, we had grown up together in every way possible, and to me, that was the definition of a sister. We fought like sisters and loved unconditionally like sisters. Nothing else truly mattered, except the meaning of the actual word.

I also often wondered if I had other siblings related by blood. "I'm taking you to lunch today," I told her. "Where should we go?"

"Oh, I love when you treat!" she squealed, looping her arm around my elbow. Clara has remained true to herself throughout her life. She was, and still is, sassy and spunky, through and through. "A new diner just opened up a few blocks down. Want to try it out?"

"That sounds great," I told her, as waves of anxiety buzzed through me as if I had caffeine injected into my veins.

"Something is wrong. What's the matter? Tell me," she said. I didn't realize it was so obvious that what I wanted to talk to her about was really weighing me down. Plus, I wasn't prepared to just say it right there on the street.

"Oh, nothing is wrong. Don't worry. I just wanted your opinion on something," I told her, hoping it would give me a few more minutes to build up my confidence.

"It's about a man. I already know," she said.

"Clara, why in the world would you assume such a thing?"

She glanced over at me with a smirk against her cold-kissed, pink cheeks. "Your eyes opened wider when I said the word 'man.' I know you, Annie. You can't hide anything from me."

She's making this harder by the minute. "We can't talk about this outside. It's too cold," I said, sharply.

Clara grabbed my arm and pulled me into a record store we were passing. "There, now we're not cold, so tell me," she pleaded.

"We need to be somewhere private," I continued, begging for more time, knowing I was losing the battle with each blink I took.

"Excuse me," Clara shouted toward the back of the store where a clerk was sorting through some labels. "Do you mind if my sister and I look through some of your records while we have a private discussion?"

The man looked around with an unexcitable expression. "No one else is in here. Feel free to chit chat all you want. Just don't touch the vinyl."

"Of course. We would never," Clara told the man with a wave of her gloved hand.

"Only part of what I wanted to talk to you about has to do with a man," I told her.

"Oh, good God, you finally have a man in your life. I didn't think the day would ever come. I'm so happy for you, Annie. What's his name?" Her hand was clutching mine with a level of excitement that could have broken my fingers.

"His name is Fisher," I began.

"Oh, he sounds handsome," she said, fanning herself with her clutch.

"Clara, stop, please."

"Where did you meet him?" She asked, trying to sound casual as she flipped through a row of 1940s jazz records.

"I haven't met him, exactly. Not yet," I continued.

"Well, that's ridiculous and impossible. Did you just make him up?" Having a serious conversation with Clara had never been an easy task in our younger years. She was typically one to think in a straight line and had trouble veering off in any other direction.

"He lives in Prague. We have been writing to each other for two years."

She let the stack of records fall toward the back of the rack, and I nervously looked toward the clerk, hoping he didn't hear the racket from his pristine records. "Oh, wow, like a pen pal? You know, I always wondered how people found pen pals. How did you manage to find this Fisher character?" Clara asked me.

"Be careful," I muttered. "I mean, with the records."

She tapped the top of the rack gently and contorted her mouth into a look of concern. "Oops, I'm Sorry."

"Clara, Mom and Dad are not—"

She looked at me with wonder. Her big blue eyes were unknowingly extracting the pain from my soul. I couldn't tell her. It would crush her if she knew I wasn't their real daughter or her real sister. She lived in this bubble of happiness, and Mom and Dad spent their lives trying to protect my heart by keeping the horrible truth from me, and in the same way, I couldn't just destroy her innocence for no reason.

I changed my mind at that moment. It was a secret I had to keep to myself.

"Mom and Dad are not ... what?" she asked, nervously.

I looked around the store for a moment, collecting my thoughts —forming my lie. "They aren't going to let me go to Czechoslovakia to meet Fisher. There's no way I can tell them. I'm leaving next Wednesday. I wanted to tell you because I wanted someone to know where I will be, but I need you to promise me you won't tell them. Please?"

Clara went deathly quiet and began walking toward the front door of the store. "You can't just leave the country and not tell them," Clara said. "What if something were to happen to you over there?"

She pushed the door open and waved her hand in the air. "Thank you, sir," she shouted to the clerk, her words sounding hollow.

"Please, Clara. I need you to understand how important this is to me."

She stopped dead in her tracks and turned to face me. Clara and I were the same height when she was wearing heels, and I had on flat shoes. We were exactly two inches apart, but we were looking each other straight in the eyes at that moment. "How can you ask me to cover for you when you're doing something ridiculous? I love you. I don't want you to go to a foreign country without telling Mom and Dad."

"I need you to trust me," I told her. I wasn't giving her anything else to go on. I just needed her trust, and I needed to trust her.

"Do you love him?" she asked.

Love? I hadn't considered the thought. Fisher and I had been engaging in intellectual conversations about war, peace, and everything in between. He was a missing child of the Holocaust too. I met him through the list of supporters I received from the Terezín

Memorial. He was incredibly supportive, and the only one who responded to the few letters I sent. I'm not even sure if my other letters reached the intended people since I got a few of them back in the mail with *Return to Sender* stamps. "I don't know, maybe. Can you love someone through exchanged letters?"

"I'm not sure," she said. "I haven't tried."

"Please, Clara." For some reason, I needed her approval at that point. I knew what I was doing was wrong, especially since I didn't have a good plan to board the plane without a passport. I would have happily purchased a ticket with the money I had saved for the trip, but I didn't have valid identification. Therefore, I had no choice but to find a way to sneak on. It was not going to be easy, but I needed to go to Prague. I needed to see where my birth parents were from, and where I should have grown up. I needed to see where I was living before I was rescued. I was sure it would fill in some blanks as to who I was, but I couldn't tell Clara that part.

Clara closed her eyes, and her long lashes fluttered over her cheeks as she swallowed loud enough to hear. "Fine. In the name of love, go. Find happiness, but you better come back here, Annie Baylin, or I will come after you myself ... *and* tell Mom and Dad. Do you understand?"

"I promise. I will only be gone a week."

"You need to write to me every single day," she continued.

"Letters probably won't get to you until I get home, though," I argued.

"I still want to know what every second is like, and you may forget by the time you get home."

"Okay, fine."

"Please, Annie, please be safe."

"I will." I was as unsure about the trip as Clara was, but my gut was telling me to go.

~

WHEN I RETURNED to my apartment back in Manhattan at the end of my weekend-long stay with Clara, I took the last letter from Fisher out from the top drawer of my writing desk and laid it out to read once more. I wasn't a rule breaker, but I needed to reassure myself that the trip to Europe was worth the trouble I could get into.

My Dearest Missing Lady,

I can hardly believe this is the last letter I'm sending to the other side of the blue sky, all the way to the United States, before I finally get to meet you. I figured out that we have been exchanging letters for one year and eleven months. Between the two of us, we have sent ninety-nine letters. How have we had so many words to share, yet I won't recognize you when you step off the plane? It has my mind puzzled.

I hope your weekend with your dear sister goes well, and I do hope she understands your desire to visit Europe, with the possible mention of my existence. I will be interested to hear your decision on whether or not you told her about your friend from afar.

On another matter, I remember you mentioning your appreciation for schedules and organization, so I hope you don't mind, but I took it upon myself to act as a tour guide for the duration of your stay here in Prague. It's important that you see all the beauty, as well as the ashes, we spoke about.

I must be honest about something with you because I fear it will be harder to do so once I set my eyes on you. In the last week, I have wondered what your voice might sound like. I have wondered if your "slight" New York accent is truly slight. Being the writer you are, I have considered what your reasons may be for your bland self-descriptions. Your words have managed to make me feel every emotion possible throughout the last two years, yet you have claimed to be simple looking, plain, and neutral. Well, miss, I suspect your humbleness has gotten in the way of reality, but there is only one way to resolve the mystery you are to me. I will happily determine whether you are as simple as you claim to be.

Surprisingly, I don't feel apprehensive about meeting you, as the strangers we have called ourselves, because I'm certain I will feel your presence the moment you are near me. I know your heart well, and somehow, I think I would recognize it out of a whole bunch of other hearts. Your soul, too—it's most definitely brighter than a clear blue sky.

I want to give you a telephone number you can call in case of an emergency. It will connect to the local market down the street from my home, but a friend of mine works there, and if you request me by name, they will fetch me immediately. Just tell them "the missing lady" is calling for me.

I'm hoping you will be daring enough to share your name with me once we meet in person. I have compiled a list of possible names, sheerly for the joy of seeing whether I was able to guess correctly.

Dear, I wish you safe travels. I will be awaiting your arrival on October 3rd at the airport here in Prague.

I have one last thought before I finish this very last letter before I meet the "missing lady." I hope I don't disappoint you when we are no longer strangers from opposite ends of the blue sky.

Sincerely,

Fisher Benson

THE LETTER SMELLED like fresh grass, and I wondered how a weak scent could stick to paper while traveling so far across the world. Maybe I imagined the way he might smell. Our exchange of letters left me with a vivid image of how I thought Fisher might look. That part was, in fact, my imagination, though, because he looked nothing like I thought he would.

He described himself in various ways, but none of the descriptions were detailed enough to paint an immediate picture. The image I formed in my head developed over time as I grew to know more about him and his life.

Fisher and I were born less than a month apart from each other, and though our lives had taken similar paths, his history was quite different from mine at the time.

Reading the letter once again confirmed my decision to take the flight to Prague. Therefore, I spent the next two days packing as many articles of clothing as possible into one bag, including a few outfits Clara had lent me. I spent the other minutes leading up to my trip praying I wouldn't find trouble throughout my travels, despite the foolish way in which I planned to go.

13

1962 - NEW YORK CITY, NY AND PRAGUE, CZECHOSLOVAKIA - 20 YEARS OLD

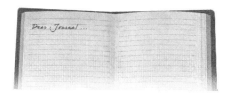

I DIDN'T SLEEP a wink the night before. My nerves kept me awake, and they were still on a high while I was walking through the airport. I had constructed a plan to board the plane without a ticket or identification, but I wasn't too sure how strict the process of checking in might be. I read stories in the newspapers about traveling abroad on an aircraft, so I did my due diligence in looking the part, as well as acting in a certain way—a way in which I wasn't necessarily used to. I didn't consider myself an upper-class woman. Though I was fortunate enough to have my job at the art gallery and was compensated enough to afford a small living space in Manhattan, saving money and purchasing expensive clothes were more of a wish than an occurrence. It took me almost a year to save the money for the airplane ticket until I read about the proper identification requirements needed to board an airplane. I couldn't apply for a passport with a fake birth certificate. It was dangerous to tempt fate by initiating that process with the government. I was afraid of deportation, and Mom and Dad would likely be held responsible for bringing me into the country illegally. Of course, it was purely my speculation, due to the lack of available information, but I was trying to avoid unnecessary trouble.

My heels click-clacked through the terminal, and it was sooner, rather than later, that I spotted the sign for the outbound flight with a destination of Prague. I had been eyeing that flight for the previous few weeks, in the little travel agency down the street from my apartment, which allowed me to preplan everything. That particular flight wouldn't be reoccurring for another two weeks, so I arrived early, though it wouldn't help much without a boarding ticket.

I waited until a woman dressed in a neat uniform called for boarding. I spotted over a dozen people walking through the door behind her before I made my approach. I jogged up to her, nearly twisting my ankles in the heels I was wearing. "Goodness, are you all right?" the woman asked.

"No, no, I'm so sorry. My family already boarded the flight. I told them I had to use the ladies' room, but I thought I had my boarding pass on me. One of them must have it in with theirs." The lies pouring from my mouth gave me a rush, one I wasn't sure I should like.

The woman placed her gloved hand on my shoulder. "Don't you worry about a thing. I think I know which family you're talking about. Go on in. I'm sure they're worried about you."

"Thank you so very much," I told her, while fanning myself to hide the sweat forming all over my body. Of course, she thought it was nerves due to being separated from my family, but in any case, I was certain it would be clear sailing from there to Prague.

The airplane was not overfilled, and I didn't have trouble finding a seat next to a family of three. I wanted to hide all suspicion for any of the staff members working on the airplane.

They didn't seem concerned with my presence at any given time throughout the long flight. I hate to say the process of

96

sneaking onto that flight was easy, making me wonder how often other people did the same thing for various reasons.

As the hours passed, I felt a sense of ease from my fear of being caught as a stowaway. Instead of focusing on the consequences, my thoughts began to center on the pungent scent of cigarette and cigar smoke. I had never been aboard an airplane before, and though I had an idea of what to expect, I thought the trip would have a more sophisticated feel to it, especially since I read about the proper flying attire. I knew I would reek of smoke once I disembarked from the plane, but at least I was on my way to where I wanted to be.

Food and drinks were served in abundance, and between my several naps and journal entries, the hours were ticking by, but every minute felt like an eternity before we arrived at our destination.

I had managed to remain lucky throughout my scheme of flying internationally, and the moment I stepped off the plane, I felt free of the trouble and fears I would have to face once again for my return to the United States. However, I promised myself I wouldn't think about that process until it was time.

The passengers deplaned on the tarmac, where guests of passengers stood waiting in a sectioned-off space about a hundred yards from the airplane's exit.

My tired legs carried me the distance toward the crowd, and I recited the words from Fisher's letter, reminding me we had no way of truly recognizing each other's faces.

In my last letter to him, I said I would be wearing a blue, A-line coat, black patent knee-high boots, and a burgundy scarf. I didn't know what he would be wearing, though.

Sudden thoughts of what he may look like were fogging up my mind. I wanted to stay positive about the idea of meeting the man whom I had become quite attached to throughout the prior two years. The person I was didn't care much about another person's looks, but at that moment, I became fearful that he may be so hideous, I couldn't bear to look him in the eyes. That would have been horrible, after all that time spent exchanging letters and flying across the world.

I probably did deserve some sort of punishment after sneaking onto an airplane without much concern. Therefore, I was certain I would pay a consequence sooner or later for my behavior.

"The beautiful missing lady in her burgundy satin scarf." A deep, raspy voice startled me from behind. His words were well enunciated, but slow, as if he were trying his best to speak clearly. I didn't turn around right away. Fear of the unknown was holding me hostage, and the trepidation prevented me from moving my body an inch in any direction.

From the way he sounded, my predetermined image of Fisher changed from a slender man to one with more meat on his bones. I'm not sure why I imagined he would be tall and thin. It didn't make sense to assume such a thing, considering he worked long days on a farm.

"Fisher?" I questioned, still facing away.

"Yes, miss," he said, with less of a boom to his voice that time.

I don't know why I couldn't get myself to turn around faster. I wanted to hold onto my preconceived thoughts for just another minute.

"You must be afraid of what I look like, yes?" Fisher asked, but with a hint of sarcasm to his question.

"No, not at all," I replied, which wasn't exactly the truth, but I was also scared of falling a little deeper for him. Unless of course, he looked like a rat; then I might have a problem. "Looks are merely skin deep. I don't care if you're missing an eye, or your nose." It was how I had managed to think of people throughout my life, and I had to say it out loud to remind myself, as well as informing him of how I should be feeling inside, rather than the opposite.

"Well, I can tell you it takes two good working eyes to see the fine details of your beauty, even if only from behind your head. You also smell like vanilla, and it's lovely."

The way Fisher said vanilla made the thought of the scent and taste more exotic than I had ever known it to be. The one word was enough to unhinge my frozen body, so I could finally face the man I knew better than any friend I'd ever had before. I knew English was not his first language, but his letters were written perfectly. I could hear the struggle, even though it sounded beautiful.

I gasped unintentionally after I turned around and got a quick look at him, immediately blinded by his exquisite charm and handsome physique. He looked like no one I had seen before. I tried to take him in, inch by inch, as quickly as I could, but it was impossible. It would have been like trying to see each piece of art in a museum within a short period of time. That would be quite impossible.

His hair was dark, longer for a man. He had a mixture of curls and waves tucked behind his ears, which scooped upward above his square shoulders. Fisher's eyes were the color of cinnamon, deep set, and darkly shadowed by his thick, but tamed eyebrows. His nose was long but squared off at that tip, which was complementary to his wide, dimpled grin.

He hovered over me by almost a foot, it seemed, and though he was slender, he was not thin. He had a broad frame and a narrow waist, which I assumed came from a farmer's daily regimen. He was dressed in worn clothes, a plaid shirt, and tan-colored pants with patches of dirt stains.

Fisher must have caught my gaze as I noticed the dirt because he looked down to see what caught my eye. "I just came from work. I hope you can pardon my looks. I wanted time to shower and clean up, but I was worried I might be late. We had a—ah—big load of eggs to send out today, and it took much longer than I thought it would."

"No pardons necessary," I told him, feeling the need to fan myself. My next thought was horrifying. What if he was disappointed in the way I looked? The thought hadn't crossed my mind until that very moment.

"You are as lovely as I imagined," he said. His cheeks turned a faint shade of red, and I felt mine react in the same way. "I am a bit nervous. As I'm sure you know, I'm not one who usually has a lack of words, but my spoken English is not perfect, and I feel like you have stolen my ability to talk."

"I'm a bit nervous, myself." After two years of feeling like there wasn't enough paper in the world to suit the amount of words I needed to share with Fisher, I was also short on thoughts at that moment.

"Come, let us leave the crowd of travelers, shall we?"

"Yes, please, I'd like that." I didn't tell Fisher what it would take for me to fly across the seas. I was afraid of what he might think of me, so I kept the details about purchasing an airline ticket to a minimum.

"I want to hear all about your trip. I've always wanted to fly, but the cost is brutal, especially for a farmer. Still, someday, I will. I will see that sky up close."

"It was beautiful, though not as smooth as I imagined it might be. It was quite a bumpy ride, to be honest."

Again, our conversation fell short as we made our way toward the airport's exit. Fisher looked over at me every few seconds, but I wasn't sure if he was checking on me or appraising me. I had a thought that he may have just been saying kind things, since I had flown so far, but I figured time would tell. Plus, I couldn't lose sight of the fact that I had another significant purpose for my trip besides meeting Fisher.

I was home.

14

CURRENT DAY

"I HATE that I felt like I was home when I got there," I tell mom.

"Home is where your family is, Annie," Mom corrects me.

"I didn't mean home in the sense that my house and family were there. I meant it in a habitat kind of way. It was where God intended me to be. Was it not?"

"Ladies," Charlie interrupts. "I don't mean to interrupt, but it's almost lunchtime, and if I don't get there on time—"

"We know." Mom and I mirror each other in response.

"They have corned beef sandwiches today," Charlie continues.

"I won't keep you," I tell them, taking my bag from beside my feet. "I'll be back tomorrow, same time as normal." When I stand from the chair, a sense of weightlessness fills me like it hasn't before. My secret had been long overdue for sharing, just as well as Mom's.

"You are never 'keeping us,' Annie," Mom says, as she slowly stands from the seat she made on the wooden coffee table. "Annie?"

I stand as well, greeted by the warm sun filtering in through the partially opened blinds. "Yes, Mom?"

"I'm glad you took that trip. I wouldn't have agreed to it, but I'm sure it was something that offered you peace of mind."

"It gave me more than peace of mind. It showed me the truth. In some ways, seeing it was harder than hearing it, but in other ways, it was necessary for understanding."

"I'm not sure I follow," Mom says. "If you went all that way and found some understanding, why were you uncertain about your given name?"

"There was no way to confirm who I was, so I researched the three possible families with a child born on the same day as me, finding some information, but nothing definitive."

Mom's lips tighten into a firm, straight line. "I see," she says. "I'm sorry you weren't able to find any bloodlines. If you had just told me—"

I shake my head. "You were in denial, Mom, and you were set in your ways of keeping me safe from the truth. If I learned anything from you over the years, it was never to waste a moment arguing with a woman who has far more worldly knowledge than I ever will."

"Well," she says with a sigh, her hand pressed to her chest. "Be that as it may, I can say one thing with certainty ..."

"What's that?"

"I may not have given birth to you, but I will selfishly own some claim over teaching you to fight for what you believe in, even if it's against your parents' wishes."

I walk a bit closer to where Mom is standing, needing to embrace her small body. "What I did was wrong. Sneaking onto an airplane and leaving home without a word to you—I won't forget what desperation led me to, and I'm sorry for that."

"Darling," she says, pinching my chin between her fingers with her firm grip. "We have all done things we aren't proud of, but not everything we set out to do will coincide with society's regulations. Some rules are intended to be broken. It's your life, Annie. I have told you countless times to paint what you see in your mind because no one can argue with an artists' entitlement to see the world in a different light than everyone else."

"You have, and I tried," I say, softly.

"You succeeded, my dear." She leans forward and places a kiss on my cheek. "I'll see you tomorrow, sweetheart."

"Until tomorrow, kiddo," Charlie says with a quick wink, waving Mom toward the door with urgency.

Mom rolls her eyes and shakes her head. "Men."

I follow them out into the hallway, closing the door behind me. They walk, hand in hand, muttering to each other, then laughing about whatever was said. Charlie places his arm around Mom's shoulders and squeezes her.

It's hard to believe she has known Charlie all this time but went so long without him. Life isn't fair, but some things are certainly worth waiting for, I suppose.

"Please, please, please, tell me you brought home some sandwiches from the deli. I ran out of pastrami and salami yesterday, and I forgot to mention it to you," Fisher says as I step inside the front door.

"You know, you sound like a starved child," I tell him. "You also know I have my phone, read your text message, and responded, right?"

"Is that what I think it is in the bag?"

"Fisher," I groan with laughter.

He stands up from his recliner and makes his way over to me with a cocked brow and his head tilted to one side. "How did things go with your mum?"

"Were you trying to distract me?" I ask him, handing over the bag from the deli.

"No, I've been worried sick about you for the last three hours, and I texted you for a sandwich, but I really just wanted to make sure you were still upright."

I slap him against the arm. "Fisher, you know my mother is elderly, and she would never lay a hand on me, you nut."

"I was worried, just simply worried, okay?"

"Worried that I was going to find out I was someone else and not love you anymore?" We've been together for so long, I can usually read his thoughts before he's finished thinking them through. I can only imagine what crazy thoughts have been lingering in his head.

"It's been so long, Annie. The number of 'what-ifs' running through my brain has had my stomach in knots since you left."

I place my hand on Fisher's back, staring up into his beautiful, cinnamon brown eyes, then urging him toward the kitchen. "By the way, I went grocery shopping yesterday and replaced your sandwich meats," I tell him. "Next time you text message me for an 'utter food emergency,' check the refrigerator first," I say, chuckling at the adorable way he has always acted when feeling nervous.

"Right, that," he says. "Anyway, I need to hear everything, Annie—everything. You can't leave one part out."

"I promise," I tell him.

"You still love me, right?" he asks.

My head falls to the side, and I gaze up at the look of concern on Fisher's face. I don't understand why he would think anything could make me stop loving him. I place my hands on his face, realizing how cold they must be since he's so warm in comparison. Fisher places his hands on top of mine in response, still giving a questioning look.

"You're freezing," he says.

"I'm warm because I'm home with you," I explain. "Fisher, sweetheart, learning my given name doesn't change anything between us. Even if I learned my name during my trip to Prague, it wouldn't have changed what we have—or what we've grown to have. You and I—we're a completely different story. You know that."

Fisher places a soft kiss on my nose and pulls me in against his chest, wrapping me with a firm embrace. "You are my world, Annie—my whole world."

"I always will be, no matter what we go through." He places another kiss on the top of my head and takes a seat at the table, pulling the plastic bag toward him.

"That's dinner," I confirm. "I just told you the deli meat is in the refrigerator. Your mind is worse off than mine today. My goodness!" I tend to the refrigerator and retrieve the sandwich meats, then the loaf of bread from the bread box. As soon as I place everything down on the table, Fisher redirects his focus onto the food. He eats when he's nervous. It's a good thing he's naturally calm spirited, I guess.

I can't keep my recently learned information to myself any longer, though. I can't wait until Fisher's had the chance to put his sandwich together before I spit it out as if it were something spicy on the tip of my tongue. "Lucie Sigel is my birth name. My birth mother was executed in Theresienstadt."

Fisher covers his mouth, and his eyes widen in response to the influx of information that will be harder to digest than the sandwich. It doesn't sound like much when said out loud, but it is clarification for a lot of my life's gaps that he has endured along with me. It's a mystery that has defined much of my life.

"It's not that I'm surprised," he says. "I—it's—we assumed wrong, didn't we?"

I didn't think I was Lucie. I never had. The other two babies born the same day had relatives I was able to find photographs of. Zaila's family had darker skin by more than a couple shades, so I had a hard time believing I could be blood related to them. There were no photographs of anyone in Lucie's family, and there wasn't a last name listed. I wanted to believe I couldn't be her, only because I knew it was highly unlikely I would find any history or relatives.

Annika, though ... some of the photographs I found from her family had viable similarities, ones I could match up to my features. I was sure my name was simply shortened to Annie, even though Mom had never taken shortcuts, and if she were trying to protect me, I had a hard time believing she would merely shorten my name and keep the rest of the information hidden. Still, it was the name I had in the back of my mind.

"I'm not Annika Baron," I confirm. "I'm Lucie Sigel."

Fisher looks a bit lost, or like he's replaying my words in his head for clarification. "We know your name, sweetie," he says with a sound of distress.

He drops the food from his hands and rushes out of the kitchen, moving faster than I've seen him move in months. He's gotten a bit lazy since retiring from the fire department, and there has been a lack of spunk in his step, but he can still move when motivation hits.

"Where are you going?" I call out.

He returns a moment later with his laptop. Neither of us have touched the darn thing in months. I'm not big on technology, and it took Fisher far too long to learn how to send a text message, never mind finding his way around a computer. We have the laptop because my niece, Emma, gave us her hand-me-down when she bought a new one for herself. She told me to use Google when I'm looking for information or want to write, but I haven't been looking for much recently, and I still prefer hand writing my thoughts.

"How does this thing turn on?" Fisher says, plugging it into the wall.

"The power button, dear," I reply.

"Very funny ... would you be so kind as to show me *where* the power button is?"

Once the laptop is plugged in, a green light illuminates, acting as an arrow to the power button, but I reach over anyway and press it for him. "There you go."

"Gee, thanks," he says with a chuckle.

"What exactly are you planning to do with the laptop?"

"I'm going to Google your name," he says, as if it should have been obvious. It is obvious, though I'm suddenly not sure I'm ready to see what shows up on the search pages. I'm afraid I'll be disappointed when the search returns with no information.

"I don't know ... Fisher. I'm not sure I want to know anything more than my name right now."

Fisher doesn't respond to me. Instead, he continues the search, and my stomach begins to churn, so I take a seat next to him, but I continue to keep my focus away from the laptop's screen. "I don't think I want to know if you don't find anything. Just don't say anything, and close the stupid thing back up, okay?"

"I think your birth dad is still alive, Annie. At least, it looks like he is." For someone who has a hard time using technology, he has figured out how to use the search button pretty quickly—so quickly, my brain hasn't caught up to what he just said to me.

"I'm sorry, what was that?"

"Your mother's name ... was it—"

"Lea—" I try to say her name but stumble.

"Leah Sigel," Fisher completes my words.

"Yes, Leah Sigel," I confirm.

"Leah and Benjamin Sigel of Litomyšl, in what was then Bohemia. They had a daughter, Lucie Sigel, but they were taken to Theresienstadt as prisoners, shortly before their daughter was born."

"Where did you find that?" I shout. I have spent years and years searching for answers on Lucie and Annika. I never gave up researching either of them, but nothing ever came across for Lucie, though I didn't have a last name until now.

"It was an article written by your birth father. The passage I just read was his biography blurb."

"My father was a writer?" I ask, feeling an extreme tightness in my chest. It's hard to breathe. I pull my blouse away from my neck, feeling strangled by the air around me.

"He was a writer as of March, this year. I can search to see if he has written anything since."

"Wait," I gasp. "What does the article say?"

"Annie, you look pale," he tells me. I can feel the blood draining from my face. This is impossible. There are so few survivors left in the world now. How can he be one of them? How can I be one of them? How could we have gone our whole lives being two of them, yet never knowing each other?

"It's not possible," I say again, but out loud this time.

"What isn't possible?"

"It's not, Fisher. It's not."

"Annie, you need to sit down."

"I can't breathe," I tell him. My throat feels tight, and my chest is heavy, like there's a weight resting on it.

"Annie!" he shouts.

15

1962 - PRAGUE, CZECHOSLOVAKIA - 20 YEARS OLD

DAY ONE IN PRAGUE

I COULDN'T fathom how a place encompassing so much beauty was used as a prison to hold thousands of innocent people. Fisher has been kind enough to take me on a sightseeing tour of the area. He promised not to skip anything, even the unimportant landmarks. We were saving Terezín Memorial for later in the week, since he felt I needed time to adjust after traveling so far.

I reached into my handbag and pulled out a small piece of notepaper I had been holding onto for several months. "I'd like to see this neighborhood, if it's in our travels," I said, handing him the address.

"What's there that interests you?" Fisher asked.

"It took me a while to find the information, but this is where my mother grew up."

"Amelia, right?" he confirmed which mother I was talking about, but he shook his head immediately after asking. "Obviously, that's who you were talking about." I had no other information on my birth mom.

"Yes," I agreed with a smile, to show I wasn't sensitive to the confusion of having two mothers. After the last couple of years, the thought had become somewhat normal in my head.

"Oddly enough, my parents didn't live too far from this location either, so I've visited the area many times, curious as to what life could have been like if I had not carried on as a missing child."

"Do you mind if we sit for a moment?" I asked. My legs were becoming tired from the hours of walking we had done, and my shoes were not the best for cobblestone roads or distance, but we had at least dropped my bags off at The Inn, where I was staying for the week.

"Of course not; I don't mind," he said, pointing ahead to a clearing. We strolled to the nearby bench that was nestled between some trees, overlooking a picturesque field filled with wheat and flowers. "You must be—eh, uh tired, or exhausted?" I could tell he had been struggling with his English throughout that day, which he did warn me about in our letters. He said the writing was easier since he could look up words and reread what he wrote, but speaking out loud was different and more challenging, though he wasn't too shabby for just learning English within the prior few years.

"Tired or exhausted, both work just fine," I told him. "They mean essentially the same thing, and yes, I am very tired, but I don't want to waste a moment here."

I fixed my coat over my knees and pressed my palms into the soft wood of the bench to stretch my arms. "Fisher, I'm curious about you. We've spoken for so long, yet I feel like there is a greater part of your story I haven't heard yet. Am I correct?"

Fisher pulled in a deep, contemplative breath and settled back against the bench. "I have told you most of what I know about my past. Other parts I left out are just—those moments I still know nothing about," he explained.

"So, your mother was taken away, and your father tried to

escape with you, but you said your father didn't make it, which left me a bit confused. How did you survive as a baby if a soldier caught your father?"

I gazed at him as the words finished pouring out of my mouth. The questions sounded more forward than I intended, but I could tell he was as numb to the puzzle as I had become. Questions were simply words that may or may not have resulted in an answer. There was no effect or consequence because there wasn't an answer that could make much difference.

"Ah, yes," he said, meeting my gaze. "You asked that question, but I failed to respond, yeah? I did have a reason for brushing around the subject."

"I see," I responded immediately, not wanting to push for an answer he may not want to give.

"As soon as I was old enough to write my name, I was forced into a—ah note, or a—ah contract to abide by the privacy of the home that was caring for me."

"The home, meaning the family who took you in?" I tried to follow, feeling as though I missed a fact along the way.

"I wasn't taken in by a family. It was more of a group home that took care of orphaned children. According to what I was told, my father had attempted our escape just a short time before April in 1945."

"Liberation?" I confirmed.

"Correct. There are only a few known cases of people managing to escape the camps, and we weren't any of those lucky ones. It's been said that any person who attempted an escape was immediately … you know …" he slid his finger across his throat, and the visual packed a punch.

I was trying not to ask too many questions, for fear of overstepping my bounds. I also realized he knew I *was* one of the lucky ones who was saved through a successful escape. I wasn't sure how I would feel toward him if the tables were turned, but I concluded that the result wouldn't have been much different. We both lost our parents. "After all the effort it must have taken to try and save you, the thought must ..." There were no positive words to use, and I couldn't think of the right statement. I was tongue-tied at the thought of knowing what his father went through for him, only to be taken away.

He shook his head. "I was still lucky. After the camp was liberated, I was taken by one of the few nurses who took care of the separated children, and I was left with that home for orphans. It could have been far worse ... far, far worse."

Fisher was left with no one. I wasn't. "You were never adopted?" I could assume that, based on the lack of information he offered on the subject. Even if he wasn't allowed to speak of the orphanage, he would mention a family taking him in ... I would think.

"No one who wanted to take in a child, had the space, money, or time, and Jewish children over the age of two weren't wanted as much as a new baby. Some were adopted, but to be honest," he said, cupping his hand around his mouth, "I don't think I was a very pretty baby. I was a bit chubby, from what I was told."

"That's terrible to say. Chubby babies are as adorable, if not cuter, than non-chubby babies," I argued.

"Be that as it may, I wasn't adopted by a family, so I lived at the orphanage until I was old enough for work. That's when I quickly took matters into my own hands and started the farm work. The owners allowed me some space above one of the barns, and I made do for a couple of years until I saved up enough money for a flat."

In comparison, I looked like I had won a big contest—one that was composed of riches and the pleasures of a first-world country. "Your journey is quite amazing, seeing as you are sitting here with a smile on your face."

"I'm alive," he said, simply. "That ... is the amazing part."

I was enamored by his strength, and curious how a child could be so determined to survive without any low-hanging fruit to reach for. "What did you dream about back then?"

"Dream?" He countered with a look of surprise. At first, I wondered if he didn't understand what I meant by a dream, but he was quick to prove me wrong. "I was living a dream. What else could I dream about?"

Confusion struck me. He had nothing, yet he had to find his own way. "You were an orphan. How could that have been a dream?"

He unfolded his arms and stretched them out along the back side of the bench. With a sigh of contentment, he continued, "You see, dreams are what find us when we experience the unimaginable. This moment ... right now ... is a dream, Annie."

I twist my body to face him, intrigued by his statement. "This moment is a dream?" I questioned, feeling as though I were floating off the bench.

"Most definitely," he said with confidence.

"I love the meaning you are using it for, but aside from this moment being surreal, don't you think a dream is like a subconscious wish? If so, how could you control such thoughts?"

"I suppose you're right, in theory. A dream is what we consider to be hope of a future possibility, but if I had survived through hell and got to keep all my fingers and toes, I knew I shouldn't be selfish enough to dream of more—not when I felt grateful for what I had. I—ah, considered that between God and the universe, I was meant to live, so in return, I made a conscious choice to let life determine what else I was destined for."

"Wow," I said, feeling at a loss for words and unable to respond to such an intelligent explanation.

"It is like a good book, Annie. When you're halfway through the excerpts, you don't want to imagine what words exist on the last page. It could ruin the entire story. I don't know about you, but I want to experience the last page after the journey. Right?"

He was staring out into an endless wheat field, seemingly lost in his thoughts. As for me, I was feeling caught between Fisher's words, wondering how someone who was left to survive with the mere essentials could be so intelligent and worldly. "You're truly brilliant," I told him.

Fisher broke his stare free from the blur between the sky and land. He looked over at me and smiled shyly. "No, I am not brilliant. I have just had a lot of time to think about life."

"Your thoughts are poetic," I told him. They gave me chills all over my skin, even though I was warm inside my coat.

"I'm glad I found your name," I told him. "I felt lost when I learned where I had come from. I was desperate for understanding and a sense of belonging. I knew it wasn't a feeling I would experience at home, not with the truths being hidden and locked away."

Fisher stood up from the bench and offered me his hand. "Come, I want to show you something."

As if I were in a trance, I didn't think twice before handing him my gloved hand. He wasn't wearing a coat, and I could feel a chill from his fingers seep through the thin material covering mine. His grip was strong and confident. It made me feel safe and less alone.

"When I registered myself with the memorial after finding out I was still marked as missing, they asked me if I would be willing to be a support contact for others in the same situation. At first, the idea didn't sit well with me. It was hard enough to comprehend what my life had become and why, so I wasn't sure if I was capable of helping anyone else. However, I had wished there was someone to help me through those rough years of brutal realization, so I offered to help, knowing what that could mean."

"You did a good thing, Fisher. People need a supportive person like you."

"That was the odd thing, though. Three years passed before I received a letter from a person seeking support," he said.

Three years? I had assumed children of the war must have been showing up more and more as time passed and our generation grew in the understanding of what happened. "Well, it's nice that you were there for that person when the letter came in, even if it was three years later. I'm sure they were relieved to have you in their life."

"Oh, yes, I think she was relieved. She was a sweet girl ... lost ... and trying to find her way in the world. What gave me a chuckle though, was that the girl I was offering support to ended up helping me more than I think I helped her."

We were walking uphill during our conversation, and my breaths were strained from the resistance, but I was too interested in what he had to say, to interrupt and explain to him that I was wearing the wrong shoes to climb such a steep hill. "I doubt that. I'm sure your conversations with her were more meaningful to her than you seem to be giving yourself credit for."

"Who knows? I just felt a kindred bond with her immediately. It was like our souls were meant to be connected. Maybe we were supposed to be in each other's lives from the start, but the war damaged that opportunity. It proved to me that if there is such a thing as a predetermined plan for our lives, that lonely girl was supposed to be a part of mine."

I stopped walking, feeling something different from I had a moment earlier. I began to wonder who he was talking about. He never mentioned a girl to me before. I suddenly feared he was a serial support mentor who reeled women in with his caring words. "What was her name?" I asked.

"Oh, she wasn't sure what her name was."

It was then that I realized I still hadn't offered him my name. "Where did she live?"

"New York, in the United States."

"I see," I said, feeling a flutter in my heart, considering the possibility of helping a man who had graciously put himself out there to help others, when he was in the exact same situation, if not worse. He seemed like an angel.

"When I finally saw her for the first time, I knew that connection I had felt through our words was something more. It was like dynamite. My heart swelled like it had never done so before. She was the most beautiful woman I had ever seen in my life, and for a moment, I wondered if I was imagining things."

"The most beautiful woman?" I asked with a raised brow, as we continued walking up the hill.

Fisher placed his hand over his chest. "My goodness, she had these exotic eyes, shaped like sideways teardrops. Her face—oh my, the creamy complexion of her skin accented the redness of her perfect cupid-bow lips. She was so—ah—regal looking, a sight of perfection, really."

I placed the tips of my fingers over my lips, wondering what "cupid-bow lips" meant. "I didn't tell you my name yet, did I?"

We reached the top of the hill between my question and his response. In the same moment, I realized why he wanted to take me up there. It was just a simple hill, but it overlooked the entire city of Prague. "No, I believe, I'm still referring to you as the lady without a name," he snickered.

I tried to hide the smile, forcing a puckered sensation in my cheeks. "This is beautiful," I said.

"Yes, this kind of beauty is rare," he replied, looking only at me. "You, however, are far more beautiful than a city."

I was too nervous to look at him. It was much easier to keep my sight set on the golden sun liquifying into the city skyline. I found the picturesque scene mesmerizing, knowing it was so chilly throughout the day, yet the rays from the very same sun were so hot, they looked like wavering oil slicks of air bouncing off the horizon. "My name is Annie Baylin, but that isn't my given name, as you know."

"Annie," he repeated, "beautiful Annie."

It took me a moment to find the courage to look over at him, but when I did, I saw the blurry reflection of the city in his eyes. "I want to say it takes more than a few lovely compliments to capture my attention, but no one has ever said anything quite like you just did … if you were, in fact, speaking about me being the first person to reach out to you for support."

Fisher placed his hands on my shoulders as his eyes tilted toward his temples, forming the look of a smile without moving his mouth. "You are the first person to reach out for my support. You are also the beautiful, nameless woman I was describing. Annie, I wanted to tell you how attractive you were before I saw you. There is so much beauty inside your heart, I couldn't fathom the possibility of seeing anything different on the outside. Of course, I refrained from writing compliments on your looks, in fear of sounding odd."

His laughter eased the tension building within my nerves. Being so close to a man I had just met in person seemed inappropriate, yet I knew him, and I knew him well. My thoughts felt like a garbled mess in my head. "I don't feel worthy of the nice comments you have been showering me with," I told him.

"Worthy? You are standing here in front of me because you found a friend in me. You are the first person to find *me* worthy, or so you stated in one of your letters. That places you at a fairly high standing in my book."

"Well, then I suppose we're both worthy of each other's company. I just—I'm not sure I'm good enough—"

"Annie, with all due respect, please stop talking." I should have been able to foretell what was about to happen, but I was so caught up in his words, his thoughts, the sights, and where the day had led us, that I didn't consider the next moment in time.

The warm sensation of his lips lightly pressed against mine, causing a startled gasp in my lungs. His mouth was so soft, and his touch was gentler than I could have imagined. I was frozen, unable to move. I could only focus on my pulse racing, my heart pounding, and my stomach felt like it was twisting and turning. Fisher's hands reached up and cupped my cheeks. The cold sensation of his skin felt foreign against the heat building inside me, and I hoped I was offering him the same kind of warmth.

I didn't know a kiss could be the connection of two souls finally uniting in a way they were destined to be, but the instant Fisher's lips touched mine, his theory of fate made sense to me.

Time seemed to stand still while we held each other in what felt like an undeniably needed embrace. We were both shivering against each other. The air was certainly a bit crisp, but I wasn't shaking from the cold. My chills were caused purely by the excitement I felt throughout my body.

I pulled away when it felt necessary to catch my breath, and I covered my mouth with the back of my hand, wondering what might have happened to the lipstick I applied several hours earlier. He tugged my hand away and ran his thumb under my bottom lip. "Still perfect," he said.

"I've never felt this way before," I told him. "I'm warm and cold at the same time, and I feel like this isn't real. I feel like this is a—"

"Dreams are what is happening in the present," he said, responding to the statement I didn't complete. Fisher placed his arm around my shoulders and pulled me in front of him. "If you're curious about dreams and surreality, look toward the horizon."

The sun was almost completely gone, except for a faint glowing line that separated the sky from the city. "One ... two ... three," he whispered in my ear.

The lights in the city began to light up, what seemed like one at a time. "How did you know that would happen at this very moment?" I asked quietly, afraid my whisper was too loud for the peaceful silence around us.

"When the sun sets, the city lights up with a type of grace that can only try to compete with the sun."

"I don't know if I can ever return home after this," I told him. I had never seen such a sight, and I had grown up in New York City. Maybe, he would feel the same way about the sights in America, but the foreign feeling of everything in front of me and behind me, was overwhelming—spellbinding.

16

CURRENT DAY

A GENTLE STROKE along my cheek pulls me from a state of exhaustion, and I open my eyes, quickly looking around, as I don't recall falling asleep. I'm even more startled when I don't recognize where I am. "What's going on?" I ask, peering down at my arm that feels oddly constrained. There's tape and— "Why is there an IV in my arm?"

I look around, finding Fisher by my side, holding my free hand. "Shh, it's okay," he says with a calming smile.

"Am I in a hospital?" I know I'm in a hospital. It's evident by my surroundings, but why am I in a hospital? That's what I really want to know.

"It was just an anxiety attack. I overreacted," Fisher says.

"You overreacted?" I repeat.

"You blacked out, sweetheart. I caught you, thankfully, but you scared me."

The memory of what caused my blackout is coming back to me. The thoughts are creeping into the depths of my soul as if they are emerging from the dead.

My name.

My birth father.

Comprehension.

I push myself up to a more comfortable seated position. "You didn't call my mother, did you?" If anything in the world could give me a heart attack, it would be the thought of her panicking because she doesn't have control over this situation.

"Annie, I didn't just meet you or your mother yesterday. There isn't anything she could do unless I pick her up, anyway, so there was certainly no point in worrying her."

"Thank God," I say with a long exhale.

"I might have called Clara, though," he says, wincing. When did he develop all those fine lines on his face? When did we reach a place in our lives when we have to worry about having heart attacks, rather than anxiety attacks? I don't feel that old. I don't want to be old. I want to go back to the time where I had a full life ahead of me. Better yet, I'd rather go back to a time when everything in my life was free of mystery, but I'm not quite sure when that would be.

"Why would you call Clara?" I ask him, unable to hide my frustration.

"Well—"

"How's my favorite patient doing?" Jackson, my nephew-in-law, walks in with his normal ear-to-ear grin.

"Do you say that to all your patients?" I ask him.

"Aunt Annie, please throw me a bone here. Thankfully, only one of you are in my hospital at a time, so I can call each of you my favorites. As for the other patients, though, it makes them feel better to know I'm caring about them, so—"

"Yeah, yeah," I say, shooing my hand at him.

"Your blood work all came back normal. Fisher says you've had a lot of overwhelming life events happening lately, so I believe you experienced an anxiety attack. I'm going to suggest the name of a therapist for you to speak to, so you can stay on top of your stress level, okay?"

"Whoa, whoa, hold your horses, mister. I don't have anxiety."

Jackson presses his lips together and folds his hands behind his back. The look on his face tells me he is waiting for me to take back what I said. "Annie, you fainted from an anxiety attack, right?"

"I'm having an off day. I'm allowed to have a day, Jackson."

Jackson pulls his stool up to the side of the bed and sits down. "I'm not telling you what to do. I'm just making a suggestion and giving you a name," he says.

"You told Emma I was here, didn't you?" I ask him.

"She's your niece and my wife. If I didn't tell her, and she found out later, do you know what I would be having for dinner tonight?"

"Emma doesn't get angry at you," I correct him. "She still gazes at you like you walk on water."

"Oh, she gets mad at me, Annie. You know what she does when she's mad? She makes meatloaf for dinner. Yeah, so, trust me … she gets mad."

"What's wrong with meatloaf?" Fisher asks. I look over at Fisher with a raised brow, finding him looking back and forth between Jackson and me. "What? I don't get it."

"Emma isn't the best cook," I tell him.

"Plus, I hate meatloaf," Jackson adds in.

"I've never had a bad meatloaf," Fisher says.

"Fisher, you would eat the hospital food here and say it was the best meal you've ever had."

"Is there any food here? I didn't get to eat my sandwich, and I'm still hungry." Fisher is asking Jackson, and I'm nodding my head with embarrassment.

"No, we're not looking for food. We're leaving," I announce as I tear the blanket from my legs. "Where are my clothes?"

Before anyone can answer me, Emma and Clara come running, frantically, around the corner. "I told you two not to come down here. There's nothing to worry about—she's fine," Fisher says.

"It's Annie," Emma and Clara say in unison.

"It's so hard to tell they are mother and daughter sometimes,"

Jackson says with a chuckle. I'm glad he hasn't gotten tired of the family drama yet.

"You should not be getting worked up, Emma. You could put yourself in early labor. My God," I tell her.

"She's not going into labor anytime soon," Jackson argues. "Our little girl hasn't dropped yet," he says, cooing at Emma's stomach. The sight of the two of them makes my throat clench, but not for a reason either would understand. I need to leave before another anxiety attack comes out of nowhere.

"I want to leave now," I tell everyone.

"Annie, what caused this?" Clara asks.

"Nothing, I was just—"

Fisher is peering down, twiddling his thumbs, looking quite guilty because he cannot lie, not if his life depended on it. I don't know how he manages to keep secrets, but lies are a completely different story. "What is it?" Clara asks Fisher, rather than me.

"It's not the best time," he says.

"Are you okay?" Clara asks me, panicking as she nearly throws herself on top of me. "Are you sick?"

"If I was sick, you would have just finished me off. Get up, Clara." How a grown woman manages to act younger than her daughter sometimes, blows my mind, but Clara hasn't changed much since she was Emma's age.

"I will tell you everything later, okay? I just want to go home and rest. I am fine. That's all that matters."

"You know she won't sleep until you tell her," Emma says.

"You didn't tell Mom, did you?" I ask Clara.

"No ... no, of course I didn't." Clara tucks her golden hair behind her ear, which means she's lying.

I breathe another sigh of relief. "That's wonderful. Now, please leave so I can get my clothes on. I will call you later to talk."

"Promise me?" Clara asks through pursed lips as she crosses her arms over her chest.

"I promise," I mutter.

Jackson wraps his hand around Emma's wrist and places a kiss on her forehead. "I'll be home in a few hours. Next time I tell you not to worry, please listen to me, baby ... love of my life ... sweet-ums." The uneasy smile on his face tells me he's probably been walking on eggshells around Emma lately thanks to those feisty pregnancy hormones. She has been an emotional basket-case for the last seven months—the poor thing.

"I was worried," she says, sheepishly.

"Everything and everyone is fine. Go put your feet up, please. I love you," Jackson tells Emma.

"Love you too," she says, grabbing Clara's hand. "Come on, Mom. We are not wanted here any longer." Emma pulls Clara toward the door while looking over her shoulder at me, comple-menting the look by scrunching her nose up and sticking out her tongue.

"This family needs to take the show on the road. I've never seen a family with this kind of drama before I met you guys," Jackson says.

"Yeah, well ... you should feel lucky to be a part of this crazy family now. There's a lot of love," I tell Jackson. As I say what I feel, the reason for blacking out earlier seems less critical when I hold the two situations side by side. Family—those who have been by my side forever. Birth dad—it would be amazing to meet him, but we are, in fact, strangers that will never have the kind of bond I have with this crazy group of people I love.

"I am the lucky one to be taken in by all of you," Jackson says. The humor resting in my head would like to tell him to wait another year or so and see how he feels then, but he does seem to fit in well with us. Plus, it has been a full year since he and Emma tied the knot, so I should cut him some slack. "A nurse will be in shortly to remove the IV, and you can go home once she discharges you. Take it easy tonight, though, okay? Go home and relax. Get some rest."

"Yes, doctor," I sigh.

"I hope you don't get meatloaf tonight," Fisher tells Jackson, "but I'm so hungry, I'll bet I'd love some of Emma's cooking right now." He sounds like that's the only thing he's heard in the last ten minutes. It wouldn't surprise me much, though, since Fisher has gotten good at blocking out the drama my family tends to create. He's unfazed by it all, which is probably why our marriage has held up so nicely.

When the room clears out, Fisher seems to snap out of his meatloaf thoughts and joins me on the bed. "Sweet pea, we've been together for most of our lives. I hardly remember life before you. Please listen to what Jackson said, and talk to someone. Please, Annie. You're the love of my life, and I can't—I won't be able to go on without you. You have to understand me. I need you to take care of yourself. You are all I have, okay?"

I place my hand on Fisher's stubbly cheek and sweep my thumb back and forth, feeling the tickle along the length of my palm. "Okay," I tell him. "I always have and always will do everything and anything for you, and if me going to talk to someone is that important to you, I will."

He leans forward to place a kiss on my forehead, then inhales sharply and pulls away. "You know what I want more than anything right now?" he says, looking at me tenderly.

"What's that?" I ask him, watching his wandering gaze skate across the ceiling panels.

"I want meatloaf, Annie. I'm getting us some meatloaf."

"You and your meatloaf addiction—" I comment. "It's been a while, huh?"

"Meatloaf is a comfort food, and I'm not the one who put the idea in my head," he argues.

"Not this time," I reply.

17

1962 – PRAGUE, CZECHOSLOVAKIA - 20 YEARS OLD

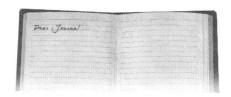

DAY ONE IN PRAGUE

THE MOMENTS FOLLOWING our first kiss stayed with me in my memories, throughout my life. Maybe it was because I only experienced one first kiss, but if I had dreamt of what a kiss might be like ... that one would have exceeded all expectations.

My body felt like it was overflowing with glitter—like a snow globe that had just been set down after being fiercely shaken.

My feet were no longer bothering me as we retraced our steps down the steep hill, and Fisher's hand was no longer cold because it was holding mine.

I didn't feel apprehensive with him like I had earlier. I felt like we had gone from strangers, to the very best of friends and more, within hours that day. Though, our friendship had been blossoming throughout the previous two years through our written words. Our kiss was like the lick of an envelope, sealing in all the certainty we were seeking since we first exchanged letters.

SHARI J. RYAN

The moments we shared that night were causing me to forget the reason I had flown across the world, but at that moment, Fisher was enough of an excuse to go anywhere. I felt things I had never imagined before, and my emotions were nearly uncontainable.

"I should be a gentleman and walk you to The Inn now," he said, as we reached the bottom of the hill.

Disappointment shrouded me with the thought of saying good night, or maybe goodbye, for that matter. I knew there was a chance that our kiss made him feel differently about our friendship, possibly opposite of what I was feeling, and I had to keep that in the back of my mind before I got too far ahead of myself. He surely had to have more experience with kissing and romance than I did. What practically swept me off my feet today might be a common occurrence for him. "Of course," I said, unsure of how else I should respond. It didn't want to sound desperate or pushy.

"If that's what you want for the evening, I will walk you there now," he continued.

I stopped walking. I was too focused on trying to understand what Fisher was saying, other than the words I understood. It seemed like there was a different meaning aside from what I heard, but it may have just been in my head, wanting to hear things differently.

"Well, what is it *you* want?" I turned the question around, hoping to earn a straightforward answer.

"If I can be completely sincere with you, I'd like nothing more than the pleasure of taking you out for dinner tonight. Furthermore, I would also like to take you to Old Town for a Trdelnik."

I could feel the smile beaming across my face, even though I was trying to compose myself. I wanted to spend more time with Fisher, more than I wanted to do anything else in Prague, which felt silly since I was on a mission to find my roots. I guess the heart has a way of speaking louder than the mind. I learned that lesson a time or two. "That would be lovely," I told him. "I'm not sure what you mean by a turtleneck, though. In America, a turtleneck is part of a shirt."

126

Fisher threw his head back and held his stomach as he laughed. The sound of his laughter was heartwarming. It was full of happiness and joy, yet I had no idea why he was laughing so hard.

"First, I know what a turtleneck is. We call that kind of apparel, Polo Necks, here. Second, I said, 'Trdelnik.' It's a pastry—one Czechoslovakia is known for."

I was happy it was dark out because I could feel my cheeks burning with embarrassment. Fisher's accent was undoubtedly thick, and I was still doing my best to understand him when he spoke fast, but I misunderstood that word. "Oh gosh, I didn't understand correctly," I told him while covering my mouth with the back of my hand to hide my face.

He reached across his chest and gently tugged my hand away from my mouth. "You are sweet ... please don't hide your beautiful face again."

With a chill from his flattering words, I took in a lungful of the crisp, pine-scented air and peered up at the starlit sky.

Everything around me felt so surreal—even the sky. Outside of the town, it was easy to see millions of stars above us. I had never seen so many stars, nor seen the sky look so big, not after growing up in a busy city like New York. It was quite hard to see stars there with all the blinding city lights. I don't think I realized what I was missing until that night. "I'm sorry. I don't know what we were saying. I got distracted by the sky—I've truly never seen so many stars lit up at once before," I told Fisher.

He lifted my hand—the one he was holding—and pointed toward a mass of stars in the center of the dark sky. "I suppose you haven't seen the Milky Way before then, have you?" he asked.

"No, I'm embarrassed to say that part of me thought the glowing imagery formed by stars in the sky were only myths," I said with a chuckle.

"No, no, the sky goes on forever, Annie. You know, I've spent many nights trying to understand why and how the human mind is not capable of comprehending the proximity of infinite space.

SHARI J. RYAN

It's hard to imagine that every living organism in the entire universe exists beneath this very one sky."

His words melted into my soul, warming me from the inside out. Just hearing his thoughts out loud, rather than on paper, was like listening to the most entrancing fusion of melodies. I wanted to ask him question after question, dig into his thoughts, understand his reasons, and process his personal sense of reality. "That thought never occurred to me," I told him. I had never looked at the sky as such an enveloping part of our world. He was right, though. I knew from that moment on, I would never be able to look at the sky the same way again.

"The sky has always offered me comfort, so in return, I'm quite thankful for it, yeah?"

"I—you're thankful for the sky?" I asked, curious to hear more of his reason. I wondered if the sky was part of his religious beliefs, something bigger than himself to believe in, like God.

"Well, yes, it's the one part of my world that holds all my pieces together in one place. My family, the life I left behind, the friends I've made along the way, those I lost, your letters over the last two years, and now ... your beauty ... and you."

"I see," I said, sounding short. I was breathless from his statement, but at the same time, I wasn't sure I could feel the same way as he did. The emotions I was feeling were exciting but also frightening.

"It's okay if you don't agree," he followed. "It's my personal thought, not yours."

"I don't know," I said. "If I can't be with the ones who are gone, I feel like we're not under the same sky."

"To each their own, Annie. You are entitled to your thoughts, and you can be entirely correct, but personally, and with all due respect, I prefer to think of our sky as one."

I smiled and nodded my head for the sake of not arguing with his opinion. I wasn't sure why I felt so strongly about such a silly thing—the sky, of all things. It's not like we would ever find an answer to prove either of our theories. In any case, I admired his

128

firm belief and hoped he appreciated mine in the same way. "I'm suddenly very hungry," I told him, changing the topic before someone went too far with their heartfelt opinion.

"Right, supper. Annie, please tell me ... do you like meatloaf?"

"Meatloaf?" I squawked.

"Oh no, do you hate meatloaf?"

"No, no, it's just that people eat meatloaf at home all the time. I assumed you ate different types of meals here."

"Well, sure we do, but meatloaf is my favorite. I can't ever seem to get enough of it, really."

His fondness for meatloaf made me giggle. "You must have some incredible meatloaf here if you enjoy it that much."

"Oh, the meatloaf will not let you down. I promise you that."

"Okay, meatloaf it is!" I told him. For the first half of my life I kept a kosher diet per Mom and Dad's wishes, but as we grew older, they allowed Clara and me to make our own decisions on our religious beliefs and practices, so long as we didn't fail to appreciate the meaning of all the parts that made us who we are. While neither of us chose to keep a kosher lifestyle, we still held tightly to our other traditions.

I was going to ask Fisher about his preferences, but knowing he didn't have a proper upbringing, I was afraid he may not have had many religious beliefs or traditions. I decided that conversation would be a better fit for another day.

Without a second to spare, Fisher tugged my hand and pulled me a little quicker down the street. "We are almost to the edge of Old Town. It's where my favorite pub is." I liked the fact that he wasn't interested in showing off with extravagance like a man in New York might do. I wanted to eat the same foods as the locals did. If meatloaf was a favorite of his, I couldn't imagine disliking it.

The orange flickering lights in the small town greeted us as we entered a village-like area. The pub on the corner, where we were heading, looked like it had been around for a while, which matched the charm of the surrounding shops. "I already adore it," I told Fisher.

"We haven't stepped inside yet," he said. "You can't proclaim your appreciation for something you haven't experienced."

"You do have a point," I agreed.

"You can adore the pub after you try the meatloaf."

I couldn't help but laugh. Meatloaf, of all things. It wouldn't have been my guess if someone asked me what his favorite food was. I realized the topic of food never came up in our letters, and I wondered how it hadn't since we talked about so much.

Fisher reached for the bronze handle and opened the door, bowing a bit, as an invitation for me to walk ahead of him. He was such a gentleman, especially for as young as we were.

The variety of scents claimed my nose almost immediately. I was overwhelmed by the combination of aromatic spices filling the air, but what was most pungent, was the beer. There was a sweet smell overall, and it seemed to stay with me as we walked by the few people scattered around.

"Ah, these folks are just waiting for takeaway. I think there's a small booth down there," he said, pointing to the back of the pub. "It'll be a bit quieter back there too. That way we can hear each other better."

Fisher took my hand back within his and led us toward the table he had his eyes set on. It was cornered beneath two large windows, overlooking the cobblestone street that was lit by a faint glow from the gas lamps lining the curb, which blurred into the dark distance.

Fisher helped me remove my coat, and I tucked my gloves into the inside pocket just before he hung my belongings up on the wall hook near our table.

We made ourselves comfortable in our seats, and suddenly, we were face to face with one another again. He was very ... dreamy, for lack of a better word. Gazing at him made my pulse race. "I feel like I've known you my whole life," I told him. It honestly felt that way. I had been in Prague less than a day, and it felt like a place I could call home.

"It seems like it," he said. "We've shared so much. It seems like I know your family, how your apartment is set up, and what it must be like to work in the art gallery. Your life has fascinated me from the day I received your first letter."

"Speaking of family," I began. "I did tell my sister I was traveling out here to meet you. I left out the other details, but she promised to keep the information to herself." I felt nervous, confessing the way I tidied up before I left home. Fisher didn't agree with the idea of me leaving my country without telling anyone in my family. It was hard to explain why I was sure Mom wouldn't have wanted me traveling to Prague.

"I'm glad you told your sister," he said, while placing his hand over his heart. "I'm worried your parents wouldn't like me much if they found out you came over here without mentioning your plan, though. Do you talk to them a lot?"

"Oh, yes, I'm very close with my entire family. We have Shabbat dinner every Friday night and sometimes brunch the last Sunday of each month." I knew what his next question was going to be. I had already planned my answer, though I was beginning to regret my plan of avoidance for dinner with my family that coming Friday. Mom wasn't a fool, and it was hard to play her for one.

"What are you going to do this coming Friday?" Fisher asked. I was scheduled to stay in Prague for just over a week, which would mean I only had one Friday night to worry about.

"Clara, my sister, will handle it," I told him.

Fisher looked displeased with my answer. "I see," he said. "You'll have to forgive me for my intruding questions, but I do have another."

"What is it?" I unintentionally set my gaze out the window, breaking eye contact with the man who was making my insides melt like warm candy.

"You mentioned that you didn't know your given name or

your birth parents' names, correct?" He was only asking to be polite because he knew that was my initial reason for reaching out to him.

"Correct," I responded with a sharp inhale.

"How did you get here?" Fisher asked softly. His question was followed by laughter filled with the subtle sound of discomfort. I assume he was concerned for how I was going to answer his question. "I just mean, you must not have any birth records, and I know customs can be a little tricky without identification, right?"

I glanced around, worried someone else could hear our conversation even though it was very hushed. I was hoping to avoid the topic of sneaking onto an airplane, but in truth, I had no other choice if I wanted to visit. "There was no other option," I said, being vague.

"Annie," he said, leaning forward to hunch over the tabletop. "Did you do something that could get you trouble?"

The word trouble and my name had never been in the same sentence. Before, I was a good girl and did as I was told, followed the rules, and obeyed and respected Mom and Dad. "Possibly, but I'm a smart girl. I'll be all right."

"Do you know what happens to people who toy with international affairs?" Fisher asked.

"I'm sure they would get into a great deal of trouble if they were caught," I replied, trying my best to keep my chin up while I felt the confidence draining out of me like a leaky faucet.

Fisher placed his hands on his head, and his eyes widened. "You can't go home the same way you came. I can't let you do that."

I placed my hands down gently on the edge of the table, reminding myself to keep my voice low. "Fisher, I have no other choice."

He nodded curtly, seeming angry, but in a silent way. It hurt to think I was disappointing him, but it was nice to feel worried about at the same moment. My heart and mind were at odds with each other, and I didn't understand the meaning of that phrase until then. "Okay, we'll figure this out before you leave. For now, though, let's focus on the time we have together. I'll make sure you get home safely. I promise."

"You don't have to worry about me," I told him. I shouldn't have to become his problem, even if he was kind enough to be concerned.

"Quiet," he snapped. "I don't care about many people in this world, Annie, and believe it or not, I cared about you long before I was graced with your gorgeous presence today. Therefore, I will worry about you going forward from this day, too, because you are already very special to me, and believe it or not, you're my closest friend. Do you know that?" I do know that. We had been each other's closest friends for almost two years at that time. There was no one else I wanted to spend my time writing to, or even speaking with in person. Every little thing that happened in my life during those first two years, good or bad, Fisher was the first person I wanted to share it with, and I had felt the same reciprocation from him, as well.

With a moment of peace allowing me to settle down, I unwrapped the scarf from around my neck and placed it down neatly beside me.

"I guess we've been bundled up all day, huh?" he asked.

"It's colder here than at home, and I didn't think that was possible," I replied.

Fisher smiled coyly as his focus settled on my hands. He reached for my right hand and held it tightly between his. It was the first time the skin of our hands touched. The gloves were shielding a lot of the warmth he had to offer earlier. "Just as soft as I imagined," he said. He lifted my hand and held it up against one of his palms, grinning at the size difference. "I didn't imagine your hands would be so small and petite compared to mine, though. They're quite perfect for holding," he said.

Again, the man could make my cheeks burn with heat at such a simple compliment. I was eating it up, enjoying our time together more and more as the minutes passed.

I wasn't sure how long we had been sitting in the booth, silently staring into each other's eyes, but it seemed like a while had passed before a woman greeted us. She was a bit of a frazzled mess, with her hair in a loose knot that didn't hold all her dark strands in together. She appeared tired, and her apron was stained with several different colors, showing how long her shift must had already been. Still, she had an abundance of happiness swimming within her big hazel eyes as she held out her small notepad, ready to take our order.

Just then, I realized I hadn't seen a menu. Maybe it was near the entrance, and I missed it.

"Fisher, I see you brought a friend tonight?" the woman said. She gave him a quick wink, and I'm sure she saw the blush stain my cheeks in response. She was an older woman, and I wondered if she might have worked at the pub her whole life. Along with the scattered food stains, her apron was also decorated with branded patches that were sewn into a pattern of disarray along the white material. I suspected the pub must be a homey place for many people; it already felt that way to me.

"Yes, Madam Rose, Annie is my good friend. She's from America—New York City, in fact."

"America," the woman hooted. "My oh my, we don't see many of you around here. It's a pleasure to serve you this evening. I apologize for not sharing our available meal options with you sooner. We stopped using menus here about twenty years ago when most of our customers became nightly patrons."

She was full of life and loud, overcompensating for the nearby conversations. "Fisher was telling me how wonderful your meatloaf is," I told the woman.

She looked over at Fisher with a raised brow and cocked her head to the side. Then she slapped the back of his head with her notepad. "You buffoon, no one comes to Prague to eat meatloaf."

"No, really, I would like to try it, if that's all right?" I asked.

Fisher's face broke into a large smile, displaying his pride in the small fact that I ordered his beloved meatloaf. "Well, it is a favorite here, so I'm sure you will enjoy it."

"I'm sure I will," I told her.

"To drink?" she asked me.

"Oh, I—water is just fine, thank you."

"I'll have whatever Pilsner you have on tap tonight, Madam Rose," Fisher told her.

"Very well," she said, jotting it all down.

"You know, I'll try the Pilsner as well," I said, keeping my eyes set on Fisher.

He smirked at me with a look of approval. I did enjoy the taste of beer, though I had only tried it a few times. In any case, I was sure it was good to try new foods and drinks while I had the chance.

"I'll be back with your drinks in a flash," the woman said, then winked at Fisher again as she turned to hurry away.

In return, Fisher rolled his eyes. "She acts like a mum to me. I've been coming here a long time, and she's so nosy that she knows more about me than most around here. She's a sweet woman, though. Rose and her husband took me in a couple of times when I was searching for a new flat to rent."

"She does seem very nice," I told him. It's nice to know someone looks after him, even if it's from afar. Growing up without a real family must have been difficult, though I wonder how much he realizes that, since it's the only life he's ever known.

"Is this odd to you? Us, this moment?" he asked.

I couldn't tell if he was having a hard time with the reality surrounding us. One minute, I was a stranger behind words, the next ... it was as if we had never gone a day without speaking. "No, it feels right," I said, sounding a bit shy at that moment.

It did. I stood by my terrible decision to sneak onto a plane. Otherwise, I would never have met Fisher, and I would never have tried the meatloaf he had been raving about for nearly an hour straight by that point.

"Good, I feel the very same way," he says, while sweeping the back of his hand against his forehead. It was just a way to express his relief, but I didn't think he was really questioning my feelings at all. As I think back on it, things developed quickly between us, but people genuinely get to know each other much faster when there is only conversation being exchanged. Being in each other's presence was a simple confirmation of what we had already been feeling.

Rose returned twice more in the following moments. The first time was to place down our beverages, and the second was to deliver our meatloaf, laid out on massive platters with candied carrots and a heap of mashed potatoes. Each plate looked as though it could feed a family of four, and I wasn't sure why he didn't suggest one dish for the two of us. However, I learned the answer to that question shortly after I took my first bite.

The meatloaf was quite tasty. It wasn't how I predicted it to be. Any serving of meatloaf I had before that night was a bit dry in the center and never had much seasoning or taste. It wasn't my favorite meal, but I was certain I would order that dish again. Prague knew how to make a good meatloaf.

While trying to guess which ingredients were used to make the inside taste so juicy, I heard a fork scrape against a plate. I was shocked and a little in awe to notice that Fisher had eaten every morsel of the large-sized meal in less than five minutes. "Wow," I told him. "I don't think I've ever seen anyone eat so quickly in my life!"

He lifted his forest green, linen napkin from his lap and wiped it over his mouth. "Oh, I'm so sorry. I've always been a quick eater. The orphanage I was in—if you didn't eat fast, the older kids would snatch the food. I can assure you, I only let that happen once."

The more I heard about the orphanage, the more I began to compare it to another type of prison, like where we were born. Of course, I didn't know how brutal our living conditions were, but life didn't sound too lovely for Fisher after he was released either.

"That's terrible," I responded.

"Tonight, is not about terrible, Annie. Tonight, is about finding what was lost—or who, for that matter. We were lost, but now, we're found. Right?"

His words were sweet and made sense, but in my world, I was still very much lost.

18

CURRENT DAY

"How long was I unconscious? It must have been at least an hour, which seems like an unreasonable amount of time to be unconscious from an anxiety attack," I ask Fisher as we pull away from the hospital.

"You weren't unconscious, sweet pea. You only blacked out for a moment, but you weren't thinking clearly or making any sense. The paramedics said when a person works themselves up into an intense state of panic, they'll sometimes fall into a sleepy place where they aren't completely coherent. You exhausted yourself."

"Everything seems foggy, I suppose." I set my gaze outside of the car window, recalling how vivid my dreams were while I was asleep—or unconscious—whatever they want to call it. "I was dreaming about us—when we met that first day."

"Was it about meatloaf?" he asks with laughter.

"Is that all you remember about that day, Fisher?"

"Annie, you are what I remember about that day."

"Don't sweet talk me now. You already mentioned meatloaf."

Fisher reaches into his back pocket and retrieves his ringing cell phone. "Who's that?"

"You don't want to know," he says.

"You're right. I don't." I can hear the voice, clear as day, shrill as ever, piercing through the tiny speaker on the phone.

"Amelia—Mum, she's fine. I promise you."

Fisher shoves the phone toward his shoulder and peers over at me for a quick second. "She's not very happy with us," he whispers.

"Mum, I'm taking good care of Annie. She's just fine." More shouts. More lectures. "I didn't want to worry you or Charlie."

"Clara can't stop herself," I mutter.

"Okay, I will, Mum. We'll both come to see you straight away in the morning. Okay then. Bye-bye."

"She must be losing her mind," I share my assumption. "Why can't I just be sick in peace?"

"Oy," Fisher sighs while pulling off the road into the dirt parking lot of an abandoned building. He shifts the car into park, then releases his seatbelt to twist and face me. "Annie, sweet pea, please look at me. Look me right in the eyes," he says, pointedly. Fisher doesn't like to be serious. It's a rare occasion when he is, but when he gets this way, I know there is meaning and a build-up of emotion behind it.

"What is it?"

"I know that you feel resentment—"

"What? No—" I counter.

"Let me speak," he cuts me off, mid-sentence. "I'll rephrase myself. You may not realize it, but sometimes you act as though you resent having a family who loves you more than anything else in the world. I know I don't need to remind you of how lucky you are—we are—to have the family we do, but sometimes I think you need to think about why there is a telephone chain in your family that moves faster than the damn internet. No one wants to miss a second because life can be over in as little as a second. You know this. You've lived it. Let them love you, okay?"

For a man who says the word meatloaf at least twice a day each day of our lives, he is brilliant—always has been. "You are right," I tell him humbly, while dusting the dashboard off with the tip of my finger.

"Annie, I don't know why Emma's pregnancy seems to have triggered your need to reopen all the old, dusty boxes in the attic, but watching you dive back into this dark hole in search of more answers, hurts to watch. We both had gotten to a place in our lives where we were satisfied with the information we had, but something changed, and it seems like you're suffering again."

I called him brilliant too soon, I suppose. "What in the world does Emma's pregnancy have to do with me?" As the question rolls off my tongue, the answer swings through my brain like a massive wrecking ball.

"I don't know what one thing has to do with the other, but I know you started rereading our old letters and your journal entries, and now you're finally admitting all of your buried secrets to your mother. I just never thought I'd see the day, I guess. We can call it coincidental, but you've been going on like this for the past seven months—since we found out Emma was pregnant."

I break my stare from Fisher's eyes, losing my thoughts while trying to coherently determine a good explanation. I truly don't know how one situation led to another, but I do understand why my mind took a nosedive seven months ago. Fisher knows too, so he's either avoiding the topic or hoping it's something completely different. "When did your car become so dusty?" I ask him.

"Annie," he says through a gentle murmur. "Everything is the same. The sky is still above us, and it's still blue. Remember? The sky is our anchor. The sky never changes, and neither do we."

"That isn't true, Fisher. The sky *does* change."

Fisher takes my hand and squeezes. "We aren't getting into this age-old argument, sweet pea."

"You're right. We don't need to explain ourselves again."

"I'm sure someday I'll understand your logic better. Until then, take comfort in knowing you are a very loved woman. Furthermore, if it will make you feel complete, we will go back to Prague and find your birth father. We can start the process of collecting your proper birth records too—right now."

"Thank you," I say coldly. My frustration is not toward Fisher, it's from a desire to shake my fist at the world and say things I can't take back.

"A 'thank you' is not necessary. I will do anything for you. You know this."

I nod my head. "No, I mean thank you for sticking by my side through thick and thin as you promised."

"It isn't your side, Annie. It's our side. This is our life … our world. Your sadness is mine. Your heartache is mine. Your frustration is mine."

I won't say it out loud because the words I want to say would contradict everything I have been thinking for the last seven months, but I was going to ask how I got so lucky to have him as a husband. *Lucky.* That word—lucky. How many unfortunate occurrences does a person need to encounter before they get just one lucky moment that lasts forever?

"So, you said you were dreaming about me, eh?" Fisher asks while readjusting his shoulder belt into place.

"You, not the meatloaf," I retort.

"I do remember that first week of ours. I remember it as if it were yesterday. The second day you were in Prague, you persuaded me to change all my tour guide plans because you had a personal agenda, if I recall."

I smirk at the memory. "I did have an agenda, all right."

"I remember you tried espresso for the first time. That was a mistake," Fisher says with a chuckle.

"I told you I didn't need caffeine to start my day, but you insisted." I didn't know the coffee in Europe was stronger than the coffee at home. I learned that lesson quickly.

"You were like a wind-up toy, storming through the city in heels. It was quite amusing, if I do say so myself."

"I had places to go and things to see. You, on the other hand, you were more interested in taking in your surroundings, Fisher Benson," I say with an arched brow that he will diligently ignore.

"You can't blame me. You're a sight for sore eyes."

"Was, maybe," I correct him.

"You haven't changed a bit, Annie. I only see the best version of you, which is what is sitting right beside me."

19

1962 - PRAGUE, CZECHOSLOVAKIA - 20 YEARS OLD

DAY TWO IN PRAGUE

I HARDLY SLEPT a wink that first night in Prague. My mind was wild with thoughts, hope, and dreams—the kind of dreams Fisher didn't believe in, for a reason I didn't completely understand at the time. I spent a bit of extra time fixing myself up early that morning. Fisher mentioned that he could get most of his daily work done before the sun would rise, and he said he would meet me afterward. I wasn't sure how that was possible if he was working on a farm. I thought farmers needed sunlight to do their work, but I didn't want to question his ability to spend time with me during the short time I was going to be in Prague.

When I took one last look in the vanity mirror before I set out, I realized I hadn't spent much time noticing my appearance in the recent months. My face suddenly appeared to have taken on a more mature look, and the makeup I had applied made me feel glamorous in comparison to the way I typically felt. While walking around town the day before, I admired a lot of the women passing us by and noticed a resemblance between some of their features and my own. Our eyes had a similar sideways teardrop shape, with slight diagonal lines stretching toward their ears. Mom always told me my eyes were enchanting, and a man would fall in love with them. I always thought the shape of my eyes looked like cat eyes. I never thought they were very attractive, until I saw the commonality in Prague.

In the art classes I took, I learned that a symmetrically shaped face with evenly proportioned eyes, ears, mouth, and nose constitutes abundance of beauty in a person. After learning that fact, I studied my reflection for a bit and could only see how asymmetrical my features were. I noticed that my top lip was fuller than my bottom lip, my nose was smaller than the space between my eyes, and my ears were pinned a tad higher than they should have been —all which, in my mind, painted a picture of a hideous woman. When I saw all the beautiful women strolling around town in Prague, I realized I was wrong about a pallet of perfection. It was the imperfections that made a person unique and uncommonly beautiful. That specific day, my first day in Prague, I began to feel more appealing than I ever had before.

Confidence was not something I wore often, but my aura was radiating it as I left The Inn behind for the day. Fisher was where he said he would be waiting, at the exact moment he said he would be there. Punctuality gave him another point in my book. Most men in New York failed to be punctual, always blaming a late train, traffic, or any number of other possible reasons for a delay. I would never make a man wait for me, so finding the reciprocation was a bonus.

"My beautiful, not-so-missing lady," Fisher greeted me. He was dressed a bit neater that day, wearing tan-colored pants, but they were clean, rather than covered with dirt like the day before. He was also wearing a navy-blue wool sweater with a white t-shirt poking out around the rounded collar. His hair was combed back, and he looked ready for the day. I assumed he must have taken the time to clean up after he was done on the farm. If that was the case, I didn't realize I was that worthy of impressing.

Fisher was leaning against the brick facade of a short building across from The Inn, but when he noticed me, he pressed his foot away from the wall and met me halfway across the street. Without care for passing cars or people, he took my gloved hand and touched my knuckles to his lips. "Did you sleep well?"

"Oh, yes, I did," I lied. I couldn't tell him I stayed up half the night daydreaming about his charming smile and dark, lustrous wavy hair.

"Fantastic," he said, cheerfully. "I have our day planned out. I hope that's okay with you?"

I might have mentioned in letters that I was a bit of a planner and that I enjoyed taking control of situations, but I also believe Fisher might have responded with something along the lines of the fact that he took pleasure out of the same habit. I pondered whether I should go along with his plan or speak up about my own. Fisher didn't make me feel inferior, as many men had in my past, so I felt comfortable saying what was on my mind. "What is on your agenda, might I ask?"

"May I surprise you?" he asked. I couldn't find the right words to explain to him how much I despised surprises. They made me nervous and apprehensive. They still do. I think he must have seen the look on my face because he waved his hands in the air and said, "You know what? Never mind. Let's do whatever it is you want to do. This is your trip, after all."

My desire was to acquire my research first, then enjoy the remainder of my time. However, I had a knot in my stomach from thinking about the potential of finding out more information about who I was and where I came from in that country. I'm sure the Terezín Memorial sent me all the information available, but I was hoping to gain insight by being there in person. I wanted to see the camp area and the town of Terezín. That was all the information I had about myself, and I needed to experience what I could to make it feel more relevant in my life. I needed that pain, for whatever reason. It felt necessary. "I know you wanted to wait until the latter part of my trip, but I would really like to visit Terezín today. Is it far from here?" I asked Fisher.

Fisher seemed uneasy for a moment, as if I had just told him I wanted to see a corpse, which in theory, was what I was requesting. "We can take the bus. It'll be about a two-hour ride," he said.

"Fisher, I would never want to force you to go back to the camp if you didn't want to go. I can go alone if I'm asking too much." He had visited the camp just once since he was a child. He took a guided tour when he checked in at the Terezín Memorial to search for the information on his birth parents. Since his name hadn't been changed when he was a young child, he had an easier time locating his family's information. It was frustrating to know I still wouldn't find out much during my trip, but I still had the names Terezín Memorial gave me, and I planned to collect any information available about the three family bloodlines, then hold onto the information for when I did find my answer.

"In the same respect, Annie, I could never let you go through that on your own," he said. His eyes were a bit glossed over, and he was staring through me as he spoke. "You should most definitely visit, though."

"Are you sure? I would be just fine by myself."

"I am sure," he repeated. He took my hand and began to walk, leading the way. "The bus station is just down the street. Let's see if we can get on one soon."

"Thank you, Fisher. This truly means a lot to me."

"I can understand why," he says.

I had emotionally prepared myself, or so I thought. With the little information I had about the Holocaust, I felt as though I had enough understanding to comprehend the severity of what it was like during the time prisoners were kept in the camp. However, there was not much research or information available about Theresienstadt, and I had gone to several libraries in my search. The only information I could find was that the camp was distinctly used as a holding location for transits, as well as a place for upper-class citizens and the elderly. The research didn't make much sense, but from what I could understand, it seemed the camp was used as a form of propaganda to prevent the Red Cross from finding out what was happening to so many innocent people. It didn't answer my question as to why I was brought to that camp in particular, especially since I was sure my birth parents were not elderly. They might have been wealthy, but again, I had no way of finding out.

We were able to purchase round-trip tickets for a bus that would be leaving within the hour. Fisher said we were lucky to obtain seats so easily. I understood why when I saw how filled the bus was when we boarded. I was just thankful they didn't need identification and that I was able to purchase a ticket, rather than committing another crime.

Fisher ended up dozing off for half of the trip, while I took the opportunity to stare out at the endless landscapes filled with a type of lush scenery I wouldn't find in New York. The bus stopped at several stations, allowing passengers to come and go, which I learned was the reason the tour took so long to travel a mere sixty miles. When the driver announced that our stop would be next, I shook Fisher's shoulder, startling him awake. He glanced down at his watch, then back up at me.

"I am so sorry, Annie, I didn't mean to doze off. I'm a horrid tour guide, aren't I?"

"Don't be foolish," I told him. "I loved taking in the sights as we drove by."

"Yeah, it's a nice ride," he said.

"Fisher, I'm curious. What time did you wake up this morning to go to work?" It must have been earlier than I thought. He looked exhausted, even after the long nap he took.

"Eh, about three in the morning, but I'm used to it," Fisher said.

"We didn't call it a night until nearly midnight, though. You must not have gotten any sleep," I said, realizing what he was putting himself through for me.

"You are worth the lost sleep, Annie. I enjoyed our time

together last night more than I have enjoyed anything in longer than I can recall. Please, don't be upset. Sleep can wait, I assure you."

"Will you have to do the same tomorrow?" I asked with concern.

"Yes, but I promise you, I will be okay."

"I will stay up with you, then. I will also help you with your work."

"Don't be ridiculous. I don't want you shoveling cow manure. You would smell terrible all day."

"You don't smell foul," I said.

"I showered, of course."

"I will shower afterward too then, silly."

"You are a force of nature, Annie. You truly are, you know that?"

"I'm aware," I said with a coy grin.

The screeching of the bus's brakes interrupted our discussion. "We're here," Fisher said, taking my hand and pulling me up from my seat. I couldn't understand why he was moving through the bus before it came to a complete stop, but I followed. No one else had gotten up in a hurry during the prior stops. "What's the rush?" I asked.

"You don't see many people departing the bus at this stop in the off-season for travelers," he explained as we took the three steps off the bus.

"Really? There aren't many visitors this time of year?"

"No, not with the American holidays coming up. Things are fairly quiet here now."

When the bus pulled away from the designated stop, I found we were in the center of a square with different-colored buildings surrounding the area. Just as Fisher mentioned, the location seemed somewhat abandoned, except for a few passersby and tourists here and there. It felt colder, and the trees were thinner there than they were in Prague. The upkeep wasn't the same either. There was a rundown appearance to the buildings, but I wondered if it was intentionally left in that condition to preserve the memories of what those who were imprisoned there, endured. "We can start at the memorial, okay?" Fisher asked. "It's just a few blocks down there." He was pointing with his finger but studying a map he had pulled out of his pocket.

I'm not sure I even responded to him. I was in a state of shock, feeling tiny in the broad area. My stomach began to hurt, my heart was racing, and I hadn't even seen anything upsetting yet. It was just a feeling resonating through my body. I had been in that very place once, but I couldn't remember. I never would remember. It was a thought I couldn't digest.

We walked down three streets until a sign for the Terezín Memorial came into view. The memorial looked as empty as the rest of the area. I wondered if there were residents even living there, or if the town was too full of history and tragic memories for anyone to have the desire to make it their home. When I spotted the building marked as the memorial, I was taken aback, as I didn't expect the building to look as it did. It didn't look like a memorial or a museum. It appeared more like a courthouse, but smaller.

The moment we stepped inside, we were greeted with the dismal scenery. The interior was poorly lit, and everything was sad and depressing, from the walls to the floors. Photographs and exhibit remnants covered the walls, which kept our focus moving along the path we were intended to follow.

We were greeted by a woman dressed in business attire, with her hands held tightly behind her back. My tongue felt tied in a knot when I tried to speak up. I wanted to ask her for help or guidance on where I could begin my search for information, but the words didn't come out.

"Are you all right?" Fisher asked, placing his hand on my back.

I closed my eyes for a quick moment and took in a shallow breath, telling myself that I survived hell once, and I could make it through this too. I was back there to claim my survival. I was lucky. I had been blessed throughout my entire life. "I am fine," I answered him.

"She is a—" Fisher began to speak for me, probably knowing I was having a hard time, as I'm sure it appeared.

"I was born here, in Terezín, miss. I am one of the missing children, but I'm afraid I don't know my given name. I wrote a letter here, to the memorial, about two years ago for assistance, and I was given names of the three children born on the same day I was born while in this camp. I was hoping to do some more research on the three names, so I might be able to narrow down my history a bit more. Is there any place I can do that here?" My chest felt hollow once the words all came out. I wondered if I sounded like I was speaking a foreign language, which I technically was to the poor woman. Plus, on top of that, I was speaking quickly, but they were words I had recited in my head many times.

A look of shock tugged on the woman's lips and eyes. Her reaction seemed as though she was disturbed and upset by what I said. "You were a missing child?" she repeated my words.

"That is correct. I am no longer a child, as you can see, but I am, in fact, still missing. I don't know who I truly am. I have no identification or birth record, and I have no knowledge of my family's history. It has placed my life in a holding pattern for the last ten years since I found out some of my past." I sounded robotic and possibly a little too stern with the poor stranger who was just there to do her job.

"My dear, you're an American?" she asked.

"Yes, miss, I was taken in by a wonderful woman who gave me a life I sometimes don't feel I deserve."

The woman placed her hand gently around my wrist and began walking up the set of stairs in silence. Fisher followed in my footsteps as we made our way through more areas filled with photographs and memorabilia depicting moments from the war.

The woman took us up to a closed door, which she unlocked with a key she retrieved from her back pocket. Once inside, she closed us in and pulled two chairs out from behind an old metal desk. "Please, have a seat."

She pulled out a notepad with a pen and took a seat in front of us. Her eyes that appeared despondent just moments earlier, suddenly looked wild with intrigue. "Could you tell me the woman's name—the one who rescued you?"

My body went cold and numb with the thought of someone asking for Mom's name. Not only did Mom not know where I was, but it was out of fear that I didn't tell her, knowing what reasons she would have had to keep me from visiting Prague. "I am so sorry, but I must keep that information private. I'm only here to find who I have lost."

"I completely understand," the woman said. "I'm Sarah, by the way." She held out her hand for us to shake. "It is truly a pleasure to meet you—"

"My name, now, is Annie, and this is Fisher," I responded.

"I'm also one of the missing children, but I registered as 'found' several years ago," he said. "That's how Annie and I found each other."

"You're a supporter for the missing?" she asked, knowing that there was a list of people who were offering a hand to those still trying to find their way home.

"Yes, miss, I am."

"God, bless you," she said, placing her hand over her mouth. Sarah looked as though she wanted to cry, and I wondered what her history looked like. Was she also a missing child who had a vested interest in helping others in the same situation? No matter what her story was, it must take a strong person to be surrounded by that type of sadness each day.

"I was given three names of children born the same day I was."

"Do you have them with you?" she asked.

I leaned to the side of the chair and opened my purse, pulling out the index card I had jotted the names down on. "I do," I said, handing her the card.

The woman took the paper with a shaky grip and placed it

down in front of her. "Are you going to be here for a bit?" Sarah asked.

"We were going to take a tour of the camp and cemetery," Fisher responded.

"Yes, yes, please do. If you don't mind, I would like to go through my records to see what I can find out about these women. When you are through touring the camp, please come back so I can share what I have found, if I do find something, of course."

For the first time in years, I felt hope. Someone, in addition to Fisher, wanted to help me find myself. "Thank you. Thank you very much," I offered.

"It is beyond my greatest pleasure to try and help you, dear."

20

CURRENT DAY

TIME TO GET this over with. The lecture I have coming to me probably won't make this day better than yesterday, but very little slides by Mom without an in-depth conversation to follow. "Smile, sweet pea," Fisher tells me as we lock up the house.

I force a faux smile across my face, just for my loving husband. "I want to relax and put my feet up—doctor's orders, remember?" I tell him while heading toward the car.

"Now, we both know that is not true, Annie. In all the years I've known you, I've never seen you put your feet up, or want to, for that matter."

"Fine," I say, continuing with my phony smile.

"That's my girl," Fisher says, winking at me. "Would it help if I did the talking today?"

I'm the type of woman who prefers to speak solely on my own behalf. I don't enjoy when people talk for me, especially in front of me. I'm a firm believer in handling my issues, but I'm not sure I have the energy today. Maybe I just experienced a silly anxiety attack, but the emergency of it all made me very tired.

The car ride is as quick as usual. The care facility Mom and Charlie moved into is just a short, five-minute ride down the road. It's easier to check up on them this way. Plus, Clara and Emma both work, and I've wanted to alleviate some of the stress from their plates.

The moment we walk into the botanically decorated entrance, Judy, the front desk manager, stands from her desk and jogs over to me. "Annie, Annie, Annie, your mother told me about your episode yesterday. Are you okay, doll?"

Judy is very sweet. She has been extraordinarily helpful anytime I've called to check on Mom when I haven't been able to locate her. She also puts up with Mom, which is an entirely separate reason she's a saint. "Have I told you lately, how sweet you are?" I ask Judy, placing my hands on her shoulders. She looks truly concerned, but here I am, in the living flesh, breathing, walking, and talking.

"You sure have. I don't think you let a day go by without mentioning those kind words of yours," she says. Judy wraps her arms around my neck and gives me a tight embrace. "Don't you dare leave your mama on my hands without your help, you hear?" Her laughter bellows through my ears, but my own laugh might have drowned out the sound of hers. Judy is known for making wisecracks, which makes me cherish her even more.

"I'm not going anywhere any time soon, Judy. Don't worry," I tell her.

She leans back and points her polished finger at me. Her eyes go wide, and her smile straightens into a line across her cheeks. "I'm serious. That woman would be ninja-ing her way into my brain within twenty-four hours, and I wouldn't be able to say no to her anymore. It would be bad news."

"Trust me, I know," I tell her. "It's called Jewish guilt. It's an art my mother perfected before she even had children."

"I wonder if it would work on my spoiled children?" Judy asks while walking back to her desk.

"Don't do that to those beautiful children of yours." I can't help but laugh as I walk away. *Jewish guilt.* Half of my life has been run on Jewish guilt. I never had the chance to truly understand the exact science of how it works, but it seems, once you got it, you got it. Mom has never missed a chance to pour it on nice and thick. Fisher tells me I must look past it and keep her words from seeping into my brain, but I can't stop it, or her, for that matter. Then, of course, there's Clara, who has also perfected the so-called Jewish guilt, and poor Emma gets a big dose of it daily. I've given Emma the same advice Fisher has offered me, but we all know those guilt trips aren't easily ignored.

"Mum sure makes a name for herself around here, huh?" Fisher mentions while pressing the button to the elevator.

I glance over at Fisher, noticing the look of unease in his eyes as he's scratching the back of his head.

"You're getting nervous, aren't you?" I ask him. "You only scratch your head when you're nervous."

"I'm not nervous," he says quietly as we step into the elevator that reeks of ammonia and bleach. It's early in the morning, which means the facility was just cleaned, so the scents of cleaner are stronger now than they are later in the day. It's the only thing I don't like about this facility. I do like clean, but I don't care for the scent of pungent disinfectant. I know it's necessary, but it's the one little contribution that makes the grounds feel more like a hospital setting than an elderly assisted living facility.

We arrive on Mom's floor, and I knock a couple times before hearing Charlie shout out, "The door is unlocked."

"Okay, I lied," Fisher mumbles before we walk in. "I am nervous. She can get inside my head, Annie. She's a master at getting into my head, just like Judy said. You know this."

"Oh, my goodness; I'll handle this," I tell him.

"No, no, you are my wife. You were sick yesterday. I can handle her."

"She's in her nineties, Fisher."

"Right, I got this."

I shake my head and open the door. Just as I figured Mom

would be situated, she is in her favorite antique cushioned chair with her knees pointed toward the window, and by the look of her profile, her eyebrows are a half inch higher than they normally are. It's a perfect look of anger pinned to her face—one she has perfected.

"Oh, your mother isn't talking to you," Charlie says as he moves around us to lock the door. It was just unlocked when we arrived, and we're all here, so I'm not sure why he's suddenly concerned with locking the door, but I've learned not to question an older man.

"I figured as much," I reply to Charlie.

I begin my approach toward Mom, but Fisher takes my hand and holds me in place. "I told you, I got this," he mutters under his breath.

"Mum, you look lovely today," Fisher says, taking a seat across from her.

"Mm ...," Mom responds. "Don't kiss my rear end."

Fisher looks shocked to hear her speak that way. "Told you," I sing in a whisper.

"It was my fault. Yesterday, I should have called you right away. Annie had begged me to call you, but I was too focused on what was going on," Fisher begins.

"I thought Annie blacked out? How could she beg you to call me?"

For the love of God. "Mom, it was nothing. By the time I snapped out of it, I already knew I was fine and going home. There was no sense in worrying you over nothing. It was literally ... nothing," I speak up.

"Do you know how many years I have spent trying to protect you?" Mom asks.

"A lot," Fisher mumbles. "However, you agreed to allow me to take care of her too. You told me you were confident I would be a good caretaker, remember?"

"Yes, I remember, Fisher," she replies, keeping her words snipped. "It isn't that I don't believe you are protecting Annie or giving her a good life." Mom turns her attention back toward me. "It's because ... I want to know you—Annie—are okay. I love you, sweetheart. Why won't you let me love you?"

I know she loves me. I know she has gone to the ends of the earth and back for me. A day hasn't gone by where I questioned her feelings toward me. However, Mom hasn't told any of us in her immediate family that she loves us—not in those words. She has refused to speak the word love, for a reason she wouldn't give us. There are plenty of other words in the dictionary to describe adoration for a person, so we found ways to express our emotions in other ways. Mostly, we learned to show love, rather than saying it. A word is just a word, but an action is proof.

"What did you just say?" I ask her. My heart feels as though it has jumped into my throat. It's preventing me from inhaling any air. Does she realize what she just said out loud? "You said you love me ..." I realize, in a normal world, a daughter wouldn't be highlighting such a delicate subject, but why now? How can she suddenly say something she's never been able to say before?

"Life's short; then we die. I wasted a long time fearing love, not realizing how much more I had been loving you all because I was making up for the fact that I couldn't say those words out loud. Love equaled a lot of loss for me, but then love came back to find me, so I figured ... maybe I can give it another chance too."

I make my way past Fisher and kneel in front of Mom, taking her hands within mine. "Look at me, Mom. Look me in the eyes, and listen to me. I love you, and I will say it until I'm blue in the face, even if you don't want to say it back. I don't need to hear those words because I feel them in my heart. I haven't confused the lack of those words for the feelings you have devoted to me. Honestly, I don't care how short life is, we each have our own way of expressing ourselves, and I could die tomorrow without a question in my mind about how much you love me. Although, I have a suspicion that Judy from downstairs would not want me to die tomorrow. Evidently, you're a handful."

Everyone laughs at my joke, knowing how often we've heard

Judy threaten me and Clara not to leave without Mom because she's too much for one person. Charlie doesn't seem to think that way, but while love doesn't need to be expressed in words, it can also make a person blind to certain aspects.

"Dear—Annie, come on, pull yourself up from the ground and sit down next to your scared husband, then tell me what made you so upset yesterday, will you?"

I take the seat next to Fisher on the sofa, and Charlie takes a seat on the other side of me and places his arm around my neck.

"I think my birth father is still alive," I gush without warning—without thinking.

Mom uncrosses her legs, and her eyebrows furrow in toward one another. "How in the world did you find that out overnight?" Mom's voice is so soft, I can hardly hear her, but the rest of the room is also silent ... I could likely hear a pin drop.

"Google," Fisher says.

"The Google is not always right, Annie. I do not want you getting your hopes up. Your father must be my age, if not older. The chances are so slight."

"His name is Benjamin Sigel. He's a writer, and he published an article just a few months ago." My words are stumbling and rolling into each other as I can't seem to speak fast enough.

"All this time," Mom says with a lost look in her eyes.

Charlie's hand unexpectedly tightens around my shoulder. "I wouldn't have been able to remember his name, even if I tried, but I remember Amelia—" Charlie looks toward Mom. "I remember you asked me to see if Leah's husband was somewhere in Theresienstadt. I tried to locate him, but I only remember finding out that he was transported to Auschwitz. No one survived Auschwitz, Annie," Charlie says. His eyes are full of despair. Charlie's probably wondering how my heart is handling the intense ups and downs of this revelation. I wouldn't be able to answer him if he asked me that question, though.

"Charlie," I breathe. "Not everyone at Auschwitz died. I did my research. Not everyone died." I don't know if I'm trying to convince Charlie or myself, but the historical research couldn't be a complete lie. There is a chance he's alive, and if there is even the slightest chance, I need to find out.

"Sweet girl," Charlie says, taking my hand within his.

"Please, just let me have some hope. It won't make any difference now, but if he's alive, I need to know before it's too late."

Mom pulls in a deep breath through her nose and sits up as straight as she can manage. "Do whatever it is you need to do to find your answer, Annie. I want you to know."

"Do you?" I ask with sincerity. My entire life, this other world I should have been a part of was not mentioned between us because she wanted to protect me from knowing the horrible truth. She protected me so well that I couldn't bear to cause her the same pain by letting her know I knew for so long.

"This is love, Annie. Maybe, I haven't been able to say those words, but I know what love is, and I know how to show it, feel it, live it, and offer my blessings. If this is what you want, then I want you to be successful with your search. You deserve to have what you want."

"Mom ..."

"What is it?" she asks me. Mom sounds as if she's trying to remain complacent and calm, but I can see through the act.

"Did you wonder if I would eventually figure out my birth certificate wasn't real? I wasn't able to do so many things because I didn't know who I was—apparently, no one knew who I was." I don't mean to cause any hurt by this question, but I am curious, and have been curious for a long time, to hear what she would have said if I told her I knew my records weren't real.

She intertwines her fingers and squeezes her palms together tightly. "Maxwell—your father did a fine job, making your birth record look as real as possible, especially with his access to the printers at the press. I didn't think it would ever be an issue, honestly."

I tilt my head to the side, knowing Mom very well. I'm sure she had a backup plan for when things potentially went south. "Mom, what was your backup plan?"

She shakes her head and peers out the window. "I didn't have one, Annie. If I had known you found out, I don't know if I would have made up another story and tried to fix it, or if I would have told you the truth, but I do know that the thought of telling you that your birth mother was—that I watched her—that she wasn't alive because of the Holocaust, made me sick to my stomach. It was bad enough you were born into that life, but I wanted to shield you from the horrors a child should never have to face."

I nod with understanding. I get it. I do. I would have done the very same thing for my child.

"I know," I tell her.

"I was born in the camp too," Fisher says. "Since we're clearing the air and all." He's looking around at everyone who appears as shocked as I must look since he just confessed his story that we have kept secret along with mine. "That's how Annie and I found each other. We were both on the list of missing children, except she didn't know which missing child she was until now."

"Dear God," Mom says, cupping her hand over her mouth. "I don't know how many more surprises I can take right now. How—why didn't you ever say so?"

"The coincidence would have been too much," Fisher says. "Annie and I tried our best to leave the horrors behind us, just as you wanted, and just as I'm sure my parents would have wanted. Honestly, we hadn't brought up the topic in a long time, but Annie got an itch to start her research again, and—here we are."

"You lost your parents too?" Charlie asks, but for reassurance I assume, since Fisher just said so.

"Yes, they're both gone. I was told my mother died shortly after my birth, due to complications, and my father was immediately transported to Auschwitz due to a medical condition he suffered with. I was cared for by the nurses until we were released. Then I was placed in an unorthodox orphanage until I was sixteen."

"The nightmare will never end," Charlie says. "There is not

enough good in this world to undo what has been done. To see that the war is still affecting people so many years later, is the most disheartening part of everything I witnessed."

Fisher places his hand on my lap as he leans forward to look at Charlie. "Charlie, sir, the war brought us together. For that, we are thankful." It is a simple statement, but true. We were lucky to survive, and we were luckier to have found one another, to have one another as a life-long comrade who will understand the feeling of emptiness that remains in a small part of our hearts.

Mom is lost in thought again, and I'm worried we said too much today. We are supposed to be careful with her stress level, and this is not healthy.

"I think we should make a pact that this topic is closed," I say out loud. "I will continue to seek out the information I'm looking for, but you can rest easy knowing it will not affect you or us in any way. I promise you that. Fisher and I have lived a normal life, for the most part, and that is what matters."

Neither Mom nor Charlie respond, and I wish I knew what was going through their minds, but I'm sure they need time to digest the information.

"Of course, dear," Charlie finally says as he stands from the sofa.

I stand, as well, and take his good arm within my hand. "Charlie, I know you are the one who saved Mom and me. I know what you did. Because of you, there is good that came out of all the evil. Thank you for my life," I tell him.

He swallows hard and clenches his jaw. "I would do it again in a heartbeat, Annie."

Fisher stands up from the couch and leans forward to give Mom a kiss on the cheek. "We're all here because of you," he says to her, softly. "You are an incredible woman and have been the best mum to me since Annie and I met. I could never thank you enough for the love you shared, even without knowing my past. You are the purest definition of amazing."

A tear falls from Mom's eye, and the sight of the one tear makes me feel like a jagged knife is slipping down the center of my chest. Mom doesn't cry. She does not shed tears, and I didn't know when the natural born emotions would take back their place in her soul, but after today, I see them emerging.

This means she's healing. It's about time she's on the mend.

Fisher takes my hand, and he leads us to the front door. "Annie," Mom says through a choke in her throat. "If you leave the country this time, please let me know so I don't worry, or have to find out from your sister again." Mom glances over, twisting her neck slowly to show her youthful smirk and raised brow to prove her all-knowing ways are still very present.

"Of course, Mom."

"We're going to go ahead and leave now," Fisher says, pointing to the door as if it were the safe place he needs to be.

"Send me some meatloaf if you go back to Prague, okay?" Charlie says.

"Oh, my goodness," I groan while opening the door. "You are unbelievable." I tug Fisher's sleeve to pull him out into the hall. "You've done it to Charlie, too, with the meatloaf."

As the door closes and I laugh off my quip, I fall heavily against the hallway wall, feeling more of the weight release from my shoulders—a weight that has been embedded within me for so long, and for the first time in what seems like forever, I feel somewhat free from my thoughts.

Fisher wraps his arms around me and presses my head down onto his shoulder, squeezing me the way I like to be held when my world feels like it's falling apart. He knows. "Let's see if Benjamin is alive, okay?" he whispers in my ear.

I try to stop the influx of emotions erupting through me, but I can't stop the gasp or the silent cry I unwillingly release. "I just need to know, Fisher."

"Me too, sweet pea. Me too."

21

1962 – PRAGUE, CZECHOSLOVAKIA - 20
YEARS OLD

DAY TWO IN PRAGUE

I REMEMBER WALKING beneath an archway decorated with a sign that read, "Arbeit macht frei," which roughly translates to, "Work makes you free." The very moment I tried to translate the German words, I knew it said something terrible. I didn't have to ask Fisher to elaborate because he mumbled it on the way in as he shook his fist toward it.

I remember that a part of my mind fantasized about the moment I would finally step onto the camp's grounds. I wondered if memories from when I was a baby would fill my head. I knew it wasn't possible to form memories from such a young age, but I wanted to, despite how horrific that time was. I wanted to see my birth mother's face, or something that could connect me to the missing pieces.

I didn't have the magical flashbacks I hoped for, but I did have a sick feeling in the pit of my stomach. Actually, it was more of a pain—a pain fierce enough to remember all these years later. I clutched the spot beneath my ribs and squeezed to try and unhinge the pain, but it was relentless.

"Are you okay, Annie?" Fisher asked when he noticed I stopped walking. I was directly in the center of a dirt-filled court-yard, surrounded by decaying cement blocks with door openings.

"I have a sharp pain," I told him.

"Do you think it could be your nerves?"

"I'm not sure." I tried to stretch and move in different direc-tions, hoping it would stop, but nothing worked.

"Maybe it's gas," Fisher said, as he placed his arm around my waist. The mention of gas on the second day we were spending together in person was probably one of the most mortifying moments throughout my younger years. Of course, I didn't realize the perspective I would gain in the following minutes, and how inferior that type of embarrassment might have felt if we were living in that camp as prisoners.

"Fisher!" I scolded.

"Sorry," he said with a chuckle. "It's true, though. It could be. Or, maybe it's from the espresso. It was quite strong, and you seemed to have lost that energy spark during the train ride."

"You were asleep," I remind him. "Anyway, no, no, I'm fine." I wasn't fine. It *was* probably a gas pain, but I was sure there was not a public restroom anywhere in the nearby vicinity.

"Are you sure you want to keep walking?"

"Yes, of course, I'll be fine." I continued to clutch my stomach as we moved forward.

Fisher led us in through the first open door, where we found two long rows of stacked wooden planks, three levels high. "This was one of the living quarters," Fisher said. "They crammed as many prisoners into these beds as they could. When someone became ill, the entire barrack would likely become infected too. That's how so many people died so fast."

The pain in my stomach was beginning to subside, but a wave of nausea was taking over. "Is this where we would have been?"

"I'm not sure what you mean?" Fisher asks while running his fingers down the length of the top wooden platform.

I closed my eyes and imagined a baby lying naked on one of the platforms, screaming from the cold and hunger. I imagined her lying there alone with no one around, no clue what she's missing out on, or who, for that matter. She didn't like the loneliness. The thoughts grew darker, consuming me—no baby should have been left alone in a prison, surrounded by hatred, or abandoned by soldiers who were supposed to be heroes. I needed to understand how anyone could turn their back on a baby.

My throat tightened with the thought of that baby being me. Acceptance was percolating slowly within my mind. I was that baby twenty years earlier. I reached over to the nearest wooden platform and placed my hand down on the soft, tattered wood. I could feel the baby's skin, the cool sensation of the powdery flesh. I ran the back of my knuckles against her cheek, trying to soothe her cries, but her face was hot in comparison to the rest of her body. I wondered how long she had been in tears, and alone. I thought, maybe if I held her, she would stop crying. I tried to pick her up, but instead, I fell against the wooden platform, collapsing onto it. I waved my arms around from side to side, looking for a baby, but I only found air in the empty space.

My knees collapsed, and I fell to the wooden planks below me. My throat hurt from the tightness swelling around my tonsils, and for the first time in a long while, sobs erupted from my throat— tears poured from my eyes. There was not a baby there to save. I was the baby, and I *was* saved, but I couldn't understand why I had to be saved or why was I put through that.

I felt everything in that moment; the cold, the hatred, the loneliness. It all hit me. It was a confusing way to feel, while knowing I was fortunate enough to have a loving family back at home. *It wasn't real, though.* What *was* real was taken from me before I had a chance to experience it. My fingertips scraped against the uneven splintered wooden floor, feeling the sandy dirt prickling the skin beneath my nails. I pressed the side of my face to the ground and screamed as loud as I could manage. I was screaming for the people who put me on this earth, pleading with them to come back for me.

I had forgotten I wasn't alone. I forgot Fisher was watching me —watching me break down, but I didn't care who was watching me. I was experiencing such grief that it was physically painful, and I needed to let it out.

Fisher startled me when his arms gently looped around my waist. "I have you, Annie. I have you. You're not alone." Fisher lifted me from the ground as if I were nothing more than a weightless feather. He gathered me in his arms and cautiously pressed my face against his chest. It seemed as if he didn't know whether it was okay to hold me in that way.

"Say that again," I mumbled.

"You're not alone, Annie. We're here together." The tears continued to barrel down the sides of my cheeks, and my heart pounded against the inside of my chest. I didn't think I would feel so emotional or upset being in that one space, but it was like life outside that dark barrack had paused, and I was facing a reconciliation of just how small the space between life and death was when I lived there many years ago.

"The other blue sky—it's down there," I cried. "That's where they all are, Fisher. I need to see the other blue sky. I just need to see that it exists. They're all there."

Fisher held me a little tighter and ran his fingers through my hair. "Shhh, it's okay. Let it out, Annie. You have a right to be angry and upset."

"Show me the other blue sky, please," I begged. I can hardly remember where those thoughts came from. I didn't understand what I was saying. It was nonsense. I knew there was only one sky. I knew there wasn't a sky beneath the wooden floor we were standing on, but I wanted to believe that everyone who died was down there, alive and well. Even if I couldn't be with them, I needed to know they were okay.

"There is only one blue sky, Annie. We're all here. Just because we can't see everyone, doesn't mean they aren't here."

"No, no, you don't understand. They are down there." I tried to pull away from Fisher, so I could be closer to the ground again, but he wouldn't let me go. He walked us back outside, and I didn't realize we were moving until I felt the sun warm the top of my head.

"Annie," Fisher said, releasing me from his hold. He turned me around and pressed his fingers beneath my chin so I would look up. "We're here. We're alive. We won. We're lucky. We need to appreciate that for *them*. They would want us to appreciate it. They would want us to stand in this very space where they may have suffered, and smile up at the sky. They would want us to be happy. I know this."

It was hard to let his words soak in, but after a short minute, his sentiment began to saturate the vivid agony that was burning through me. He was right, and I could see that.

His hands found my cheeks with a grip so loose, the touch nearly tickled. Fisher gazed down into my eyes with a look that captured my soul and embraced my inner inflictions. "This is how I tell the monsters we won," he said, as his lips touched mine. The sensation caused an explosive feeling within my heart. I was lost within our connected worlds whenever he touched me. Like he said, I wasn't alone. We were the same. We were claiming that spot and telling the enemy we won.

When Fisher pulled away, a shy smile tugged on the corners of his lips. Then, he peered up at the sky and squinted against the brightness. His dimples deepened, and his lips stretched out wider, forcing the creases in his face to nearly reach his ears. "They can't take this away," he shouted.

I didn't have it in me to repeat his words, though I felt them in my body. So, I followed his lead and smiled at the beautiful clear sky.

I was still wondering if I may have been right about the other sky—about there being another sky that contained the rest of our kind, but that thought may have just been a comfort to me in a way only I could understand. I realized everyone grieves their losses differently, and I was just at the beginning of coming to terms with mine. Fisher began his grieving process many years earlier and had more time to embrace his destiny.

"I don't think I can go any further here," I told him. I felt like a coward. It wasn't like me to give up on anything, but the thought of visiting any more parts of that horrid place was what was hurting my stomach.

"I didn't get much further the last time I came. This isn't a museum; it's a memorial, and you aren't proving anything to anyone by making it all the way through."

I had convinced myself before I visited Terezín that I would not give up. I would see it all, but I quickly came to realize that once I saw them, those sights would always stay with me. That was precisely what Mom had been protecting me from.

22

CURRENT DAY

IT HAS BEEN a month and five days since I was able to claim birth records and fill in the missing records with the registrar of missing people from the Holocaust. It was a lengthy process, which I will happily never go through again, but for the first time in my life, I'm a real person, with an authentic birth certificate and a passport, rather than a state-issued driver's license provided after a year of letters explaining my situation, proof from my childhood school records, and the Rabbi from my temple vouching for me. Mom assisted in this process but claimed that she didn't understand why my illegitimate birth certificate was not valid. She had to keep some truths to herself since she had no way of obtaining my actual birth certificate without admitting to the crime of stealing a child from another country, and maybe the memories are still too strong for her to revisit.

I assume a crime such as that would be a cause for arrest and possible prison time, but maybe not at this point in her life. In any case, it wasn't a risk we were willing to take. I spent years researching the laws and rules on identification and immigration, but it has become harder and harder to find what I was looking for without holding a red flag above Mom's head.

As these past few weeks have unfolded, Mom finally began to realize a lot of what my missing identification caused, including the validity of my marriage to Fisher, which still isn't in accordance with the law. Mom now knows that we only had a ceremony, but the papers were not signed because we couldn't prove my citizenship.

Fisher went through a lot of hard work to become a citizen of the United States, and it was no thanks to me.

I assumed the process of correcting my information with the Registry of Motor Vehicles was going to be more difficult than it was, but that part went smoothly. I left Mom's name out of my case, claiming I didn't know who brought me here or how I got to this country. Lying was terrifying, especially with the slight differences in my story when trying to obtain various records, but the thought of what could happen to an elderly woman was even scarier. Surprisingly, my answers, or lack thereof, sufficed. However, I still fear the day an immigration officer will knock on my door, seeking more information, but if there is anything I have learned through the years, it's to fear one day at a time, and today is not the day I need to worry about.

Through my research, I also obtained birth records for the man responsible for my life—Benjamin. There is not a death record on file, which means he should technically be alive. We learned he has been a resident of Pilsen, a town outside of Prague, since the war ended. I even have a current street address. I considered calling him to start the process of introducing myself, but since he is such an elderly man, I feared the many possible outcomes of what might happen during a simple phone call. Therefore, Fisher and I decided to finally return to Prague.

Mom and Charlie wanted to join us on this trip, but I couldn't risk traveling abroad with them, especially Mom, with her history of heart problems last year. Plus, I think it might be best that we do this on our own.

"Are you nervous?" Fisher asks as we slide into a rental car we signed for at Prague's airport.

"Not if you can manage these tiny little roads with this oversized car. I know you like to take your wide turns," I say, playing off my apprehension with a joke.

"You're making jokes—you're nervous," he corrects me.

"I'm excited, Fisher. It's taken a lifetime to have a life to claim, and now I want to sit back and enjoy everything that comes with it."

"That makes perfect sense, sweet pea."

I pull out my cell phone and open the driving directions I saved. It was hard to tell online, but I believe the address is of some type of retirement home, which is good since a man Benjamin's age shouldn't be living on his own. Although, I suppose there is a chance he hasn't been living alone. Maybe he remarried and had a family after the war. *If that were the case, I wonder if he ever thought of me.* I shake the thoughts out of my head. I've promised myself to stop questioning everything because there is no way of knowing the truth until I hear it.

The car ride is going by much quicker than I thought it would. It looks like we're only a mile away now. I'd rather not admit to the rush of anxiety aching through me, because Fisher will lecture me again. He's worried about my health now with these new discoveries, so I'm doing my best to show calmness, even when I'm not feeling the same way inside.

Fisher glances over at me and smiles sweetly before taking my hand from my lap. "See, I think they widened the roads. Nothing to worry about," he says.

"Oh, my gosh, I don't think that's the case, but yes, Fisher, sweetheart, you can still drive perfectly here. Would you like a reward for your heroic achievement?" I tap his hand with my other. His goofy personality never falters, not once in the years I've known him.

"I would, as a matter of fact. You already know what my reward is, though," he says with a sigh.

"Yes, I know—meatloaf at the pub. Are you sure the pub is still there? What am I saying? I'm sure you managed to use the internet long enough to check for that answer," I tease him.

"I did use The Google machine to find that answer, and yes, they are still in business. They even have an online menu, which shows a beautiful meatloaf entree, so there is nothing for you to worry about, my dear."

"Thank goodness. I was very worried, to be honest."

"Don't play with my emotions like that, Annie."

"We're here," I tell him, pointing to the retirement home I saw on the 3D map before we left. "This is it. There's a parking lot over there."

Fisher slowly pulls into the gravelly lot and parks next to a row of cars. The "what if" questions are begging to be spoken out loud, but I know they aren't necessary.

We step out of the car and meet around the front, taking each other's hands at the same time. "Okay, I'm a bit nervous," he admits, as he tugs on the white collar of his shirt poking out from beneath his pewter-gray sweater.

"What? Why?" I ask him.

"I don't know. We have both gone our whole lives without knowing our birth parents, and now you're about to meet one of yours. It's surreal. Have you considered how bizarre this is going to be?"

"Trust me, it's all I have considered," I tell him.

"You look lovely, by the way. You know I love that shade of burgundy on you. It's the same color as the scarf you wore the first day you arrived here back in 1962. You're still just as radiant, sweet pea."

"Thank you," I say sharply, giving him a questioning look. Now isn't the time I'd expect compliments on my casual sweater that I have worn many times before today.

"What if he doesn't—"

"Fisher," I stop him. "You are the one who has told me to stop questioning everything."

"You're right. Let's go inside, shall we?"

"How come you didn't make mention of my blue jeans?" I ask him.

"I'm sorry," he says. "Your blue jeans are radiantly blue today."

I swat my hand at his arm and pull it in toward me as I loop my hands around his bicep, so glad to have Fisher by my side at this moment. As we continue walking toward the entrance, I feel a rush of adrenaline moving through my legs, carrying me across the lot and through the doors of the building. The reception desk is free of other people, except for a woman sitting behind it.

A familiar sickness is brewing in my stomach and threatens my throat as I open my mouth to speak. "Excuse me, I'm hoping you can help me. I'm looking for Benjamin Sigel."

Please, let him be here. Please, God, tell me this isn't a mistake. Please. The woman stares at me for a long moment, seeming a bit dumbfounded, which is not a good sign of things to come. I can feel it in my bones. We just came all this way for nothing. That can't possibly be true.

"Are you a relative of his?" she asks. "You'll have to forgive me, but you don't look familiar."

"I—" I try to speak, but the words don't form on my tongue.

"Yes, she is his daughter—separated at birth," Fisher says.

The woman, who looks to be around our age, places her hand over her chest and slouches back into her chair. "You're Benjamin's daughter?"

"Yes," I manage to say through a heavy exhale.

"He's always spoken about losing his daughter in the war. He likes to tell war stories a lot."

A hiccup bucks in my throat. "So, he's here? Right now?" I don't know if she understood my question as it was hardly audible.

"Uh, you see, he's not currently at this location."

"Why, where is he?" My hands have landed on the countertop, and I'm gripping so tightly that I hope the strength in my hands is enough to hold the rest of my body upright.

"I'm so sorry to be the one to tell you this, but—"

"He's gone?" I choke. "Please, don't tell me he's gone. I just called the Department of Records here in the Czech Republic, and they told me he was not dead. There has to be a mistake."

"Madam, I didn't mean to upset you. He is not gone, but he is with hospice right now. He has been ill for a while, and he asked us to make him comfortable."

"Hospice?" I repeat.

"Yes, it's just across the way, on the other side of the parking lot. You can visit with him over there, if you would like."

I peer over at Fisher, seeing the same lost look in his eyes that I feel in my chest. "We didn't miss him, Annie. He's still alive," Fisher says.

"He's very much aware of his surroundings," the administrator says.

"Thank you," I offer as we both turn around, probably looking like a pair of zombies.

"He's still alive," Fisher says again.

I can't find the words to respond. I just need to focus on walking and breathing as I cross the parking lot to the other building. The stone wall on the outside appears to be a mile away, but my feet carry me as if I were walking on air, and we make it to the building in what seems like one long-held breath.

When Fisher reaches for the door handle, an orange monarch butterfly lands on a plant next to the door. The wings are fully erect, and it seems as if the beautiful insect is looking directly at us, trying to send a message. Fisher peers over at me with a small smile. "There ... now we know it's okay. Everything is going to be okay," he says, pulling open the front door.

Once again, we are greeted by the smells of a hospital, but the setting is nothing like a medical facility. It feels more like a spa inside, which soothes the pain and nerves jittering through my body. We approach the front desk, and once again, we ask for Benjamin Sigel.

"Of course." The gentleman asks us if we're family, just as the other facility did.

"Yes," I answer simply this time.

"He's having a good day today," the man says. "Follow me. I'll take you to his room."

Fisher reclaims my hand as we walk side-by-side down a salmon-colored hallway, finished with white trim and dark wooden floors. The paintings that line the walls are abstract but beautifully arranged. It seems like a nice place to die, I suppose. It's certainly better than the alternative.

The gentleman gently waves his arm toward the partially opened door of room 111. "Enjoy your time with him," the man says.

I nod, hoping my gesture will suffice as a *thank you*, and I pull in a deep breath that's accompanied by the scent of bleach and soap.

We step inside the room, similarly decorated as the hallway. A man about Mom's age is lying in the bed, flipping through a newspaper. He has a full head of white and gray hair, and he hardly has a wrinkle on his face, which I think is a bit unusual for an elderly man.

"Excuse me … are you Mr. Sigel?" I ask, walking in a little further toward him.

The man looks down at his watch before responding but then peers up at Fisher and me. "I guess that's still me for now; not sure how much longer, huh?" he responds with laughter. "How can I —?" He stops talking mid-sentence and his mouth falls open from what may be shock because he looks like he's staring at a ghost.

I should have laughed at his joke, but I couldn't figure out how to react. I'm staring at the poor man as if I've forgotten how to speak again. I swallow to push away the influx of thoughts. "Would you mind if I took a seat?" I ask.

Benjamin looks over at the guest chair and back at me. "Of course," he says, breathlessly. His chest is rising and falling so quickly,

I'm afraid of talking too quickly. Yet, I'm also worried I'm not talking quickly enough. Tremors run through my body as I take the chair, pulling it up toward his bed. Fisher positions himself behind me and rests his hands on my shoulders for the support I desperately need.

"You—um—I'm sorry, you look like someone—" he begins.

"Mr. Sigel, there isn't exactly a simple way to say this to you, but ... I'm Lucie Sigel."

The newspaper drops to Benjamin's lap, and his hands follow. His mouth falls open, and I suddenly realize I hadn't considered the possibility of what my confession might do to him in person, never mind the phone. I should have thought this through. I could give the poor man a heart attack. I don't know if that's what's happening, or if he is in shock.

He shakes his head around for a moment and widens his eyes as if he's trying to focus on me. "Lucie ... that was the name my wife and I were going to give our daughter—"

"I am your daughter—we just never got to meet." His hand lifts back up from his lap, his arm is trembling, and his fingers shake as he places his hand over his mouth. Benjamin's eyes fill with tears, and he hasn't blinked since I spoke.

"I spent my life wondering about you," he says, softly. "There were no records of a Lucie with a last name. I didn't even know what day you were born once your mother was taken from me, and there wasn't a speck of information on where I could even begin to find you. It was unknown whether you were dead or alive, but I prayed. I prayed every single day that you—made it, somehow."

"Your prayers were answered. I made it," I tell him. My eyes burn from the tears working their way through the backs of my eyes.

"You have my eyes," he says. "You have your mother's small nose and her beautiful lips. You look exactly like her, Lucie."

Lucie ... no one has ever called me Lucie. "I look like her?" I say, trying to make my words clear, but they sound muffled through the tightness of my tensed jaw.

"You could be her, if I didn't know better."

I can't help touching my face as if it would give me a sense of connection to his words, but I wish I could see for myself. Benjamin's words floated around me as I gazed around the room, spotting a framed picture on a small dresser below his television. A flutter of apprehension sloshes around in my stomach, and I stand from my chair, feeling a magnetic pull toward the picture frame. I take the few steps across the room and gently reach for the photograph.

"That's my Leah," Benjamin spoke softly. "Your mother."

I lift the framed photo, my hands shaking uncontrollably as I hold it up in front of me. Leah couldn't have been more than twenty years old here—she was so young. My mother had long, silky dark hair with large, voluminous waves draped over her shoulders. Her eyes were big, beautiful, and they seem so full of life and possibility. I can tell we have the same nose and lips, just as Benjamin said. I feel the connection, and I'm just looking at a simple old photo. It's as if there is another world between us now.

"Keep it," Benjamin says. "There's another one over by the window with the two of us. Take that too."

"Oh, I couldn't possibly …"

"Please," he insists. "I won't have much use for photos soon."

My eyes are burning from holding back my tears. This doesn't feel real. After all these years, I'm finally holding the images of my biological parents in my hands. "Thank you," I whisper. "Thank you, so very much. I will cherish these forever."

"It's nice to hear I will be remembered after I'm gone, Lucie. I suppose I can say my dying wish has been granted." Benjamin struggles to smile, and it appears as if he's trying to hide the pain.

I return to my seat with the framed pictures and sit back down in front of Benjamin. "What are you dying of?" I ask softly, as gently as possible. It doesn't exactly matter, but it was the next unplanned question to come out of my mouth.

"I have been dying of a broken heart since 1945, Lucie."

My face strains to comprehend the meaning of his statement, which I'm not sure I understand. "How?"

"Shortly after I was liberated, I had some undiagnosed medical conditions that came as a surprise. Somehow, I survived the war with a literal hole in my heart. I wasn't expected to make it past the first year of my life, or even make it to ten years old, never mind fifty and now past ninety. God wanted me to test the odds of life, I suppose. However, it has become a struggle to keep up now. The hole has gotten bigger, and surgery is no longer an option, so I can't do much of anything but wait it out."

"A hole in your heart," I say again. Fisher's hands clench my shoulders, and I know what he's thinking, and it is exactly what I'm thinking.

"You have an American accent," he says.

"I was rescued after Leah passed away, and I was taken to America. I was given a wonderful life by a loving family," I tell him.

"Hearing this brings me so much joy, Lucie." He clutches his hand over his chest, and the skin on his forehead wrinkles with what looks like concern. "Could you pull that rolling table over for me?" Benjamin asks.

Fisher reaches for the rolling bed table, pulling it over the bed and up to Benjamin's chest.

He reaches to his opposite side and retrieves a notepad and a pen. "Oh, just one second, please," Benjamin says while jotting down some words on a piece of paper.

We wait for a long couple of minutes, and I'm utterly curious about what he is writing down. Benjamin finally folds up the paper and hands it to me. "If the woman who raised you is still alive and well, please give her this note. I want to thank her for what she did for you. It's the very least I'm able to do, but I need her to know how greatly I appreciate her giving you a life that I wasn't able to offer you."

I feel stunned by his thoughtful gesture. He seems like a wonderful man. It's a shame there's no more time to get to know him. It's a shame life has worked out the way it has. I take the note from his hand and slip it into my purse. "I will see that she gets this," I tell him.

"Good. Thank you." He looks sad but relieved at the same time. "Please know, if I knew of your whereabouts, I would have come for you. I did want to give you a good life. After a while, though, I had to assume you were gone, like my Leah. My only hope was that if you had somehow survived, you were experiencing a good life." He tries to smile, but his lips quiver at the attempt to be happy. "Is this your husband?" Benjamin points to Fisher.

"Yes, sir, my name is Fisher Benson. Your daughter and I met when we were twenty and have been inseparable since. I have done my best to give her a good life, as well."

I glance up at Fisher and mouth, "You have given me everything."

"This is just—this is simply incredible. Any kids? Do I have grandkids?"

In an instant, without warning, my world pauses again. My breath disappears from my lungs, and I'm left struggling for air.

My head nods to say yes, but the word *no* echoes around us in this small room.

23

It took me two years of marriage to lose sight of my sins. I never shared my feelings out loud, but the thoughts spun like a lump of clay on a spinning wheel, revolving so fast, everything I had pieced together repeatedly falling apart, again and again. I was about to give up the battle of having a proper identity, and I was going to stop considering the possible outcomes of confronting Mom with my truth.

Mom must have assumed the fake paperwork Dad had made for me when I was younger, worked. It was hard to tell if it was denial on her part, or an abundance of faith that no one would take a closer look at the validity of my papers. I knew if I brought this topic to her, she would live in fear, misery, and defeat, and after all she had done for me, that was the last thing I wanted. I knew my appreciation for the life she provided me should be enough.

For a while, I thought I could slide by without the proper paperwork officiating my life. It's not like I wasn't alive and real. Papers were just papers. I had gotten good at finding a work-around, but I fell short when it came to applying for a marriage license.

I could have risked using my fake birth record, or I could stop tempting fate and accept that my relationship to Fisher was bound by other means. However, living together out of wedlock would not have been acceptable to Mom and Dad. Therefore, I needed to make the appearance of our wedding real—as real as it felt, and still feels. To me, I'm officially Mrs. Fisher Benson—Annie Benson.

We had our wedding, but it wasn't a legally binding commitment as everyone thought it was. Only Fisher and I knew the truth.

Fisher became a citizen on his own, through hard work at the fire station. Mom and Dad didn't know the truth about Fisher moving to the United States to be with me. Therefore, they were led to believe we met in New York at the art gallery I worked for.

However, the lie I was living kept growing. I felt like it was only a matter of time before everything was out on the table. I was beginning to lose sight of who I was, which scared me, since I didn't know the person I was born to be, either.

"Annie," Fisher said, as he wheeled me through the halls of the hospital. "Are you doing okay, sweet pea?"

"I'm fine," I lied. I was scared out of my mind. I was about to have a baby, and I didn't know the first thing about being a mother. How could I be a mother when I didn't know how to be an actual person? That was the root of my web of obsessive thoughts, although the hormones probably weren't helping at that moment either.

"I wish I could stand beside you," Fisher said. I had a hard time agreeing to the doctor's birth plan when we spoke at the appointment before I was scheduled to be at the hospital. He made it clear that husbands were not allowed in the delivery room. I didn't care for that policy. It's not that I was particularly fond of the idea that Fisher would see me in such a compromising position, but I wanted the comfort of him being there.

Whenever we went through anything scary, we had done so

together. Plus, he wasn't like most other husbands I came to know. Sure, he did work many hours and came home incredibly dirty and tired, but he never showed me a lack of appreciation. Fisher never expected dinner to be on the table when he got home. He didn't expect the apartment to be clean, or his mail to be waiting for him. He didn't expect anything. Instead, each day, he came home from work and looked surprised that I had made him dinner and cleaned our home. Every single day, he tried to show me how grateful he was for what I did while he was at work.

My days at the art gallery had become few and far between, especially during the pregnancy, since they didn't want to be responsible for anything happening to me while I was on my feet for such long spans of time. However, I felt great every single day of my pregnancy. I didn't experience the common side effects I read so much about. My doctor told me I should consider myself a lucky woman since I had the privilege of enjoying my pregnancy. I certainly did feel lucky.

By the time I reached my third trimester. I was relieved of my job at the gallery, which was for the best, since I would have needed to take a lengthy leave of absence anyway. Though Mom had already stated her declaration of being our baby's full-time caretaker, I argued with her a bit because I was determined to learn how to be a mother without full-time help. We were living in a time when women were capable of handling more than we had once given ourselves credit for, and I was determined to prove that.

"I won't even know what's happening," I reminded Fisher. The hospital hallway felt endless as we continued rolling along toward the maternity ward.

"I know. That's the problem. It worries me, Annie," he affirmed.

I grabbed his arm, holding onto him gently. "In just a few short hours, we're going to be a mommy and daddy. That's all we should focus on. Besides, my parents and Clara will be sitting with you to keep you company."

"Right," he said, continuing to push ahead as we followed a nurse carrying a clipboard.

All I could think about at that moment was ... who decided to put the maternity ward on the farthest side of the hospital?

"How many arguments do you think I will have to break up between your mother and Clara while I'm chewing my nails off?"

"Oh," I laughed. "Just tune them out. They are good at resolving their daily bickers."

"What a day this is going to be, sweet pea."

"It's going to be the best day. The very best," I told him.

The moments became blurry from that time on. Whatever medication they gave me was causing me to get drowsy. Apparently, it caused me to forget some of the details that led up to the time I was placed under anesthesia too. I was not given the option to remain awake like mothers are today, but I suppose that was par for the course of medical practice in the sixties.

I woke up feeling cold, out of sorts, and queasy. It was terrible, as I remember it. I didn't feel like my eyes were even completely open when a bundled baby was placed gently into my arms.

The words, "It's a boy," brought me out of my haze in a way that made me feel like my body had been zapped by an electrical current. He was, indeed, a boy—nearly identical to Fisher but with my eyes and lips. He was the most beautiful little person I have ever seen in my entire life.

Fisher's hand seemed to come out of nowhere as he placed it down on top of mine. When I glanced up at my sweet husband, he was crying—tears of joy. I had never seen Fisher cry prior to that day, and the sight of his tears made me feel like I would be crying for days. "He's our little boy, Annie. He's ours." Fisher's voice was raspy and broken up. He was truly elated, and there was pure joy pouring out of him.

I couldn't manage to respond. I could only smile down at the two big eyes staring up at us as if we were his universe. He *was* ours. We finally had a family—a real family—one tied together by blood.

"What shall we name him, sweet pea?" Fisher whispered near my ear.

Fisher's question had entered my mind daily from the time we got the result of my pregnancy test, to my initial blood work. Truthfully, I had fallen in love with a name almost immediately, but I sat with it and let it grow with me. I wanted to share my thoughts with Fisher at the right moment, which happened to be the moment we laid eyes on our little boy. "I have been thinking of the name *Sky*. You know, like the blue sky. I want him to have meaning and purpose in his life. I want him to be the piece that ties everyone and everything together."

"I think that's brilliant, Annie. Brilliant. *Sky*. You are holding the sky in your hands. We must take good care of him because he has a big job to do," Fisher cooed, while lightly touching the tip of his finger to Sky's nose.

"May we come in?" I heard from the door. It was Mom. Behind her, I could hear Clara squealing with excitement, and then I heard Dad clearing his voice with what sounded like unease.

"Of course," I said, beaming through my words.

"Oh my God, Annie," Mom said, boisterously. "Look at those eyes—such a perfect face. Oy, I'm getting choked up."

"Sweetie—" Dad said with glossy eyes. I never saw him get emotional like he did that day.

"It's a boy," Fisher announced.

"Well, I can tell," Clara cooed. "He is just the most handsome little boy I have ever seen."

Mom leaned over my bedside and placed a kiss on my forehead and held her lips there. "I'm so proud of you, sweetie. Look what you did," she whispered. "He's simply perfect, isn't he?" She then placed a kiss on Sky's tiny nose. "Welcome to our crazy little family. I'm your grandmother!" Mom couldn't stop smiling at Sky. It was obvious she fell in love immediately, just as I had.

"I want to hold him!" Clara shouted, a little too loudly.

"Clara," Dad scolded her silently. "Fisher probably hasn't even gotten to hold his son yet. We were just coming in to congratulate them. We can visit more later, okay?"

Clara groaned. I figured she would understand someday, so I let her mood go unnoticed. Dad switched spots with Mom and gave me a kiss on the cheek. "He's just wonderful. Finally, another man in this family," Dad said.

"What about me?" Fisher asked.

"Yeah, yeah," Dad joked with him.

"Very funny," Fisher responded. The two of them were constantly jabbing each other with crude jokes. It was nice that they had a good relationship, though. It was important to me that Fisher was as close to my family as I was.

"Mr. and Mrs. Benson," a man's voice boomed from the doorway. He was a doctor, one I figured was there to visit Sky and to make sure we were both doing well.

"Oh, hi, doctor," I greeted him. "I'd like you to meet Sky Benson." I held him up, to show off his perfection.

"He's a cute one," the doctor said. "Congratulations to you both, and little Sky, of course." The doctor's words sounded monotone, like he was just making his rounds and had already seen a hundred babies that day. I could understand his job probably got boring after a while, but to us, our lives just got a whole lot better. We were floating on a cloud, and even a dud of a doctor wasn't going to bring us down.

"Are you here to check on us?" I asked, wondering why he continued to just stand there, looking at us.

"I am," he said. "Folks, would you mind stepping out for a moment while I—"

"Of course!" Dad exclaimed while wrapping his arms around Mom and Clara and guiding them out of the room. They did not want to leave. At that moment, I had a feeling I didn't want them to leave either. I just wasn't sure why yet.

As soon as everyone was out of the room but us and the doctor, he continued to speak. "I would like to have a word with you both, if you don't mind?"

"Of course, what is it?" Fisher asked without taking his eyes off Sky.

"Well, you see ... I have a bit of a concern," he said. The word "concern" seemed to suddenly highlight all the pains inside my body at that very moment. The medication was wearing off, and I felt like I was about to burst into flames. The doctor immediately noticed the change in my facial expression. "Oh my, are you uncomfortable, Annie?"

"Yes, very," I answered the doctor.

"Nurse! Could you please find Mrs. Benson something to control her pain?" The doctor shouted into the hallway, then returned to my bedside. "As I was saying, about my concern, I—I don't want to jump to any strong conclusions yet, but it seems your son—Sky—may have a slight congenital abnormality. We need to run some more tests before anything is conclusive, but we wanted you to be aware of the situation."

"What?" Fisher said, on behalf of both of us. The wind had been sucked straight out of my lungs, and I couldn't respond, or even speak. My baby—he was right there in my arms—perfect as anything. Sky couldn't have some sort of birth defect. I was sure the doctor had to be incorrect with his suspicions. "What could be wrong with a baby merely an hour old?" Fisher continued with the questions, ones I would have asked if I were able to think as quickly as he was.

"Sky was in some distress when we delivered him," the doctor said, then lifted his hands toward us as if he needed to hush our concerns. That is exactly what he should have been doing, but not by silently gesturing that we should be calm. "I assure you Sky *is* stable now, but while we were giving him extra oxygen, we took a couple of blood samples to make sure everything was okay."

"Okay, so, did the tests come back normal?" Fisher asked, sounding hostile. Fisher had typically been the calmer one of us, but he was turning red in the cheeks, and as for me, I felt like punching the doctor square in the jaw. Maybe I would have if I had figured out how to move without writhing in pain.

"Unfortunately, some of his results were not in the average range we like to see. Honestly, I can't tell you how this will affect Sky yet, but I assure you, we will do whatever we can to narrow down our concerns to facts as quickly as possible."

"He's fine," I snapped. "How dare you walk in here like you're someone important, then tell a new mother that there is something wrong with her child? You must be some monster, like one of those—" I clenched my teeth together firmly, trying to stop the words threatening to erupt from the depths of my sour stomach. "Like one of those—" Fisher placed his hand on my shoulder, gripping me firmly. "Sweet pea, you're still under some anesthesia. Let's allow the doctor to run some more tests before we say anything hasty. I'm sure it's all a mistake."

Fisher didn't mean what he said. I could see it on his face. I knew every single one of the faces he made when he felt a different emotion. He was scared out of his mind that the doctor was right.

So was I.

A WEEK in that hospital came and went. Mom, Dad, and Clara visited often, spending a lot of that time reassuring Fisher and me that the doctors didn't know what they were talking about, that I shouldn't listen to anyone, and that I should only focus on the good. I felt the need to appease them with a nod or a shake of my head because they were clearly in denial, as I wished to be.

I can't even remember how many tests were performed on Sky, but it seemed like there were more bandages and tubes around him than his little body could handle. He was quiet and observant. He didn't cry much unless he was hungry, which made him quite amazing for a baby—perfect. Despite the doctors' warnings, statements, and diagnoses, Sky was the definition of perfection. That was what I tried to focus on. However, every time I would think of him as perfect, a voice inside of my head reminded me that I was told otherwise.

"Are you ready to take Sky home with you?" one of the nurses asked as she was checking his vitals.

"I'm a bit nervous I'm going to do something wrong," I told her.

"Well, all new mothers feel that way. You're going to do just fine, Annie." That particular nurse was there a lot. She was one of the regulars coming in and out of my room throughout that week. I feel like we bonded a bit, especially when she shared stories about her daughter who was born six weeks early and suffered developmental delays because of her prematurity. That lovely nurse made me feel a little less alone, even though Sky's diagnosis was different. It was going to take a miracle to change the mindset I had—the one where solid ground meant raising a child for eighteen years or more until he was sufficiently capable of surviving on his own. I had to adjust my thoughts to raising a child until he didn't need me any longer—no official end date.

"Felicia," I said, addressing the nurse. "I want to thank you for the time you spent with me this past week. It was very helpful. I am, by no means, *okay*, but your words will stick with me forever."

"Annie, I gave you my phone number, and I expect you to use it. This is just between us ladies—moms. If you need a friend, I'm here."

"You're wonderful. Thank you," I told her.

"Of course. You have your surgery scheduled for Sky next week, so I will see you then. Make sure you get some rest, you understand?"

"Yes," I told her.

I glanced over at Fisher, who had finally fallen asleep after a week of forgoing any opportunity of rest. Unless he passed out from exhaustion, he forced himself to stay awake. I know he was scared something would happen to Sky if he dozed off for a moment. I tried to assure him we would be okay, but Fisher was grieving with a new type of pain, just as I was. There was no way to know how to navigate through that time. We handled our feelings through instinct.

"Fish," I whispered, hoping I wouldn't startle him awake. He was probably comatose by that point, after sleeping four solid hours. I couldn't move too far with Sky asleep in my arms, so I nudged his chair with my foot. "Fisher, we can go home now."

Maybe it was the word "home" that brought him back to life, but he gasped as if air had been pumped into his lungs. "What? We're going home?"

I smiled as hard as my face would allow those muscles to move, while the inherent sadness I felt, tugged against my attempt. "They just gave us all the discharge letters. We can go." My voice sounded exactly how I was feeling inside. There was no point in trying to hide the reality of the truth.

"Okay, I'm going to go pull the car up front. You stay put. Will you be okay for a minute?"

"Fisher, sweetie, we're fine." We're not, but the answer to his question would still be the same. For a moment, we would be okay.

"Okay, okay. Just—I will be right back. He shook his head around to snap out of his sleepy haze as he jogged out of the room.

I looked down at Sky, watching him watching me, and wondering what was going on inside of his little head. I ran my fingers through the few sprigs of dark curls he had and sang him a lullaby I remember Mom singing to Clara when she had nightmares.

> Good night, my beautiful baby,
> Good night,
> May God watch over you.
> Good night, sleep well, beautiful baby,
> May you dream sweet dreams.

AFTER SLOWLY SINGING THE WORDS, trying to hold back my tears as

Sky closed his eyes, Fisher returned like a bat out of hell with a wheelchair. "What is the emergency?" I asked him in a whisper with a quiet chuckle. It was the first time I had made any attempt to laugh that week, but Fisher looked ridiculous. He was sweating and out of breath, and the people around the hospital were probably confused when they saw him running with an empty wheelchair.

He stopped to think for a moment, as if he hadn't considered his reason for rushing. "I'm not sure. I'm just nervous, I suppose."

"I know," I agreed.

"Okay, here we go now, yeah?" He took Sky carefully from my hands, curling his arms around him, and carrying him like he was a fragile piece of fine china. Fisher looked terrified every time he held him, but he never denied an opportunity to hold his son, which made me fall more in love with him than I already was.

With some dull aches and pains, I pushed myself off the uncomfortable hospital bed and made my way over to the wheelchair. I hadn't imagined a day where I would be wearing such an unattractive outfit like the pinstriped nightgown-looking dress I was sporting, but life at that moment was about comfort.

Once I was settled in the chair, Fisher gently passed Sky back over to me. He was still asleep and content. I could have watched him sleep for hours and never get bored. I imagined what his dreams were like, but then I remembered Fisher's words about dreams, and thought maybe it was best if we all thought that way going forward. It was most important to make each of Sky's days as good as they could be, so he wouldn't feel the need to dream of anything better. That would be our mission.

24

CURRENT DAY

"I SUPPOSE my grandchild would be all grown up by now, huh?" Benjamin says, with a struggling hoot of laughter.

"Yes, sir," Fisher says, before I can answer.

"Well, boy or girl? Name?" Benjamin continues to question.

"A boy—Sky," Fisher says, seeming quick to answer the questions, and I'm getting the hint that he doesn't want me to say any more about Sky than what he is saying, but is that the right thing to do? Benjamin is on his deathbed.

"How nice," Benjamin says, leaning back into his pillow with a dazed look in his eyes. "It's ironic that we go through life wondering what could have been, then it's a surprise when you find out what was. I often wondered if my life was full of challenges I needed to meet and accomplish throughout the time I was alive. Then, I considered how unfair life could be to offer only cause and purpose, while never providing insight or reason. I have tried, and tried again, to understand the meaning of everything I have experienced, but even now, I'm not sure I can comprehend it all."

"I've always enjoyed writing," I tell Benjamin, in response. "It's truly the reason I came to meet Fisher." I squeeze Fisher's hand because it's the truth. I'm not sure I would have been motivated to write so many letters to a stranger over the course of two years if I didn't truly enjoy the experience writing brought to me. "You were a writer too, right?"

"Oh yes, I spent my life writing. I have a couple of published books, in fact."

"I would love to read them," I tell him. I didn't see the books when I was searching for information on Benjamin, but I need to find them.

"I used a pseudonym. The books will be found under the name, B. Sigel."

"I look forward to finding them. I have dreamed of writing a book," I admit, knowing I have never admitted that thought out loud before, not even to myself. The idea has always seemed too daunting to attempt.

"You should, Lucie. You should. I am sure you have quite a story to tell the world." The way Benjamin is speaking sounds as though the words are coming on their own, and he isn't here with us in the present moment.

"I spent most of my life wondering about you and Leah," I tell him. "I wanted to imagine my life in a way that wasn't affected by the Holocaust. I wondered where I might have grown up, or what life would have been like, for that matter."

Benjamin smiles slightly. "I have spent many years wondering the same. Leah was the love of my life, as were you, even though I never got the chance to meet you. I loved you from the moment you made your presence known inside your mother's—Leah's—small belly. She walked around as though she were carrying you on the outside, while you were still comfortably resting inside. We lived here, in Pilsen. We didn't have much, but we made the most of our lives and what we did have. I had big plans for our family. I was determined to become an artist and sell my work all over the world, but I lost my desire to paint once I lost you and your mother."

A numbness has taken over my entire body. The words he's speaking seem like a story out of a book, rather than the dream he once had for his family—for me.

Dreams don't always come true—sounds like Benjamin's story lines up with Fisher's theory.

"I'm sure I would have had a lovely life here with you," I tell him. Part of me would like to ask if he remarried and had any other children, but the other part of me would like to pause the story where it is and live on without knowing the rest—since the rest doesn't involve me.

Benjamin turns his head and looks at me with sadness in his light brown eyes. "I am so grateful you flew here to meet me, Lucie. I'm sorry we couldn't have met sooner in life, but I believe and hope we'll be together again sometime in another life. Throughout the course of my life, it became clear that I needed to learn something very important—the meaning of life and every-thing found within it. I have learned to love, lose, and the value of intangible belongings. Life isn't about the hate. It's about the growth from experiencing hate. I survived every odd there was, and it doesn't seem like an achievement, but what my heart has survived—that is something very few can claim."

"You are very wise," I tell him. "I couldn't agree with you more. I feel the same way. I'm not sure I experienced the same pain as you, but in my way, I have suffered a great deal of loss with the time it has taken me to find myself. I'm not sure what the lesson was in my situation, but I feel stronger for what I have been through."

My words are just words. I don't feel what I'm saying because it doesn't make sense inside, not like it sounds when speaking. I can't pretend like I don't feel as though I wasted too many days of my life piecing together a puzzle that would eventually come together as a blurry image. I can't seem to understand the reason for the losses I've experienced.

"Lucie, my dear, there is one thing I wish to leave with you. Even though I never thought I would get the chance to say this, I'm grateful I do know what I needed to learn—even in my final moments here."

"What's that?" I ask, pulling my chair a bit closer to his bed.

"Embrace it all. If you do, your soul will move on to experience a lesser task of appreciating the horrors we faced. I believe those we lost will return in our lifetime in one form or another to let us know they are okay, and hopefully they are getting another chance to experience what they should have. When you see a new life, and feel a connection, consider the deeper meaning. We're all here in this world, but we may be unrecognizable to the naked eye. It's the connection inside that will draw you to your origins."

"Wow," Fisher says. "That's incredible; I never considered the thought."

"It has gotten me here, to this point, where I feel fulfilled enough to leave this journey behind. Now that you have come to see me, I know this life is complete for me."

The knot in my throat won't allow me to say much, even if I had words worthy of following his. Instead, I stand up and lean over to hug the man that should have spent his life with me. I place a kiss on the stranger's cheek and whisper, "Thank you," in his ear. Words form, and I believe it's the only proper response to offer after the wisdom he shared. "You have given me more in the last few minutes than I could have asked for in my lifetime."

"We are blessed," Benjamin says. "Thank you, son, for taking care of the little girl I never got to care for." Benjamin struggles to lift his neck as he nods toward Fisher.

"It has been my pleasure and will continue to be," Fisher says.

Benjamin takes a deep breath and slowly leans back into his pillow. "I'm going to go now," he says. "I should do so alone, though."

His words send a set of chills up my spine that travels through my limbs and face. I don't know whether to feel upset or satisfied, but Fisher is helping me out of the chair and taking me away from what I had been tiredly searching for so long. "Goodbye," I offer.

"No, Lucie, it's not goodbye. It's until we meet again, yes?"

"Until next time," I repeat, but beneath my breath, choking on my own air.

This isn't fair.

The world is a blur and spinning around me as Fisher takes me from the room and guides me back down the hallway and out into the fresh air, tears trickling down my cheeks. We don't speak as we make our way to the car, or as we travel to the hotel where we are residing for a couple of days. I don't know how to process it. I can't handle any more.

It's too much.

It has always felt like too much.

How has he been able to accept a reality in which he loses everything, yet still find beauty at the end? I don't understand. I thought I would feel like less of a stranger to myself once I gained my full identity, and meeting my birth father was an unexpected blessing I never expected to experience, but now I feel more lost in my head than I ever have before.

Why was I punished so severely? What did I do to deserve so much loss? I am grateful for a loving husband and family, which is more than many people can wish for, but the big picture shows so many shadows of empty spaces that should have taken up space in my life. I feel like a balloon filled with water but covered with tiny pinholes—so many pinholes, I can't possibly stop the water from eventually draining out completely.

"Annie, I need you to speak to me, sweet pea," Fisher says as we pull into the parking space at our hotel. "You don't look well, and I'm worried."

"I'm not well," I tell him.

"Okay, do you feel sick? Are you upset? Talk to me, sweet pea."

"Yes," I respond.

Fisher steps out of the car and runs around the front toward my side. He opens my door and reaches in for me, but I don't feel his hands on my body as he pulls me out. "I need to get to you a doctor," he says.

"No," I argue. "I need you to give me time and a little space. Please. Take me to our hotel room and go to the pub like you wanted. Then, I'll be ready to go home when you come back."

"Annie, we're supposed to be here for another three days. Do you want me to change our plans?"

"Yes," I tell him.

He's appears distraught and confused, just as I am.

"Please."

"I'm not going to leave you like this."

"Please," I say again. I can't see right. Life is blurry. Life isn't real. This isn't real.

"No, Annie, I'm not leaving you to go to a damn pub."

"I just need to lay down," I tell him.

Pricks of cold sensations run up my arm that he's holding onto, and I feel as though I'm on a moving escalator as we make our way inside the hotel lobby. I can't smell the sweet aroma of pastries from the bakery off to the side of the elevator toward where we're heading. I can't smell the flowers we're walking past either.

The bronze elevator door opens, and I touch the metal, seeking a sensation I'm familiar with, but there is numbness within my fingertips. "Are you anxious?" Fisher asks.

"No," I respond, feeling like the word is as elongated as a long exhale.

The doors to the elevator close, and I see the reflection of us in the shiny metal, but the figures look distorted, like a radio wave. Is this how everyone sees me too? I switch my focus from the reflection to the buttons lighting up one by one as we ascend toward our floor. I can see the numbers, but when I concentrate on them, everything else liquefies. My brain feels broken. Maybe a human mind can only handle so much in one lifetime until it shuts down from overheating.

The elevator doors open, and we glide down the carpeted hallway, greeted by the swirling chevron wallpaper that's watching us as if we are significant figures.

Our room is bright, filled with sun and white fabrics and wallpaper. The decor is white too. Fisher helps me to the bed and removes my shoes, one at a time, then pulls the plush blanket up to my neck. "Just rest, sweet pea. Everything is going to be okay." He places his cool hand on my forehead and runs his fingers through my hair.

"I let myself go. I'm sorry," I tell Fisher. Ever since life turned upside down, I struggled to keep up with the speed we were moving. Instead, life sped by and left me standing in the center while everything continued around me. Now, I'm here, and I want to go back to the time when my life should have begun. Why don't we have that option? I want to do things again.

"Annie, you aren't making any sense. I'm calling a doctor, okay?"

"No, please, I'm fine. I just need my mind to catch up to the thoughts."

"Annie, I think you're having a breakdown of sorts. This situation isn't healthy, after your last episode. I need to make sure you are okay. You are my wife, and I am caring for you the way you would care for me, right?"

"Fisher, I am all right. Believe me. I just need to digest things."

"Things?"

"I need to understand."

"Understand what, Annie?"

"Lucie, I'm Lucie. I'm not Annie."

The scent of Fisher's cologne stings my nose, as it's the first smell I've encountered since we left the hospice. I can feel his warmth lying beside me and his embrace holding me tightly. "I was afraid of this," he mumbles.

"I needed this," I remind him.

"You're confused, sweet pea. I was afraid this would happen when we came back here."

"We're home, Fisher."

"No, Annie, no, we're not home. We are in the place we were born. We are in the place that offered us pain and grief. We are not in the place that offered us safety and happiness."

"There is no place like that," I respond.

"Is this about Sky?"

"My world is beneath the sky ... and above it. I don't understand," I tell Fisher.

25

1972 - BOSTON, MA - 30 YEARS OLD

IT WAS JUST another typical morning in our small house outside Boston, Massachusetts, where we decided to settle down shortly after Sky was born. Fisher accepted a fantastic job with the Boston Fire Department and had moved up the ranks quicker than we thought he would. He was in love with his work, and I was in love with spending my days caring for our child, as a mother and housewife. I didn't think I could find such pleasure in tending to our house and preparing meals daily, but being the caretaker for my boys felt like what I was placed on this earth to do.

Six in the morning to six at night, five days a week, Fisher would be at the fire station, which meant Sky and I had a lot of free time to fill. Being one who appreciates routine, I had set the tone early on after Fisher accepted his position with the fire department. I would wake up at five in the morning and prepare breakfast for Fisher before he left for work. Just as Fisher was ready to walk out the door, it was time for Sky to start getting ready for school, so Fisher spent a few minutes each morning with his miniature twin boy, telling him a story or two, or going over baseball stats. Fisher and Sky had a mutual passion for the Red Sox, so that was what their conversations often revolved around. In any case, it was wonderful that they had that time in the mornings for Fisher to cherish throughout his long work day.

Once Fisher left, it would be time to start breakfast for Sky. As he got a bit older and became school aged, he had specific requests for his morning meal. Every morning, he requested pancakes or waffles, and whichever it was, it had to come with a lot of maple syrup.

"Is it okay that he's trading baseball cards on the school bus?" Fisher asked as he left Sky's bedroom.

"I haven't heard otherwise," I told him. "I'm sure it is just fine."

"Okay, well, he has a Tony Conigliaro card. He needs to hang onto that one."

"Tony Conigliaro?" I asked. Unlike the two of them, I didn't know much about baseball. I was probably one of the only people living so close to Fenway Park, without a passion for the game. After long days, I preferred to unwind and let the revolving excitement from the day sizzle out, but during baseball season, there wasn't a night when the game wasn't blaring through our television.

"Okay, I will make sure he does not bring Tony Conigliaro on the bus."

"The card, sweet pea, not the player, himself. He's not here," Fisher jested and poked my side with his elbow.

"Very funny," I told him. "Smart aleck."

"Is your hair a lighter shade of brown today than it was yesterday? Maybe I'm just imagining things?" Fisher asked me.

"I did get my hair done yesterday when Sky was at school," I told him, running my fingers through my long waves.

"I love it. You are gorgeous, Annie. I still wonder how I got so lucky to have the perfect wife. Plus, it doesn't hurt that you're the talk of the fire station somedays. Do you know how many of those men would kill to be your husband?" Fisher was just joking around, but he wiggled his eyebrows after his statement, letting me know he appreciates and agrees with their opinion of me. He wasn't the jealous type, though. He preferred to think of himself as lucky, instead.

"Oh my gosh, what in the world are you talking about?" I slapped him with the dish rag I was holding.

"You have no clue how beautiful you are. Someday, you'll see what I see."

"I'll see that you've lost your mind?" I asked with laughter.

"Annie, Annie, Annie, you know … I like those jeans too … they're certainly accentuating your perfection."

"Fisher Benson!" I squawked.

"You can't blame a man for noticing his wife. What do you expect when you walk around the house like that?"

"I'm wearing bell bottom jeans and a white blouse. I can hardly see the thrill."

"It's thrilling to me," he says, wrapping his arms around me and kissing me as if he hasn't seen me in a week. He leaves me with a soft feathery kiss on the back of my neck—the spot he tends to when he has *other* thoughts on his mind. "Hold onto that kiss until tonight. I have more to share."

"Oh, do you now?"

He slapped the palm of his hand against my backside and offered me a wicked smile as he grabbed his coat from the edge of the sofa. "Love you, babe."

"Be careful today. Don't forget your lunch. It's in the refrigerator."

"Ah, see, Annie? What would I do without you?"

"You would be hungry, my sweet Fisher." I offered him a prideful smile as he walked out the door, feeling the meaning of a dream.

A dream.

I should never have thought I was living a dream.

People eventually wake up from dreams.

Just as Fisher pulled out of our driveway, Sky's bedroom door opened, and he came out into the kitchen, dressed and almost ready for school. Since he was getting older—seven years old at that point—the mornings seemed to bring fewer challenges, since he was becoming more independent. "Good morning!" he said through a quiet cough. "Did you hear about the game last night?"

"Sweetie, you know I don't watch the games," I shooed my hand at him. He knew I didn't understand a thing about baseball.

"Yeah, but Dad said one of the plays would probably make history because it broke records," he said through a cough, filled with his excitement for the baseball game he didn't even watch the night before because it was on too late at night.

"Oh dear, are you coming down with a cold?" I asked him.

He shrugged. "I dunno. I feel okay. Maybe it's just a cough." He looked a little pale too, and I was sure his cough was the start of a late fall cold. As he opened the refrigerator to grab the carton of milk, I placed the back of my hand on his forehead, feeling an abnormally high warmth.

"Okay, mister. Hold your horses. I need to take your temperature."

"I can't miss school today, Mom. I'm trading cards with Jameson on the bus, and I think he's giving me his extra Yaz card."

"You're not trading your Tommy Conigliaro card, are you?" I responded.

"His name is *Tony* Conigliaro, and no, I would never do something so crazy. Besides, Dad would cry," he said with a chuckle.

He was probably right. Baseball was a very emotional topic back then. "Okay, just making sure. I still need to check your temperature, though. If you have a fever, I can't let you go to school, Sky. You know that."

"Yeah, yeah," he said, plopping down at the kitchen table. "I really do feel fine, though. You don't have to worry, see?" Sky stretched a smile across his face from cheek to cheek. The cute dimples poked through his cheeks, and his eyes widened just like Fisher's. Even his freckles stretched when he smiled that hard. He was a happy little boy, and I took credit for that happiness.

I retrieved the thermometer from the medicine cabinet in the downstairs bathroom and returned to the kitchen with it. Sky was used to my neurosis, checking him regularly to make sure he didn't have a fever or anything else of the sort. In fact, he enjoyed making fun of me for my constant state of worry. I preferred that he made fun of me rather than worry the same way I did, so I laughed along with him when he poked fun.

Sky waited with his mouth open, and I slipped the glass rod beneath his tongue. "Mrmph try lumf sum."

I laughed and shook my head because without fail, every time I put a thermometer in Sky's mouth, he would try to talk, knowing full well I had no clue what he was trying to say. It was just another way of making light of the subject. "You know, I was thinking the same thing. We should go shopping for new shoes after school today."

"Nooo," he mumbled. "I hay shoing."

"You hay shoing? I don't understand," I joked with him.

He grumbled in return as I checked my watch for the time. "Okay, let me see." I took the thermometer out of his mouth and checked the mercury level, finding it to be as I expected. "One-hundred and two. No school for you," I told him. Thankfully, a fever meant he only had a common illness that could be treated with antibiotics, or rest and liquids. Regardless of the ailment, though, he needed to be seen by his pediatrician, per our lifelong guidelines.

"I'm going to guess you have some silly fall virus. What do you think?" I asked him.

"I'm probably just dying," he said, casually.

"Sky, that is not funny," I replied, through an unnecessary shout.

"We all have to die sometime, right?"

"Stop it," I argued.

"I'm kidding, Mom."

I wrapped my arm around his neck and pulled him into my waist before kissing his head. "I'll call the doctor. Do you want pancakes or waffles?"

"I'm not hungry," he said.

"Sky, there has never been a day in your life that you haven't been hungry. It must be strep throat. Does your throat hurt?"

"A little, I guess." A little meant a lot. Sky had a knack for downplaying the truth. It was probably out of fear for worrying me, though.

"Okay, well, stay put so I can call the doctor."

It took a few minutes to get through to the doctor's office and a few more to speak to a nurse about Sky's symptoms. She mentioned that strep throat had been spreading like wildfire in the local schools.

I called the school to let them know Sky would be out sick today and straightened up for the few minutes I had before it was time to leave for his appointment. His doctor's office was excellent about getting us right in since we were regulars.

I could tell Sky was feeling lousier than he was letting on because it took him a little extra time to get himself into the station wagon. He seemed sluggish, but nevertheless, he was sluggish with a smile.

"We'll get you all fixed up with some antibiotics, and you can be back at school in a couple of days, kiddo. Nothing to worry about." He didn't exactly look worried, but I was concerned enough for the both of us, which meant I had to constantly remind myself to stop worrying.

"I'm not worried," he said, reminding me I was saying those things for my benefit. "Can I still go to the trading store later? They got a new shipment of cards in, and I was hoping to look at what they got. I saved my money up from cleaning the car last weekend."

"Sure, honey, I'll take you on the way home from the doctor's, okay?"

"Thank you!" he said, perking up a bit more. He didn't love school as much as he loved his friends at school. He was very popular, and I admired him for it, since I was never much of a socialite while growing up. Sky and I were different in that way, but he looked like me, talked like me, and owned the meaning of sarcasm and dry humor the way I always had. Our house was filled with a constant stream of laughter from the three of us continually attacking each other with jokes, puns, and riddles. There was never a sad day.

The doctor's office was only a couple miles down the road from our house, and we lived in a small enough area that it was never overly crowded when we went inside. I was thankful for that, considering the number of times we were down there each month.

Everyone knew us by name, and Sky would often walk around the front of the desk and steal an empty chair next to the receptionist. She would let him draw pictures on her sticky notepad, and I would sit in the waiting area, reading a magazine. It was a good way to make that office a place Sky didn't despise. I suppose the same went for my feelings on the building too.

"This man is dyn-o-mite," I could hear Dr. Walker singing his tune as he walked toward the waiting area. "Where is the groovy dude I'm supposed to see right now?"

"I'm right here, Dr. Walker," Sky said with laughter.

"No way, man, did you get a job here?" Dr. Walker was older than me by a least twenty years and sounded ridiculous while trying to sound cool to the kids, but I guess it worked, since Sky loved that guy to pieces.

"Come on back into my medical pad," Dr. Walker said as he stepped away from the front desk. "Cool man's mom? You coming?"

I shook my head and chuckled while placing my magazine down. I turned the corner and followed Sky and Dr. Walker down the hall. "Thank you for seeing us so quickly, Dr. Walker," I said.

"The pleasure is all mine, Mrs. Benson. Nice threads, kid. You got some far-out style, you know that?"

"I try," Sky said while rustling his fingers through the back of his auburn moppy hair—the hair he refused to let me cut. His long locks reminded me of the way Fisher's used to look when we first met. He had great hair, and I couldn't argue with his plea to keep it.

We settled into one of the small rooms down the far end of the hallway, and Sky jumped onto the table as if it were out of habit, which it was. I took my usual seat in the corner and sat quietly as Dr. Walker went through the motions of his routine checkup with Sky.

He checked his throat first and recoiled at the immediate sight. "Yikes, I don't think I even need to run a throat culture. You have fuzz growing in your throat, dude."

"Seriously? Like, real fuzz?"

"It could totally pass for a fur ball. Do you have a cat I should be worried about?" Dr. Walker joked with him.

"Nah, Mom gets sick around cats, or so she says." Sky gave me a sidelong glance, calling my bluff on being allergic to cats. I just couldn't handle a pet, a child, and a husband. I knew when to call uncle, and I did.

"Does she, now?" Dr. Walker asked, looking over at with a coy smirk.

I looked down at my freshly painted rosy nails and hummed to myself. "So, what do you say, doctor? The usual antibiotics?"

"Let me finish checking things out, and I'll get you two out of here. Sky is going to need a lot of rest, television, comic books, and soup. Sorry, kid." He held his fist up to Sky to pound it. I often wished Fisher could experience the joy of sitting through a half hour or so at the doctor's office, for as often as we came, but his job hardly allowed for those times to match up.

I tried to ignore the part when Dr. Walker held the stethoscope up to Sky's lungs. It was the part I hated the most. I closed my eyes or looked out the window, but there were no windows in that exam room, so I could either close my eyes or stare through the wall behind Sky's head.

I couldn't do either because Sky was looking directly at me that time. Maybe he was waiting to see what I would do, or perhaps he was starting to wonder why I acted unsettled every time Dr.

Walker listened to his chest. Fisher and I explained to Sky that he had a special heart that needed to be protected more than other people's hearts, but we never got into detail about the longevity of his condition. Neither of us wanted to scare Sky or force him to live in a constant state of stress. However, he wasn't entirely in the dark since he couldn't play baseball or do some of the other activities the other boys his age were doing. He didn't ask many questions, but I imagine he wondered why he was different in that way.

"Can you take a few deep breaths for me, Sky?" The mentality of our cool, young, hip Dr. Walker was gone, and in his place, was a professional that I had learned to trust with Sky's life with over the years. I could almost hear the man's thoughts just by the way he would switch his way of speaking. "Good job, Sky. Now, one more time."

"Okay, my friend. Why don't you go bug Ms. Holly out front for a lollipop while I get a prescription written up with your mom."

"Boss!" Sky said as he jumped down from the table. He gasped when his feet hit the floor, as if he had accidentally knocked the wind out of his lungs, but as usual, he straightened his back, pulled in a deep breath and shook it off. He didn't think twice about it when his body hiccuped.

"You have something bad to tell me," I said pointedly, as soon as Sky was out of hearing range. I could tell by the look on his face.

"The murmur is back," Dr. Walker said without skipping a beat. There's a struggle in his lungs too. His resting air intake is very high."

"Is it bad?" I knew it was bad. I don't know why I even asked. Of course, it was bad.

"We need to get him over to Children's Hospital right away and find out more."

My tears were instantaneous. I had been such a strong person before I had Sky, but since he was placed on this earth, under my care, my strength had diminished two-fold. "It may be time for surgery again, so we can repair the hole, but we need to check with a cardiologist."

"Is it because of the strep throat?"

"That's just a coincidence."

"I'm scared," I told him.

"Be strong, Annie. Call Fisher, and be strong together. We'll get through this. I'll meet you over there, okay?"

I took Sky away from the front desk in a swift motion as if the time it took to arrive at the children's hospital would depict his outcome. That wasn't the case, however.

As we walked away, I heard Dr. Walker tell the receptionist to cancel his other patients or reschedule them with a different pediatrician in the office.

Things were bad.

Dr. Walker was following me over to the hospital. He was coming with us. He hadn't ever done that before. I couldn't figure out what was so bad about that time, versus any other times, but I was beginning to assume the absolute worst.

26

CURRENT DAY

IT HAS BEEN a week since we flew home from Prague. It has been a week since I have spoken a word out loud, but the voice inside my head is so incredibly loud I can't make it stop or soften. I feel as though there are different voices of people I know, or knew, speaking at the same time in a crowded room. They're all reminding me of their advice. They are all acting as though they have been through what I have. They are all making it seem as though they know me better than I know myself. So many times, throughout my life, people have said to me, "I don't know how you are so strong. You keep pushing forward with your chin up. You never let anything get in your way. You're a warrior."

I'm not. I'm not strong. I'm not a warrior. I have been struggling with my emotions for most of my adult life. I have kept my thoughts to myself, for fear of drowning Fisher with my feelings, or bringing Mom into a world she thought she had protected me from, but I can no longer fight the thoughts, the demons, or the warriors in my head.

If I open my mouth to speak, I fear they will all come out at once, and I don't know what will happen then.

There hasn't been much for me to do this past week besides sit on my couch and stare through the black screen of my television.

I have been wondering if I'm dead, and my family is sitting here mourning my death. I wonder if people know when they are dead. Maybe it's just a continuation of life, but one-sided. If that were the case, I would hope to see some of my loved ones who have slipped away before now, and I don't see anyone except for my immediate family members who are all still alive and smothering me.

I have not been left alone once. Three or more members of my family have been continuously sitting around me ... morning, noon, and night. If it's nighttime, they sleep sitting upright while I put myself to bed. I would tell them to go home if I could, but I'm sure that would hurt them. No matter what I do, I will hurt someone.

"Did you speak to the doctor again this morning?" Mom asks Fisher.

Fisher isn't focused on what Mom was saying, though. He jerks his head around as if he were sleeping with his eyes open. "I'm sorry, could you repeat that?"

"Have you spoken to the doctor this morning?" Mom repeats.

"Yeah, I'm just waiting for the callback," Fisher says.

"Have you made a decision?" Mom asks.

I find it shocking that Mom is asking Fisher if *he* has made a decision about my well-being, when she usually finds a way of taking partial control over the happenings in my life—not so much in a negative way, but in a bit of an overbearing, loving mother, way.

She's a mother who is always concerned about the wellbeing of her children, whether they are young or old, and she constantly proves her love in the only way she knows possible. She just may not understand the stress and implications sometimes involved, so

I've reminded myself countless times that her strong-natured opinions have grown from love and knowledge.

"I have," Fisher says.

He told me this morning what his decision was, and I would like to disagree, but he's probably right. The doctor gave Fisher the option of admitting me to a rehabilitation facility with a focus on psychiatric care, or waiting a little longer to see if things change at home.

If I could, I would lie to everyone until I'm blue in the face and say I don't need any help, but after this past week, I'm not sure there has been a time in my life where I didn't need professional help. I have tormenting emotions locked away in the darkest cavities of my mind, and if they don't find a way out, soon they may take over the good parts of my mind too.

"You're going to admit her, right?" Mom asks.

"What? No. You can't just throw her in a looney bin," Clara shouts.

"Clara," Mom says softly. "Please."

"I'm going to have her admitted, yes. She will have the ability to check herself out after a month of therapy. I won't hold her there against her will after that time, of course. She is of no harm to herself or others, but I want her to get well. That's what's important right now," Fisher says.

"I think that's a wise decision," Mom agrees.

"I second that," Charlie says, with a sigh that sounds full of distress.

"No," Clara shouts again. "You can't put her in one of those places. She was fine just a week ago. She will snap out of it like she always has before."

"Clara, when has Annie snapped out of the pain she has endured throughout her entire life?" Mom asks her.

When has this happened to me before? It hasn't. I don't think so.

"I'm not sure, since I was just informed of a truth I should have rightfully known much sooner than now. Annie might have needed help, and I wasn't there during the times she must have needed me the most. Do you know how that makes me feel?" Clara asks. Anger is seething through her words, and I can understand why she must feel the way she does. Mom didn't tell her the truth about my identity, just as she hadn't told me. However, I didn't tell Clara, either, because I didn't want to hurt her. Now, she's hurt.

"I was trying to protect you both," Mom says calmly. "I stand by my decision."

"Protecting us from what, Mom?" Clara argues. "From knowing how incredible you are for saving a baby from a prison?" Clara stands up and begins to pace around my living room as she scrapes her fingers through her short blonde hair.

"That isn't what I was protecting her from," Mom says. Her voice is quieter now, as if she's suddenly unsure of herself. However, Mom also becomes quiet when she's annoyed or angry, and I'm quick to pick up on her shift in tones, but Clara is the one who pushes everyone's buttons until someone explodes.

We have both done our best to keep Mom calm for the past year after she suffered her strokes, but Clara has obviously forgotten the importance of living a stress-free life. Not that I have been much help lately, but I needed answers before it became too late to ask the questions. I was treading with caution, and Mom was okay taking in what I had to share. Now, I'm the one who isn't okay.

Clara isn't done arguing yet. She is visibly fuming with hot steam. Her cheeks have always turned a bright shade of red the moment something remotely irritates her. "Do you think a pair of parents who adopted a child would think it was in their best interest to keep that truth from the child? That's not fair to let someone think they are someone they are not." Clara ended her lecture by slapping her hands down against her thighs.

"This isn't an adoption story, Clara. This is an 'immigrant from Terezín stole a Jewish prisoner and snuck her over the U.S. border to raise her as another person' story."

The room has gone quiet in response to Mom's comment. I don't know if Mom realizes I can hear what is being said, but her explanation of my life is quite sad and yet, straightforward.

"I don't feel like I know who anyone is right now," Clara says.

"Clara," Charlie interrupts the growing anger. "If your mother kept secrets, I think we all know it came from a place of compassion. To live with untold stories about the people you love the most must be one of the most painful experiences in the world. I cannot imagine what she has gone through, after surviving the slight odds of escaping a war camp. Please, give your mom some slack. She has done her best with both of you girls. I can see that."

Charlie is good at stepping in when necessary and typically puts a stop to the arguments that often occur between Mom, Clara, and me. I'm not sure how much he loves the role he has stepped into this past year, but he seems to enjoy the family setting more than I would have expected.

"The doctor is calling," Fisher says. "I'll be right back." He takes the call into the other room and closes the door behind him.

"Annie," Charlie calls out to me. "You don't have to respond, but if you can, and you don't want to be admitted to this rehabilitation center, you need to let us know what is going on inside of you, sweet girl. We want to help you."

I'd like to respond. I would. I can't. I just can't figure out how to speak. The words are there somewhere. I didn't have a stroke. We ruled that out at the doctor's office as soon as we got home. He suggested I was overloaded with stress and anxiety, and that I should take it easy and just rest. He also said things would go back to normal shortly.

That doctor wasn't Dr. Walker, Sky's doctor. Sky's doctor would have told me the truth. He always told me the truth. Something is wrong with me, but I don't know what it is. I've wondered if a person can forget how to speak, but I don't think that's possible.

Fisher walks back into the living room, tapping his cell phone against the palm of his hand. "He said to bring her down. Once we get her checked in, we must leave her there."

"This is what's best," Mom says.

"Yeah so, as I said earlier, the program is a month long, but more or less time, if appropriate. I haven't been without Annie in longer than I can remember, but they said I can't stay with her," Fisher says again, his eyes filled with sadness.

Emma struggles to stand up from her chair but makes her way over to Fisher and wraps her arm around him. "We'll keep you company. You won't be alone, uncle Fish."

I'm not trying to hurt anyone. I don't want to hurt Fisher, of all people. I want him to stay with me. I'm scared to be anywhere else alone.

I try to lift my arms to get their attention, but I feel like I'm disconnected inside. I'm trapped.

When I'm pulled up to my feet, I can walk, but my legs are doing the work for me. I'm not thinking about walking.

"Come on, sweet pea," Fisher says. He meets me at the couch and weaves his arm around my body, helping me up to my feet. Again, they move on their own, and I'm heading toward the door now. I want to say goodbye to everyone, but I can't.

"I'm coming with you," Charlie says.

"It's okay, Charlie ... really," Fisher says.

"No, I'm coming," he argues. "Clara, stay with your mother, please. Emma, stay with your mother." I think Charlie just told Mom, Clara, and Emma to stay put in one room, for longer than they already have. They're likely going to end up in another argument, which I don't want for Emma, who is far too pregnant, and Mom, who is far too elderly. Normally, I would say something.

Normally. Nothing is normal. Nothing has ever been normal to me. I don't understand the meaning of the word.

The minutes in the car pass by in a similar blur as the trees and buildings appear. It doesn't seem to take very long before we are walking into a nice-looking building, surrounded by gardens and beautifully manicured lawns. There are even some butterflies flying around. That's a good sign, I suppose. The building looks as though it's made up of old cobblestone, but when we walk inside, everything is brand new, from wall to wall, and from floor to the ceiling. There's even a waterfall pouring off the side of the far-right rock statue. It's calming.

"I'm checking my wife in—Dr. Marek should be expecting her," Fisher says.

"What is her name, sir?" The woman speaking from behind the front desk is dressed in baby blue scrubs. Her face is clean of product, and her hair is neatly pulled up into a perfect ballet bun. Even her voice sounds like one that might belong to an angel.

"Annie Benson," Fisher replies.

"Of course. Dr. Marek did call to let us know she will be here momentarily. If you would like to take a seat over there in the waiting area," she points toward the waterfall, "we will come over when he arrives. Does that sound okay to you?"

"Yes, doctor, thank you very much," Fisher says, meekly.

Fisher places his hand on the small of my back and guides me over toward the circle of cream-colored velvet chairs. I take one of the seats, with the assistance of Fisher's guiding arms, and he takes my hand within his as he sits down in the seat next to me. "It's going to be okay, sweet pea. I promise you. I would do anything for you, you know that, and if leaving you here for a short time is going to make you feel better, then I will selflessly walk away, but Annie, please, please hear me when I tell you, I would rather die than leave your side for even a moment. This is not what I want."

I feel like crying, but that switch feels like it has been turned off too. The tears don't fall—not even one.

Fisher quiets down and resorts to drawing circles on the top of my hand with the pad of his thumb. I know how much he loves me. I don't need him to prove or clarify his feelings. I have never questioned his devotion.

Though they are blurry, I see two people walking toward us. I

SHARI J. RYAN

believe they are Dr. Marek and the lovely lady from the front desk, and as they come closer, I confirm my assumption.

The woman leads Dr. Marek to us and smiles sweetly before returning to the front desk. I met Dr. Marek unofficially, I suppose, just a few days ago when he was evaluating me at the hospital after a stroke was ruled out. He referred to my condition as a psychotic episode. Since I had never experienced one before, he was confident my troubles will resolve on their own, but if I were to get worse, Fisher should call him and request further assistance. I don't believe I have gotten any worse, but I do think Fisher is far more concerned than he was a few days ago.

Dr. Marek lifts one of the chairs and places it down in front of me. "Annie, I know this must be scary, especially since you can't communicate right now, but I want to assure you that Fisher has made this decision based on your best interest. I would not be here if I didn't completely agree with him. This treatment is not a result of anyone's frustration or anger with you. This is because we think you could benefit from some therapy that will help the pieces in your mind reconnect again. As I'm sure you know, it's quite hard making decisions on behalf of a loved one, so I do hope we are all on the same page."

"Yes, we are," Fisher responds for me.

I don't want to be on their page. I don't want to be here or lost in my head. I want to go home and figure things out myself, but I know that isn't a possibility any longer.

"I have informed the staff here about your history, and they are going to offer you the best care possible. I don't work in this building, but I will be by to visit you once every few days for a therapy session. I will also be monitoring your progress and reporting back to Fisher, so he is in the loop."

"Thank you, Dr. Marek," Fisher says. "Am I allowed to visit?"

"While we are in a rehabilitation therapy cycle like this, we ask the family members to keep visitation to once a week in the beginning. As we begin to see progress, whether positive or negative, we can adjust visitation guidelines. I know this must be an

220

unthinkable situation for you, but I strongly believe this is what Annie needs right now."

Fisher is having trouble finding *his* words now. He's nodding at me with disdain and a glassy look in his eyes. I'm hurting him. That bothers me more than anything else, but I can't feel much pain. I just know it would hurt me if I did feel the pain.

"Whatever it takes to make my Annie come back to me," Fisher chokes out.

"I understand your concern," Dr. Marek says. "I will give you two a moment to say goodbye before I take her to the admitted patient area."

Dr. Marek stands from his chair and slowly heads toward the front desk. My focus is locked on his movement, even though Fisher is trying to gain my attention, as well. "Sweet pea," he says, carefully turning my chin so I look at him. "I love you so very, very much, and you *will* be okay. I know in my heart that this occurrence is just another blip on the radar. Our life is full of challenges. Don't forget that we will overcome each one, together, and we'll move on to our next level of strength. You have survived the impossible, and you will survive this too." He places a soft kiss on my lips, and I hear a hiccup in his throat as he sniffles it away. "I love you, Annie."

Fisher cups his hand around my cheek and presses a smile into his downward curved lips, then stands and walks away.

I watch Fisher walk away too. I watch him make his way over to Dr. Marek. I watch them talk—talk about me—talk about how I'm broken and missing pieces that I might not find again.

27

1972 - BOSTON, MA - 30 YEARS OLD

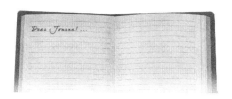

WHAT KIND of conversation was I supposed to have with my seven-year-old while we were on the way to the hospital? I have been known to wear my heart on my sleeve, which means it was hard to hide my true feelings. Sky was no stranger to my moods and emotions. He knew something was wrong without having to ask me. As I checked on him from the rearview mirror, I could see his wandering gaze was set on what we were passing by at a fast speed. He wasn't talking, which was abnormal. Sky was never short on words. He was curious and intrigued by the world around us. He sometimes wanted answers I didn't have, so we spent a lot of time at the library, finding his answers. Of course, that would only satisfy him for a little while until he came up with his next head-scratcher.

"I have one for you," I said, breaking the silence.

"Have one of what?" he asked, innocently.

"A question that will stump you," I said.

"I doubt it." He was so down and out. I wasn't sure if it was because he was worried that we were heading for the hospital, or if he was beginning to feel sicker. I didn't know what was going through his mind because Fisher and I never divulged the details of the abnormalities inside his precious little body. What did it matter? It didn't define him, and I wouldn't let it.

"How many colors are in a rainbow?" I ask him, perching my eyebrows with a questioning look.

"What is ... the number seven," he asked in Jeopardy style. We watched jeopardy a lot during the summers since the show was only on during the day, but next to baseball, it was his favorite program.

"That is correct," I told him, forcing the excitement.

"Okay. Now, it's my turn," Sky said.

"Go ahead. Give me a doozy."

"Why did Dr. Walker tell you to call Dad when we were walking out of the office?"

I told him to give me a doozy. I realized I shouldn't have suggested that, but I'm positive he was planning to ask me anyway. I could tell by the assertive way he asked. "Well, you remember how you feel like you're out of breath sometimes?"

"Yeah," he said. "So what?"

"Well, Dr. Walker wants to make sure everything is okay. That's all."

"Why does Dad have to be there for that? He said he loses— something—when he leaves work early. There's no reason for that, right?" Nothing would slide by Sky.

"Sometimes, hospitals just like to have both a mom and dad available in case they have certain questions only one of us can answer."

"You know all the answers," he said, releasing a long breath filled with exasperation.

"I know a lot of them, but not all, sweetie."

The stress was making *me* feel sick and feverish. The drive was taking longer than I wanted it to, and Sky was probably feeding off my nerves, which meant it was my fault he was speculating that something was wrong.

If I had known how long it was going to take us to get to the hospital, I would have called Fisher before I left the doctor's office, but I was in such a rush to get on the road, I didn't consider how much longer it would be before Fisher would get to the hospital. He did work in Boston, though, so I was hopeful he could get there faster than we had managed.

Just as soon as we entered the hospital, I ran to the nearest pay phone with Sky dragging his feet behind me. I reached into my coat pocket in search of a dime, and found a handful, thankfully. I dropped money into the slot and dialed the fire department, praying Fisher was not out on a call.

I waited for the call to connect and watched Sky sitting on the ledge of a small garden area. He had his finger pointed outward and was leaning in toward something I couldn't see. I leaned to the side to see what it was he was looking at, and I saw a butterfly. I couldn't figure out how a butterfly could get into a hospital, but I figured the sliding doors of the main entrance were opened often enough to let bugs inside.

I was about to tell Sky not to poke the butterfly when the phone was picked up by Paul, the firehouse dispatcher. I recognized his voice immediately, since he was probably the only one who had been smoking cigarettes for more than thirty years, and he sounded like he swallowed a rusty nail. "Paul, it's Annie Benson. Is Fisher around by any chance?"

"Yeah, yeah, he was just taking his break. Let me find him. Is everything okay, honey?"

"No," I said. Paul dropped the phone. The crash from the receiver hitting the table clattered loudly in my ear. I could hear him yelling for Fisher, which would startle him long before he picked up my call. I was hoping to keep him calm, but by then, it wasn't a possibility.

I continued to watch Sky while waiting for Fisher to come to the phone. The butterfly didn't move as Sky gently stroked its wing. It was one of the most bizarre sights I had ever seen. Butterflies don't like to be touched, yet I was watching one that did.

"Don't you wish you were a butterfly, Mom?" Sky asked. "We could just float around all day and see the entire world from the sky. I bet butterflies don't get sick, huh?"

The first question was directed toward me. Before his second question, he had already turned back toward the butterfly, not quite caring about a response from me.

"I do wish I was a butterfly sometimes, but then I wouldn't be here to take care of you, silly," I told him.

I wanted to tell him that I didn't think butterflies got sick, but before I could, Fisher picked up the phone.

"Annie, sweetie, what's going on? Are you all right? Is Sky okay?"

"Hi," I greeted Fisher. "Sky is petting a butterfly right now. It's incredible."

"Annie? A butterfly? What's going on?"

I sounded like I was in a daze, just admiring the beautiful inter-action between Sky and the butterfly. "We're okay, right now. We're at Children's Hospital, per Dr. Walker's recommendation after checking Sky's chest vitals. He told me to call you and have you meet us here." I managed to say everything I needed to say, calmly and clearly. I owed a big thanks to the butterfly for my composure during that moment.

"No," he breathed. "Damnit, no, Annie! No!" It was the only time I ever heard Fisher yell. The only time.

"We'll be on the fifth floor. I'm sure you already know where."

"I'll be there as fast as I can. Hold him, baby. Hold him. Tell him not to go anywhere. Okay?"

"Fisher, he's not going anywhere. Just, come."

He hung up the phone without a goodbye. I imagined the fire department would assist him in getting through the Boston traffic faster than any civilian would be able to travel. Fisher worries a lot. I worry too, but he worries more.

"Why was Dad yelling at you?" Sky asked as I gently hung up the phone.

"He wasn't. He was talking over a siren in the background," I told him.

With the call disconnected and the phone out of my hand, the butterfly also disappeared from our view.

"One more second, sweetie. Why don't you go over there and see where the butterfly is? I need to make one more call, okay?"

Sky wandered around the other side of the small garden as I dropped another dime into the payphone. I turned my back toward Sky as soon as Mom answered the phone. "We're at Children's Hospital. Something is wrong with Sky, but I'm not sure how bad it is. I can't stay on the phone. I don't want to scare him. I just—"

"I'm coming to the hospital," she said.

"No, no, I'll call you when I know more. I just needed to talk to you for a minute," I told her. I did want her there with me, but I had to be mature and handle the situation without stressing Sky out.

"Annie, please," she begged. "He's my grandson—my baby. Please let me come down there."

"Mom, I will call you in a bit."

"Annie!" I had to hang up on her, which just furthered my heartache. I really needed her.

I took a deep breath and turned around, while recomposing myself to hide the feeling that I was dying from inside. "Sky, come on over here, baby," I called out to him.

As Fisher told me to do, I took Sky's hand, and he let me. Sky was getting too old to hold my hand, but sometimes, if he was worried or we were at a place where no one would recognize him, he would hold my hand. I cherished those moments, knowing they wouldn't last forever.

We took the elevator upstairs as I silently questioned God. Why place me in prison on the day I was born, force me to survive, learn to live with the thought of having a happy life, then tear the rug out from below me as if I was never meant to have lasting happiness in my life. I didn't understand, and I still don't.

"Everything is going to be okay, Mom," Sky said, sounding more like himself, rather than the scared child I was talking to in the car. "The butterfly said so."

I wasn't sure how to respond to that. Sky didn't have imaginary friends, especially not at seven, so I knew he was yanking my chain. After a short minute, he smirked in response to the bewildered expression on my face, and chuckled. "Ha ha! Gotcha! Butterflies don't talk, Mom. You should see your face. You actually thought the butterfly talked to me?" He chuckled again. "Ohhh, Mom." He may have been joking, but it was a nice thought to consider.

No more than a minute after we arrived in the cardiology department of the hospital, Dr. Walker ran out from the stairwell door. He was out of breath but still put together in doctor mode. "Follow me. I had my staff contact the head cardiologist here, so he could meet with us right away."

I grabbed Dr. Walker by the loose material of his white coat. "Stop," I grunted. "What is happening?"

"I'm not playing with time, Annie. Let go."

I removed my hand from his coat, pulling my fist into my chest as if I had touched something hot. "I'm sorry."

Sky was looking at me like I had lost my mind. Maybe I had. Perhaps that's when I began to lose my ability to cope with my circumstances.

We followed Dr. Walker down the hallway until we reached a room on the left corner. "After you," Dr. Walker said, standing beside the entrance.

"Sky, man, can you remove your shirt and hop up onto the table for me?"

"Sure," Sky said. "What's happening, though?"

"We need to take a quick peek. Nothing to bum out over."

As Sky climbed up on the table, I could see his chest cavity working harder than usual to pull in air. The skin was being sucked into his chest cavity. I hadn't seen it look like that since he was a baby, before his first surgery.

Dr. Walker noticed the same thing and looked over at me. I pressed my fingertips into the side of my head and closed my eyes.

A knock on the door forced me to reopen my eyes. I didn't know if it was Fisher or the cardiologist, but I assumed the latter since I had just gotten off the phone with Fisher.

"Good afternoon, folks, I'm Dr. Klaus," he said, offering his hand for me to shake. He had a thick German accent, and there was a part of me that wanted to snarl at him and ask for a different doctor, but Dr. Walker said he was the head of the department. I was already assuming Fisher would feel the same way. I knew it was a ridiculous way to think, but I held a silent grudge against anyone from Germany. I knew the entire country was not made up of bad people, but I couldn't help thinking … what if he was one of the bad people, and he escaped as I did, then made his way over to the United States? He was at least twenty years my senior, which meant anything was possible. I felt like slapping myself at that moment, focusing on such foolishness at a time like that.

"Nice to meet you, Dr. Klaus. I'm Annie, and this is my son, Sky."

"Dr. Walker," he said, shaking his hand. "Thank you for filling me in."

"Okay, first, I'm going to have a looksie at your heart. Is that okay?" Dr. Klaus asked Sky.

"Sure, everyone listens to my heart. I have a famous heart or something."

Dr. Klaus laughed. "You sure do, kiddo."

The room was silent for a long minute until another knock on the door interrupted the listening process for Dr. Klaus. "It's just me," Fisher said as he quietly entered the room and took a seat next to me. "Hey, pal." He lifted his hand up to Sky for him to slap, which made me feel like Fisher could maintain his composure well enough for the time being.

"I'm Dr. Klaus," the doctor said, holding his hand out to Fisher. "You must be Sky's father?"

That's when I heard the expected pause. Fisher was trying to either keep words in, or convince himself that his thoughts were unjustified, as I had just done. "Yeah, yeah, I'm his Dad. What's going on?" Fisher was out of breath, but not from running to this office. He was suddenly out of breath from taking in the situation.

"I need another moment with your son, and then I will explain," he said.

Dr. Klaus checked Sky's vitals the same way Dr. Walker had, except he added in a few extra tests that didn't look familiar to me.

Dr. Klaus removed the stethoscope from his ears and looped the cord around his neck. He gave Dr. Walker a look, then focused on Fisher and me. "I am going to need to take a few pictures of the inside of Sky's chest. Is that all right with you?"

"Why do you need pictures?" Sky asked.

I should have told him. I shouldn't have kept the details of his diagnosis a secret from him. I was trying to protect him.

That's what a mother does for her child.

She protects him.

"I'll tell you what, Sky. I'm not completely sure if I need pictures, but to be safe, I would like to take them. How about, I take the pictures, and if it turns out that I needed to see those pictures, I'll answer every question you want to know. Does that sound like a good plan?"

"I guess," Sky said, looking at me with curiosity.

I should have had the answer. A mother should have the answers to their child's questions.

"Why don't you hop down and put your shirt back on. Dr. Walker is going to sit in here with you for just a moment while I talk to your parents in the hallway. Okay?"

Sky shrugged again. Seeing him like this was breaking my heart, and I wasn't the one with the broken heart.

When we stepped out into the hallway, Dr. Klaus closed the door behind us. "I'm not going to tiptoe around the subject, folks. Sky's heart is beating at an incredibly slow rate. Honestly, I don't know how he had the energy to make it up to this room. I'm sure

THE OTHER BLUE SKY

the scans I take will be more conclusive, but as of right now, his prognosis does not look promising."

My mind was going a mile a minute, wondering why this doctor, who we had just met, was giving our son a death sentence. "I'm sorry, but are you telling us that he's going to die?"

"I can't say yes or no until I have more information, but a human body can only run on a partially running heart for so long before it gives out," he says.

I knew everything he was saying.

I was in denial.

"What about surgery? They said he would need more surgeries as he got older. Is that what we're going to need to do?" I was yelling. I was furious at this German man who thought he could walk into that office and put a tag on my son's toe before he even gave him five minutes of his time.

"You a Jew hater?" Fisher snarled.

"Pardon me?" Dr. Klaus said with a look of horror and shock. "What in the world would make you ask something so absurd?"

Neither Fisher nor I had a response. Our answer was not supported by anything legitimate, beyond our profiling and fear based on the history we personally experienced.

"We'd like to talk to another doctor," Fisher said. "An American doctor."

"Despite your disgraceful rudeness, I humbly suggest you take my advice and have these scans done immediately. I am the only cardiologist here for the moment, and if I don't find out what is causing Sky's heart rate to be so slow, he will likely die tonight, no matter what. Now, would you like me to search for another doctor, or should I go through with the tests?"

"Please," I said. "Don't tell us our son is dying. Help him. Just help him," I said, gritting my teeth so fiercely, I felt pain running through my jaw.

"I'm a doctor. I am here to help children. That is what I intend to do, Mr. and Mrs. Benson. Now, if you will excuse me, I am going to call for some assistance to speed up the process of these scans.

You can have a seat in the waiting room, and we will return with Sky as soon as we are through. Is that okay with you both?"

"Yes," I answered for both of us.

I reopened the door and walked up to Sky. "Listen to the doctor. Do as the man says, and then they'll bring you right back to us, okay?" I grabbed his chin, placing my face just two inches from his. "You are the strongest boy I know, Sky. Don't worry about a thing."

"Okay," he said bravely, as he always was when it came to anything medically related. He was braver than both Fisher and I put together.

"I love you, Sky."

"I love you both too," he said to us. "Oh, and Mom? That butterfly … it really did tell me everything would be okay. I didn't say that before because I didn't think you'd believe me."

Fisher grabbed the back of Sky's head and gave him a hard kiss on the forehead. "You are perfect—absolutely perfect. I'll see you in just a few minutes, son."

28

CURRENT DAY

I THINK it has been about a week since I arrived here at this facility. The doctors said I'm getting better, but I don't feel that way. In fact, I feel worse. Throughout my life, I have done my best to keep busy, continually occupying my mind from stewing thoughts, constantly fearing the day I stopped moving and started allowing my mind to wander.

Without a choice of what to do with myself, I have been forced to let the thoughts ruminate and take over most of my waking moments. The psychiatrist who has been visiting me each day has voiced his opinion on the reason for my state of mind. He compared my mind to a body enduring a full cardiovascular workup, but without water or food. A body depends on food and water to function, and a brain depends on thoughts, memories, and dreams to operate properly. I have not allowed much of anything to run through my mind except for the current moments I live through. It's the only way I managed to cope with the past. I know Mom has done something similar, but apparently, everyone is different and handles life in their own way. The psychiatrist suggested I allow in what I have been blocking out. Acceptance may help me heal, or so he thinks.

However, like a hole in a heart, some things cannot be fixed. Or, could they?

I haven't left the chair in my room for too long, other than to use the bathroom, eat, or sleep. More of my mobility returned soon after I arrived here, which is a good sign. Hopefully, my ability to speak will be next. It's not as though I can't think of words to say. I just can't pronounce them. I have never been so confused about my own body before, and I'm a bit intrigued to see what the psyche does when in conflict with the heart. I feel like a prisoner again, trapped inside my own body.

The view from my chair is pleasant. With the fall settling in, there is a pile of brightly colored leaves scattered along the lawn outside my window. The branches are starting to become bare, and it has been a subtle reminder of time passing by. I'm angry with myself that I am wasting precious time here. In my mind, Mom is a ticking time bomb at her age, and Fisher has never been alone this long since he arrived in the United States. I can't imagine how he is coping.

One thing I have noticed during my lapse into silence is vivid images of Theresienstadt from my one visit back when I was twenty. I thought I had mostly forgotten about the things I saw there, especially since we didn't make it too far on our tour of the grounds, but I happened to remember the moment I spent in the barrack block, pleading with the dirty, wooden floor to bring back what I had lost. I should have known then that I had some unresolved issues.

I keep wondering if there is supposed to be a big picture I'm intended to understand, but for the life of me, I can't seem to wrap my head around the significant events I've experienced throughout my life.

I was born into a prison, stripped of my identity, and felt alone when I had more people around me than most. I finally learned about the type of love that only exists between a parent and a child. Then I was forced to experience a type of anguish I refused to endure again.

"Annie?" a man's voice calls from the doorway. "May I come in?"

I look over at him—the psychiatrist—to nod in response. I appreciate him asking, even though I haven't cooperated much with vocalizing my emotions. I would think that a psychiatrist would find me quite useless right now, but he seems to be extracting the information he needs by just the simple looks on my face.

"I had some thoughts last night, and I was wondering if you up might be up for an experiment?" he asks.

I think about what he's asking me, but only for a quick second. I'm certainly curious about what he's going to recommend. With another nod of my head, I agree, for the sake of learning what his idea is.

"Great. If at any point you are uncomfortable, we can stop. Just place your hand up to tell me to proceed. Okay?"

I nod once more.

"I'd like you to lie down on your bed so you're comfortable. We're going to try a method of hypnosis to see if we can help reconstruct some of the thoughts you're having difficulty with, to possibly help you regain your ability to speak. I don't know if it will work, but it can't hurt to try."

I like the idea of fixing my situation, so I can go home sooner than the month they mentioned. I stand up slowly from the chair, feeling minor aches from the lack of mobility throughout the last week. Hopefully, this will all be behind me soon, though. I want to get better. I know that's the first step to fixing a mental condition. I suppose I haven't wondered how long it can take to fix what is broken inside of my head.

I make myself comfortable in the bed and stare up at the ceiling, focusing on the textured swirls in the plaster. "I intend to help you relax to a state where you can visualize moments inside your head. I will retrace the path your life has taken with the information that has been given to me by your doctor."

I hear his words, but I'm very focused on the grooves and inconsistencies along the lines on the ceiling. I've tried meditating before, and his peaceful manner of speaking sounds like the tapes I used to play. The soothing voice, plus an imaginary landscape, is supposed to displace me from my current location and bring me to a subconscious place. According to the doctor's subtle advising words, we're supposed to be at a large field with an abundance of red tulips.

Thanks to his detailed description, I'm able to imagine this type of place.

"You experienced a terrible scare with your mother's health last year. Try to remember the joy you felt inside when you found out she was going to be all right again," he says.

I remember the moment as if it were yesterday. Throughout the journeys I've taken during my life, it's easiest to recall the recent ones.

"When you were asked to teach a class about writing and painting to underprivileged children, you must have felt accomplished and worthy, helping those who couldn't help themselves. It's a pleasant feeling when we know we have made a difference in a life." I loved teaching about my passions. I felt like I was offered a gift with that job offer since I didn't need a university's teaching degree. I poured my heart and soul into my practice with those children. When some of them came back to me years later with proof of what they had accomplished, thanking me for what I had done for them, I knew I was meant to do good in this world. I just have a hard time remembering this fact.

"Do you recall a time when you led a support group for parents who were struggling to cope with their child's disability?"

I don't want to recall that period of time. I wish I could tell the doctor to skip this part. I couldn't even help myself back then. I had no right trying to help others.

"I can see you don't like that thought. Let's move on," he says.

Exhaustion feels as though it's taking over my thoughts, and I'm having trouble concentrating on the words the doctor is speaking. He isn't asking me to recall anything, but he's switching our scenery, and I'm not sure I want to move from the tulip field.

His words have become softer and softer over the last few minutes, and I cannot hear him speaking anymore, but the landscape in front of me has changed without my permission. I don't want to imagine Terezín—this place. I don't want to see these images again. I want them to go away and disappear from my mind forever.

The camp looks different in my mind than it did when I was there. It seems odd that I would construct a different view after all this time, yet I'm still aware of how I saw it.

The camp appears to be active, with people walking around. My vision clears up a bit more, and I see I'm inside the camp's walls. Nazis are walking around with weapons in their hands. Prisoners, old, and young, are dragging their tired limbs from wherever they were coming from to wherever they are going.

There's a building labeled with German writing. Inside the building, there are very young children. They aren't doing very much besides crying or staring at one another. Another barrack block comes into sight, and it looks like the one we were inside of during our visit, except there are many women inside; it's hard to tell how many.

My vision centers on one woman. She looks similar to me. We share a lot of similar features, but she is skinny and frail. She also seems very young, especially since she is holding a newborn against her chest. She is hiding behind a dirty pile of clothes, and I do my best to see more. However, I should probably respect her privacy. As I get a better look, I see the woman smiling at her baby, whispering words I cannot understand.

She's stroking the infant's cheek over and over and peppering the baby with kisses once every few seconds. "Lucie," she coos. "Lucie-loo, I love you."

Lucie.

My mind feels empty for the moment as I repeat the name silently to myself. *Lucie. Lucie-Loo.*

I am Lucie.

I can see myself, but how? Is that my mother? My questions aren't being heard, but I want to ask the woman if she is my mother. I'm looking up at her now without a thought or concern. I hear her sweet sound and feel her touch feather down my cheek. My body is pressed against hers, but I feel so slight and small within her grip. She continues to speak, but I don't understand what she is saying.

Loud noises from around us scare me, and my heart beats hard and fast against the inside of my chest. There's yelling and scream-ing. My body aches from being pinched, and the sound of a baby's cries—my cries—reverberates within my ears. "Shh," I want to tell the baby—myself.

My mother is being taken away, and I'm being left behind.

Another person is holding me, rocking me from side to side. I can only see dirt-brown sleeves and a man's hands out of the corners of my eyes. "Hush, sweet girl," a man says. He's German. He is one of them. He took my mother away.

"Stop. Stop!" I try to yell out, but sound doesn't escape my mouth because a baby cannot talk. I could not stop them from taking my mother.

"Shh," I hear again.

I'm backing away from the scene of a Nazi holding a baby—me. I can see his young face, the swastika on his sleeve. He has a small smile on his face, as if he is happy that my mother was taken from me. "You're a monster," I want to tell him.

The nursery with other children is back in sight, and now I'm in the center of the room. There are wooden cribs, all filled with other babies. Are they just stealing their mothers and keeping them here as prisoners? What good are babies without a mother?

"What good is a mother without a baby?" I ask out loud, but still can't hear the sound of my voice. "I said, 'What good is a mother without a baby? She's dead. She's dead without her baby.'"

Another set of arms lifts me up, and I believe it's another man in uniform. Why won't they just leave me alone? This man is also smiling—he's another monster.

"Lucie," he says quietly. "It's okay. Charlie will make sure you are taken care of," he said. "I won't hurt you. I promise, baby Lucie. I'll save you."

Charlie? That's impossible.

"She's dead isn't she—her mother—my mother?" I ask, silently. "That poor baby."

I'm alone in a world where no one knows I exist, yet, I'm expected to continue as if that fact does not matter.

A bandage was placed over my life, and they said I was okay, but the bandage is superficial. The wounds inside of me are still bleeding out, killing me slowly.

"Annie," I hear. "Can you hear me?"

The voice sounds so far away, and I look around, but I only see dust in the air, and sick children. Their cries become mute, but now I hear my heart beating, along with the man's voice in the distance.

"Annie Benson, it is 2018 in Boston, Massachusetts. I need you to wake up when I snap my fingers. You are comfortably resting on a bed covered in white linen, and the sun is shining outside, creating an aura of vibrant colors through the scattered leaves dangling from the branches. You are safe here. You are loved." The sound of a snap startles me awake, leaving me gasping for air.

"Oh, my goodness," I say.

"Annie," the doctor responds, smiling at me as if I were a miracle appearing before his eyes.

I'm utterly confused and feel disconnected from my subconscious, though my thoughts feel sharp at the same time.

"What just happened?" I ask.

"You're speaking, Annie." The doctor looks thrilled, but for a reason I can't recall. I don't know why he would be telling me I'm speaking. Of course, I'm talking.

"Yes, I am. Is that okay, doctor?"

"Annie, you have been suffering from a psychotic episode for the past week. Do you recall checking into this facility?"

I glance around the room, realizing what the man is saying, also noting that I don't know who he is. Panic sets in, as if an alarm were blaring through my body, alerting me that something is very wrong right now.

"Why am I here?" I ask.

"It seems as though your thoughts were too much for your mind to bear," he says.

"What is your name?" I ask.

"I'm Dr. Marek. I've been assisting you for the last couple of weeks now. You don't remember me?"

I look at him long and hard, studying his gray hair, the many lines on his tan face, and the scar on his right cheek. I do not recognize this man at all. "I don't. I'm very sorry. I don't intend to be rude, of course."

"You have nothing to worry about, Annie."

"Where is Fisher?" I ask, feeling a sudden concern for why he isn't beside me. Fisher is always with me unless I'm visiting with Mom or running errands. We're rarely ever apart.

"He will be here in just a little while. Everything is going to be just fine. I assure you."

Everything is going to be just fine.

"He must have had to do all the shopping and laundry," I say. "How long have I been here, again?"

"Just a week," Dr. Marek says.

"A week is a long time. Do you know that my clothes must all be stained with other colors now? Fisher doesn't know to separate the colors. He's color-blind."

"I didn't know Fisher was color-blind," Dr. Marek says with a chuckle.

"He's not really color-blind. We just say he is since he hasn't been able to separate colors properly, even once throughout our entire marriage. Can you imagine that?"

"I must admit, separating colors is not my strong suit in life either, Annie. My wife gets upset with me for staining her clothes all the time."

"Men," I say with a huff.

"Can't live with us, can't live without us. Don't forget that," Dr. Marek says as he leans back into his chair.

"This is very true. You're a smart man, Doctor."

"Annie, I was trying to help you resolve the episode you were suffering with throughout the last week, and I came up with the idea to hypnotize you with hopes of clarifying some thoughts in your head. I heard you say a lot while you were semi-unconscious, which I find intriguing, but I'm curious about how much you remember?"

I think for a moment, recalling the dream I just had. I suppose it wasn't much of a dream—more like a nightmare, but it was just my imagination, I think. "I do sleep talk sometimes, Dr. Marek. I apologize if I said anything inappropriate."

"Annie, from the thoughts I heard you voice out loud, I think it's easy to conclude you are suffering from severe heartbreak. Have you lost a loved one recently?"

"Recently?" I ask, pushing myself up in the bed so I can sit up. "No, not recently, but what does time matter when a hole in a heart is not repairable, right?"

"I'm not sure I understand," he says.

29

1972 - BOSTON, MA - 30 YEARS OLD

FISHER and I had been sitting in the waiting area of the cardiology department at Children's hospital for more than an hour, and it felt like a year had passed when Dr. Klaus finally walked through the double doors with a clipboard in hand. Doctors at Children's Hospital were good at keeping a calm look upon their faces, regardless of what kind of news they were bringing parents. Therefore, it was impossible to know what was happening by just looking at him as he walked closer to us.

We stood to greet Dr. Klaus, though we both still had our biased feelings of distrust toward him. Our son was under his care, and we did what we had to in order to get through the moment.

"Would you mind following me down to my office?" he asked us.

That meant the news was bad. Otherwise, he would have told us right then and there that everything was fine. Fisher grabbed my hand and squeezed so tightly I thought my fingers were going to break off, but I needed to be held like that. I wanted to feel pain somewhere other than in my chest, but I don't think any other part of my body could hurt as much in comparison.

We stepped into his office, which was unlike other doctors' offices there. We had been inside enough of them to know how they looked, smelled, and how small each space was. There were no drawings on the walls from his patients who might have adored him. There were no family photos on his desk, showing off his children, which would might have suggested his reason for becoming a pediatric cardiologist. In fact, the only object hanging in his office was an abstract painting by Max Earnst, a famous German painter who was known for his talented ability to create surreal imagery. I had a difficult time analyzing that painting, but between the obscure faces, dark colors, and the mixture of non-complementary hues of red, I thought the painting was inappropriate to be hanging in a pediatric office. The artwork could have scared an adult, let alone a child. I was a lover of all art—the dark and light pieces— but at that moment, I didn't have a desire to see art in any form.

The artist's country of origin should not have been a contributing factor to my disdain for Dr. Klaus, but it was just another fact to hold up against my ideology. "Mrs. Benson, are you all right? It doesn't appear you heard anything I just said."

I turned my head away from the wall where the painting hung, and faced Dr. Klaus. "I apologize. No, I didn't hear you. What was it you said?"

"Sweetie," Fisher said, taking my hand back into his. "Sky needs immediate surgery to repair the atrial septal defect again."

"Then, what?" I asked, breathlessly. "Will he be okay after that?"

"Open heart surgery is always a risk, Mrs. Benson, but I would like to hope for a positive outcome."

"Hope?" I snapped. "You're just going to hope? You want to cut my son's chest open and *hopefully* fix the problem?"

"As a doctor, I cannot personally give you any medical guaran-

tees. Sky is at risk for complications since he has had several surgeries to date. I'm sorry I cannot offer you more hope."

Hope. All I could think was … *you don't have hope that a child is
going to survive. You don't have hope that you're going to do your job
correctly.* I was sure that a person either knows or they don't, and I
knew nothing was stopping that man from purposely making a
mistake during surgery on my child. "I will schedule his surgery
with someone else then," I said.

"Annie," Fisher stopped me. "This has to be done immediately.
He isn't breathing properly, and waiting could cause complications."

"I want to see another doctor," I said, furiously.

"Unfortunately, there is not another cardiovascular doctor on
staff until tomorrow afternoon," Dr. Klaus said.

"Surely, Sky will be okay until then. Will he not?"

"It's hard to say," Dr. Klaus said. "If he were my child—"

"Do you have children, Dr. Klaus?" I asked.

"Yes, Mrs. Benson, I do. If Sky were my son, I would not wait
on the surgery."

"Fisher—"

"Annie, let's step outside and talk this through, okay?" Fisher
said.

"Folks, I don't mean to cause additional stress, but I should be
scrubbing in right now. I don't know how else to explain the
importance of time in Sky's situation."

I wanted to ask him if he was a Nazi. I shouldn't have been
thinking that. I wanted to ask him if he came from a family who
hated Jewish people. I wanted to ask him if he wouldn't try as
hard to help Sky because we were Jewish. We were still living in a
time of hatred, and while there was more acceptance than there
had been twenty-five years beforehand, there were still many
people with dangerous values and beliefs.

"We'll just be one minute," Fisher said, pulling me up from
my chair.

The moment we opened the door to Dr. Klaus's office, the loudspeaker blared the words, "Code Blue … calling for Dr. Klaus … emergency C."

Fisher and I seemed to look at each other in slow motion. The announcement, the meaning, the doctor's name—it all took a little longer than a second to comprehend what was going on. By the time we were able to understand what was potentially happening, Dr. Klaus had left us in his wind. He was running down the hall, faster than we could even react. We didn't know where he was going, but we followed, hoping we would spot him around the corner.

Thankfully, we saw Dr. Klaus run into a room just as we turned down the next hall. We ran as fast as we could. Fisher was dragging me by the time we reached the door. I couldn't feel my feet or how fast I was moving. My body was numb with paralyzing fear. Fisher pushed through the swinging door, revealing Sky on a hospital bed, being revived by what must have been a dozen doctors and nurses.

"What's happening?" I cried out. "What did you do to him?"

I shouldn't have said that either.

Dr. Klaus was on the table with Sky, giving him chest compressions. It was the most horrid sight I have ever seen.

I ran to Sky's head, placing my hands on his cheeks. They were cold, but there was still a heartbeat on the monitor. "Do the surgery," Fisher said. "Do it now!"

"Yes, please, do the surgery," I begged.

Dr. Klaus didn't respond to us as he continued pumping Sky's chest with his fists. I was trying to ignore the alarm from the heart monitor, and the flashing green number that is declining by one digit at a time. "Did you hear us? Do the surgery!" Fisher shouted.

"I'm afraid it's too late," Dr. Klaus said, while trying to catch his breath between words.

"It's not too late!" I screamed. "Sky, baby, can you hear me? Sky, it's Mom, and Dad is here too. Sweetie, you need to fight. Fight as hard as you can." I didn't have a chance to get him his baseball card. I couldn't even remember which card he said he wanted. I kept telling myself I was a horrible mother. *Horrible.* "I'll get you your baseball card as soon as we can leave here, honey. Come on, Sky. Fight for me. Fight for me, baby."

His lips were slowly turning blue, but I continued to beg, not realizing that Dr. Klaus had given up his attempt at chest compressions.

Someone unplugged the heart monitor.

The alarm stopped.

Fisher fell to his knees, keeling over and shouting in grief, but I could not give up on my baby. He was my baby. I was his mother. He could not leave me. It was my job in this world to be that child's mother. I kept thinking … what good was a mother without her child?

"Time of death: thirteen twenty-five," Dr. Klaus said.

"No, no, don't you do that! Don't you call my child dead! He is still alive. Can't you see? He is still alive!"

"Mrs. Benson, I am so unbelievably sorry for your loss."

"I didn't lose anything. He's right here. Are you blind?"

"I'm sorry, again," Dr. Klaus said as he took his gloves off.

"Sky, baby, you are blue. Honey, you must come back. You have your whole life ahead of you. You're going to be a famous baseball player, just like you wanted. I'll send you to baseball practice next season. You can start right away. Sky, I will do anything if you will come back to me. Sky?"

Fisher reached for my arm and pulled me down with him, curling me into his embrace as his body shook against mine with uncontrolled sobs. "I don't know what to say," Fisher cries.

"Get up, Fisher. Talk to him. Tell him to come back. Maybe he'll listen to you. He loves you. You are his hero. Get up." I stood up from Fisher's lap and pulled on his arm, trying to get him up to his feet. Once I managed to make Fisher see our son, all he could say was … something I will never forget for the rest of my life.

"He's blue, Annie. Our Sky is blue."

"I don't want him to be blue!" I screamed. "Make him come

back to us, please. Please, Fisher. Do something, please. I'm begging you."

"You were always right, Annie. He is our sky. He is the other blue Sky. Can't you see? Sky was placed in this world for us, so we could be a part of a family again. He is our other blue Sky. See?"

I pounded my fists into Fisher's chest, pleading with him to stop. "Don't say that. Don't say that, Fisher. Do you hear me? He wasn't placed on this earth for just one reason. He was supposed to do so many good things. He was so incredible." I said the word ... was. Even though I wasn't ready to admit it, I had already come to terms with Sky's fate, just seconds after he was pronounced dead. "How could you say that?"

"He will always be with us, Annie. He is our son—the sun in the blue sky. He has a greater purpose to his life than either of us can understand."

"You are speaking nonsense," I cried out. "Our son is gone. Why would God do this to us?"

"Annie, stop," Fisher pleaded. "We got so many more years than we were supposed to with Sky. Don't you see? We were blessed. We were blessed again. We survived a war. We survived hate. We survived love, and now we are going to survive loss, but we had him—we had him six years longer than the doctors thought we would. We knew how to live, Annie. We knew how to make each of those days count, with him and for him, and we did. He taught us so much, and we will have that to keep with us forever."

"I can't," I hissed.

"Annie, I am in so much pain right now, I didn't know anguish like this existed until right this very second, but I am trying my best to make sense of this nonsense, so please bear with me while I fall apart because I don't know how to be strong for either of us right now."

All the veins and arteries leading to my heart felt like they were swollen and explosive. I could have sworn I was being strangled, as the feeling of blood rushed to my face. At that moment, though,

I saw a broken man who needed me as much as Sky needed me, and the last thing I wanted Sky to see or hear was his mom not being the strong woman he knew. I had to be strong for him. I wrapped my arms around Fisher and held onto him as tightly as I could, trying to relieve just an ounce of his pain and take it on as my own. I knew it didn't work like that, but I would do anything for the two men in my life. I still had one to protect, and I knew I would do so until the day I die.

Fisher held me too, and we both cried until we had no more energy to hold our weight up. The minutes and hours after that ending were blurry—always have been.

I don't remember them rolling Sky out of the room.

I only remember walking past the waiting room some time later, where I unsurprisingly spotted Mom and Dad. Without another thought, I threw myself into Mom's lap just as Dad stood up to catch me, in case I fell anywhere else. I couldn't tell Mom what happened. I didn't have to. If she didn't know from another source in the hospital, I think it was clear, I was experiencing a type of loss only a mother could understand.

Mom did what any mother would do for her daughter. She held me, and even though I was a grown woman, she still managed to rock me from side to side, shushing her voice—trying her best to soothe my pain.

"What?" I heard Dad mumble. Fisher and Dad must have been talking behind us. I couldn't make out what they were saying. "No, no, no. There is no way. No!" Dad was completely broken. He was crying behind me. The sound of his sobs—as horrifying as it was—were muffled, and I imagined Fisher and Dad were hugging each other, just as Mom and I were.

"Everything is going to be okay," Mom said. "I'm here. Everything is going to be okay." Her voice cracked, and she sounded unsure of what she was saying. I think she knew very well that nothing would ever be okay again, but what else was there to say? She was just trying to be strong for me, but even the strongest people in the world fall apart sometimes.

SHARI J. RYAN

I think she was in shock. I wish I had been in shock. I wish I had time to pretend like it was all a nightmare.

When Mom's shock seemed to subside a little, she helped me up to my feet, handed me over to Fisher and Dad, then walked away toward the bathroom. I know she broke down in there. I could see it on her face when she returned.

In silence, the four of us sat in the waiting room as if Sky were coming back ... as if ... we had something to be waiting for.

I don't remember leaving that room.

Part of me still thinks we are all still in there, sleeping away the time until Sky wakes up. I have told myself too many times that I am living a dream—the kind Fisher warned me of—the ones that contained broken particles of hope.

However, if there was hope alive anywhere, then I could hold on to my silly thought, and maybe someday I would learn that I was just experiencing a terrible nightmare. It's a thought I have kept to myself. It has helped me sleep at night, and it has helped me cope with my everlasting heartbreak.

When I wasn't considering the unimaginable, I was wondering how one person could be motherless and childless all in one lifetime, and yet somehow, I had continuously been considered a lucky person.

I was sure my life was a mistake.

3 0

CURRENT DAY

"I AM NOT KNOCKING on this door, because you know who I am, and you can say so," Fisher says as he storms through my door at this facility I've been held up at for a week. He plops down onto my bed and rests his arms behind his neck, sporting the goofiest grin I've seen on him in a long time. "My baby is back."

"I was never gone," I tell him.

"Oh, sweet pea," he says, while turning onto his side and caressing my face with the tips of his fingers. "You have scared me way too many times this past month."

"I am so sorry. I honestly don't know what has come over me," I tell him.

"The doctor said he tried some hypnotherapy on you. That's kind of out there for you, huh?"

"What choice did I have?"

"I don't even care how it came about, Annie. You're talking again, which means you're going to be okay."

I force a small smile across my face. "I had some wild visions while I was under hypnosis," I tell Fisher.

"Oh yeah? Do you think it was real, or just your imagination?" We've had this conversation before. We've wondered if hypnosis would help us remember things from our early childhood, but in fear of getting our hopes up, we squashed the topic and decided against it.

"I think I saw my birth mother, and what's stranger is, I saw Charlie holding me after she was gone."

Fisher strikes his head back against the bed, probably shocked to hear Charlie's name. "Did he look the way he looks now?"

"No, I didn't recognize him, not until he said his name. Then I could see the resemblance. You know, everything was a bit fuzzy, though. Maybe it *was* just my imagination."

"Maybe, but maybe it was real," Fisher says.

"Charlie told me he was going to make sure I was safe." That vision has me wondering what Mom and Charlie's story entails, and why they were separated after what they went through. I know she will take that to the grave with her, though.

"I regret our short trip to Prague," Fisher tells me. "I know that sounds terrible because it was the only chance to meet your birth father, but if I had known the trouble it was going to cause you, I wouldn't have agreed."

"I needed to see him. I would have regretted it if I hadn't taken the chance. You have to understand. It was my decision, and you supported me. This—whatever has happened over the last week— is not your fault," I tell Fisher.

"When I take the blame, it makes me feel like I'm taking the pain away from you, Annie. I don't want you to experience any more pain."

"If it makes you feel better, I feel guilty because you didn't have your meatloaf, did you?"

Fisher tilts his head to the side with a smirk. "That was pretty lousy of you. I was so angry. I didn't know how you could do something like that to me. Awful wife, you are." Fisher chuckles, but somewhere deep inside of him, I know he's a little crushed from missing out on his golden opportunity to visit his favorite pub.

"I promise to make it up to you," I tell him.

Fisher wraps his arm around me and pulls me in to his side. "Just come home, Annie. That's all I want."

"Me too," I agree.

"Oh, while you're in a good mood, I'm going to break the news that your family is waiting in the lobby for the word of approval to come back and visit with you."

"This is a psychiatric rehabilitation center, right?" I ask, simply.

"Yes, why?" he responds, seeming confused.

"My family has probably also been admitted by now," I tell him.

Fisher bursts with laughter. "Your humor is back. My Annie is back. I'm going to go get those knuckleheads and ring in the party."

I sigh and lean back into my pillow as my bed bounces from the release of Fisher's weight.

My family.

All along, I considered myself missing when I'm clearly so loved. I don't know what was going through my head, or why it has taken me so long to come to terms with the definition of what a family is—other than crazy, of course, but I've always had it.

The crowd funnels in through the door with Mom and Charlie pulling up the rear. Something is different, though.

"Emma," I call out. She's the only one I can focus on other than Jackson's beaming grin blurred out behind her. "My girl, get over here right now."

Emma struggles with a baby carrier dangling from her left arm. She doesn't even look like she was pregnant or had a baby, and it couldn't have happened too long ago if I've only been here a week. Emma sits down on the edge of the bed and places the baby carrier on the floor beneath her. She groans a little as she leans over to retrieve a tiny bundle, wrapped in the pink blanket I knitted for her almost half a year ago.

I cup my hand over my mouth as I gaze at the face of the most beautiful little girl I've ever seen. My eyes fill with tears, happy ones, and Emma hands the baby over to me.

I pull in a deep breath, close my eyes and tell myself she is not Sky, but Sky is with us, bright and brilliant above us all. I have refused to touch a baby since Sky. I never held Emma when she was a baby, and I regretted it for a long time afterward. I just couldn't bear the thought or the memory, but I'm going to push through this pain for Emma because she has been like a daughter to me, and she has given me more than I feel like I deserve.

I open my eyes, and there's a sweet baby girl staring up at me with big eyes, and long lashes for such a little peanut. She must not be more than seven pounds. "Aunt Annie, I would like you to meet Belle."

"Belle," I repeat through a hitched breath. *"Beautiful. She is so beautiful."*

"And quite loud at two in the morning," Emma says, laughing along with Jackson, who looks like a zombie, now that I'm getting a better look at him. He should be used to the all-nighters, but it's different when it's your own baby. I know that.

"How could this little peanut make that much noise?" I coo, as I stroke the side of her face with my finger. *That's how my mother showed me she loved me when I couldn't understand.*

Belle's hand lifts away from her blanket, and her fist is clenched, but it seems like she's reaching for me. I offer her my finger and she takes ahold of it. I admire the tiny hand against mine, and I notice a small birthmark on the top of her hand. I gently run the tip of my finger along the mark.

"She has a butterfly tattoo," Emma says with sweet grin and a soft laugh. "I told Belle she was too young for a tattoo, but she didn't seem to care."

A beauty mark in the shape of a butterfly.

Benjamin's words ring loudly in my ear:

I BELIEVE those we lost will return in our lifetime in one form or another to let us know they are okay, and hopefully they are getting another chance to experience what they should have. When you see a new life, and feel a connection, consider the deeper meaning.

"SHE IS AMAZING, EMMA," I tell her, while struggling to hold back my emotions.

"Aunt Annie, I talked to Fisher this week when he came by the hospital to visit me," Emma says as she turns around to face Fisher, appearing to look for confirmation about what she going to say. When she turns back to face me, she continues. "I heard about Sky, and at first, I was a little upset and confused about why no one ever told me about him, but Mom and Fisher both made it clear that you didn't want to talk about him because it was too painful for you. This family has way too many secrets, considering we're all in each other's business like twenty-four seven—just for the record."

The room echoes with laughter, and surprisingly, I join in because she is right. Secrets only hurt us. I guess we have always assumed we're protecting someone, but in the end, we aren't helping, we're hiding.

Emma waves her hand in front of her face, fanning herself, and it pulls me away from my thoughts. "Are you okay?" I ask Emma.

"I'm hot," she says.

"Hormones," I say, along with Mom and Clara, who mirror my word.

"Gosh, the three of you," Charlie says. "Do you realize it is like listening to one voice. Do any of you have your own thoughts?"

"Charlie!" Mom snaps, "Be quiet."

"Yes, darling," Charlie laments.

"Guys, please," Emma says. "I need to talk to Annie."

"You need to talk to me? Is this serious?" I ask Emma.

"I wanted to ask you something, but I'm scared to upset you," Emma says to me.

My mouth falls agape because I would never want to make Emma uncomfortable, and I have always told her if she needs to talk to me, I will be here, no matter what. Except, I wasn't this week. I wasn't there for her this week. I know she didn't need me, per-say, but I wanted to be there for her, even if it hurt me more than it would help Emma. "You can ask me anything, and I will never be upset about a question, Emma."

"Well, given the circumstances, I'm also afraid—"

"I'm okay, I promise." I can't promise I won't fall into another psychotic episode because I don't know why I fell into one after everything I had been through, but I'd like to think I'm strong enough now to control myself.

"I was going to wait until you were released, but I have to fill out Belle's birth certificate by tomorrow."

My heart is pounding in my chest, but only because I don't know what she's going to say. I'm not one for surprises, and she knows this, so I can't figure out why she's having so much trouble asking me whatever it is she wants to know. "Emma, say it," I tell her.

"Can I make Sky ... Belle's middle name? If it's too much or too hard for you, I will understand and can come up with another name. I don't want to hurt you or stress you out at all. I promise you. Please, know I am doing this out of love and because I want you to be Belle's godmother too." Emma slaps her hand over her mouth, and Jackson lifts her off the bed, pulling her into him.

"Sorry," Jackson says.

I laugh silently. "Why are you sorry? This is Emma. When she gets nervous, she talks a mile a minute and speaks faster than most people can understand. I understand Speedy Emma, don't worry."

"Sorry," she says under her muffled hand.

I shake my head and take in a breath. "You want to name her Belle Sky?"

Emma nods. "I do. I think the name is suitable and perfect, and another link between our small family."

There was never a time Fisher and I discussed having any more children after Sky. Until recently, I was sure Sky's congenital disability was a side effect of the living conditions I endured during the first year of my life, which has caused other children of the war to experience similar issues with their offspring. The doctor told me I was lucky to get pregnant after what I had been through, and I thought we had overcome the only hurdle.

For many years after Sky passed, I blamed Hitler and the Nazis for destroying my life, but last week, I found out that Sky had most likely inherited his abnormality, which can be passed down through families, in his case, his blood-grandfather—Benjamin's—genetics. Benjamin's words, "I'm dying from a broken heart," was the catalyst to all my discontent. I had done extensive research about Sky's condition. I know how common the condition is, and that there is a genetic link, but having no knowledge of our family trees, I never believed that genetics played a part in Sky's heart problems. I had been wrong, very wrong, and I had hated and placed blame where it didn't necessarily belong, even on Sky's dying day. I'm ashamed of who I became, but I'm starting to see ... it's not too late to make things right.

"Emma, I think this is the most amazing question I have been asked since Fisher asked me to marry him. I think you may have just mended a big part of my heart. I can't possibly put into words what this means to me. However, are you sure about the godmother part? I'm not going to outlive you, you know—"

Emma rolls her eyes. "One day at a time—that's how we do things, right?"

"It is," I agree.

"Yes, Jackson and I both want you and Fisher to be the godparents of Belle ... Sky."

"Beautiful, Belle Sky," I sigh. "Goodness, thank you—thank you for thinking so highly of me—of us."

"I need us ladies of the family to be a unit, and this just tightens our circle a little more, don't you think?"

"Whoa, whoa, whoa?" Charlie interrupts. "What's this unit thing all about?"

"Charlie, please," Mom hushes him.

"No, really, what's this unit?" Fisher asks.

"Yeah," Jackson repeats. "I don't know if I like the sound of this. You three—now four, do not need to be a unit. You are scary enough when you're together."

"The women of this family will all be matriarchs someday, men. It's an important role, one I teach well. So, if I were you, I'd watch your behinds, and mind your women. Do I make myself clear?" Mom says.

"Yes, ma'am."

"Yes, Mum."

"Grams—uh, you scare me a little," Jackson says.

"Good," she replies with a wink and a slap on his butt.

Oh dear, how could I ever ask for more?

"Okay," Fisher says. "The doctor said we could only visit for a little bit, and I want to make sure Annie gets some rest, so— someone go make me a meatloaf or something."

"Fisher," Clara groans.

"I kind of just meant you, Clara. Annie can't cook right now, so … please?"

Clara shakes her head and holds her hands up, jokingly motioning to strangle Fisher. "Only for you would I cook on a Saturday night."

Emma lifts Belle from my arms and returns her to her cushioned carrier, tucking her in gently. When she's done, Emma places a kiss on my cheek and whispers, "Thank you," into my ear.

The rest of the family say their goodbyes and scatter out the door, and Jackson is the last one standing there. "Do you have a minute?" I ask him.

He walks over to the side of my bed and kneels to one knee. "What's going on?" It gives me relief to know Emma is married to a doctor, but the irony of him being a cardiovascular doctor has made me wonder about coincidences that occur in life. I haven't been able to understand the odds of this man being a part of our lives, but it strangely gives me comfort.

"Can I ask you a question?" I say softly.

"Anything," Jackson replies, placing his hand on my arm.

"Is Belle healthy? Her heart ... is it whole?" I know we aren't related by blood, but Mom has her heart condition, and Dad died of a heart attack at an early age. "I don't understand why we have so many broken hearts in our family, but I just need to know—"

"Belle is the healthiest baby I have ever seen, Annie. She is perfect. One hundred percent perfect. I think ... she's made up of a lot of perfection from up above. What do you think?"

I place my free hand on my chest and thank God silently. "I think I know why Emma chose you," I tell him.

Jackson leans over and places a kiss on my cheek. "Get better, okay? You need to get out of this place, so you can get back to Fisher. That man ... he is lost without you. He's been at our house helping out a lot because he knew that's where you would want to be."

"I'm a lucky woman, Jackson. I am," I tell him.

"We're all lucky," Jackson says.

A FEW DAYS have come and gone, and the doctors deemed me healthy enough to go home if I promised to see a therapist on a regular basis. I think it's a smart decision to talk to someone indirectly involved with my life to explain my feelings without guilt or concern. I know I have endured damage that can't be undone, have wounds that will remain open, and scars that will pinch and sting from time to time—reminders of where I've come from and what I have survived.

It is Sunday morning, and the birds are chirping, which surprises me. I would expect them to be heading south by now, but it's a warm fall day.

I lay my fleece blanket down in front of Sky's gravestone and take a seat with Fisher.

SHARI J. RYAN

A morning picnic at the cemetery is what we do on Sundays. We have waffles and pancakes with our Sky.

"Okay, Sky, I have the stats for you. Listen up. The Sox are up by three games. Tonight's game seven, so all we need is this, and we'll be headed to the series again. I got you a Mookie Betts jersey and a signed baseball card. I also should have another one for you next from Benintendi. His cards are on back-order, but I'm on it. I know this isn't the official one, but I figured you wouldn't want Mookie's card getting ruined outside in case the tin gets a leak, so I've put that in a safe place for you in your bedroom. I'll leave the other one I have for you here with the others." I open the metal tin I dug into the ground shortly after Sky passed away, and drop the new card inside on top of the hundred others.

"You should have seen Mookie's diving catch the other night, bud! You would have been screaming at the TV," Fisher adds in.

"So, we have news for you, which you probably already know, but your cousin Emma named her new baby girl Sky, like you. I'm sorry I never told her about you, Sky. It was selfish, but it hurt too much."

"We're still a work in progress, kid. You were supposed to raise us into functioning adults, I think, so we've had to do a lot of the legwork ourselves," Fisher says, while gently nudging his shoulder against mine.

That's the truth.

"Anyway, I see you're busy today, shining brightly, and glowing your glorious shade of blue. I miss you sweetheart, every second, every minute, every day. I thank God, morning, noon, and night that we were smart enough to give you the perfect name because I truly believe you are the whole Sky, encompassing our world, keeping us together as you always have."

Fisher leans down, resting on his elbow, and stares up toward the sun, squinting from the rays. "I still think we should have named you Sun, son. Your mother is always making all the decisions. Don't you think you would have been cooler as the sun?" Fisher laughs at his joke, as usual. "See what I did there?" He isn't

260

talking to me. I know that exceptionally well since he knows I would close my eyes and shake my head. Sky, though, he would be in hysterics laughing.

As if he were called for, a butterfly with blue and golden colors —unique and rare, lands on top of Sky's gravestone and watches us for a minute before taking off toward the sky. I take Fisher's hand, and we squeeze until it hurts. "He's here," I whisper. Maybe the butterfly is just a figment of my mind sometimes, but Sky is alive in my heart, so to me, it's all real.

"I feel it," Fisher responds.

This is how we have survived, and this is how we will carry on. Holes in our hearts and all, there is life here and on the other side, but I'm sure now, there *is* just one Sky.

EPILOGUE

THE MEANING OF MY LIFE AS ANNIE

I HAVEN'T WRITTEN in my purple, velvet journal in many years, but after the last few months of my life, I began to remember why I used to sit down and write. My words clarify the unfiltered thoughts that have eaten away at me, thoughts that eventually made me ill.

I have vowed to continue a revolving review of my life as it happens, so I will be able to revisit where I have come from and how I've grown as a person. Maybe someday I can formulate my entries into a book and reveal my secrets to the world outside of my family so others can learn from what I've lost.

When I look back, I see how my views have changed, developed, and grown. I can learn from my times of weakness and moments of strength. If I survived once, I can do it again, and that's why I will need to constantly remind myself of daily accomplishments.

Dear Journal,

SHARI J. RYAN

When I close my eyes, I can be where I want to be, see what I want to see, and visit with who I want to visit. It has taken me a lifetime to understand the difference between a dream formulated by desire, and the subconscious process of conceptualizing a reality that comforts my soul.

I thought it was unnatural to fall asleep at night with the hope of seeing Sky, Dad, Benjamin, and Leah, but when they visit me in the night behind my closed eyelids, I'm able to consciously connect with them—visit a place and time that doesn't exist. The visions bring me peace to know they are still with me, as well as alive inside of my mind and heart. Losing the physical being of a person is a superficial pain that can slowly heal over time, by taking what they left behind and planting their seeds in the world to ensure their souls grow through other means.

I was born in hell and faced the unthinkable before I was old enough to comprehend much of anything. I don't have the memories to help answer my questions, but I have convinced myself that for everything bad that happens, there is a reason.

Therefore, I officially give up wondering what else there is that I don't know.

The Holocaust taught future generations the result of unnecessary hate—the same hatred that forced me to question a doctor who was trying to help my sick child, or doubt the love between a man who wore a symbol of death, and Mom. I was wrong to question the motives of anyone who has not proven to be guilty of the unthinkable.

Coming to this realization in recent months has given me a deeper understanding of the world I grew up in, and mostly what the true meaning of racism and the act of prejudice is. I think, most often, hate is the cause of insecurity and fear of being different. Innocent people died because of the personal fear of one man, who persuaded others to have an aversion to an entire religious culture, as well as anyone different than themselves. What that means to me is that fear is a result of the dreams and nightmares created by the imagination. The thoughts are figments of what could be, rather than what is.

It took me more time than I'd like to admit, to agree with Fisher's explanation for disagreeing with the meaning of a dream. Internally, I fought his thoughts without understanding how a person could go through life without a dream.

Then, I learned what a dream is. Though he explained it to me quite clearly, way back when, it didn't make sense until the life I dreamed of for my child was taken away before he could experience it. The dream of learning about where I was born, why I was born there, and who I was born to, resulted in answers that caused me more pain.

I have experienced many variations of anger and sadness throughout my life, but I was never taught how to cope. I don't believe anyone truly knows how to handle life and death, or anything in between, because the emotions tied to each experience are unique. Therefore, navigating life, and giving reason for all happenings, will act as a guide to help me conquer the challenges I am supposed to overcome in my lifetime.

What I learned from Benjamin, the man who unknowingly gave me life, is that some people are here for a purpose, and some purposes may take less time to accomplish than others. It isn't about the distance or time, it's about the lessons we are here to learn on behalf of our soul, rather than the bodies that act as a temporary casing for what needs protection inside. I also learned that it's never too late in life for a "thank you" or a letter of appreciation. When I gave Mom this letter, she held it against her heart and told me that she had finally received the last piece of closure she longed for. She said her heart was as full as it would ever be, and she could go on, knowing that everything she endured throughout her life, had a serendipitous purpose.

I never understood why some people would suddenly become an extremist in their religious beliefs, and while I was fearful of *showing my beliefs at the risk of reciprocating hate, I see now that the experience of having something more significant than ourselves to believe in, no matter what that may be, is more important than fearing what anyone else might think of me.*

Maybe there is someone out there who thinks I have lost touch with reality, or thinks I sound completely crazy when I talk about the life that's bigger than we see, but I used to think there were two sides to the blue sky—one that was made up of life, and the other with death. However, I now believe that we are blind to what we cannot see, which means we are all here together in unity, connected through our history under a one-sided sky. It's hard to admit I might have been wrong about my perceived view of life, but Fisher and his sophisticated ways were brought to my life to teach me how to live.

Most importantly, I have learned:

Hate brought me happiness.

Being lost, made me found.

Losing, helped me gain strength.

Surviving, fulfilled my life challenges.

Through tremendous ups and downs, I can say I have experienced the beauty of life, and I am lucky enough to be part of a family that proves unity within love, rather than just blood.

Too many times, I wished life had turned out differently, but as I grow older, I see what that might have meant: I may not have found the love, happiness, and strength I needed to appreciate what I have each day.

I never thought I would admit to being one of the lucky missing children of the Holocaust, and I think that has been my biggest life challenge.

I am lucky.

Life cannot be measured in time, but it is only a matter of time before we will all be together again.

-Annie Lucie Benson

AFTERWORD

I write to heal. It has been my therapy for many years, and it has brought me great joy, even while I sometimes feel more pain in the process.

"The Other Blue Sky" is dear to my heart because of my roots and curiosity for a part of my personal history that I will never know about. The ties to my great grandfather, great uncles, and aunts, are gone. I realize most people don't have the opportunity to know their ancestors, but the history is often brought forward through family stories.

Most of my paternal family didn't have the chance to live long enough to have a story that could be carried forward. I know very little about those relatives, and it saddens me to know they faced such horrifying deaths.

As a child, I was taught about the Holocaust by my grandmother. In fact, I was one of the first descendants who heard her stories. This was due to the fact that it took her that many years to find the ability to discuss her memories. I learned to stare at my grandmother without blinking as she explained what horror truly meant. Internally, her stories evolved in my head and developed into fears. Sometimes, I would have nightmares about reliving an experience she survived through, and my parents would find me crying and sweating on the bathroom floor in the middle of the night.

For that reason, I hid my religion. It took me most of my life (to date) to show pride in my religious background, but these books help me overcome my unnecessary fears.

My grandmother easily could have been Annie. She could have been left without knowing a family member, or even a single fact about her family, but instead, she lived through losing her family, and at a young age.

In this book, I stressed the meaning of hatred and how easy it is to experience those feelings, but also the bigger picture of what hate can cause, provides a reason for understanding between people. Just people—men, women, and children—people without religion, color, or culture defining them. World peace will not happen until all people can refer to one another as the same, and my wish, on behalf of the family I never got to meet or learn about, is that I see just a small glimmer of hope for peace in my lifetime.

Thank you for going through this journey with me!

Shari

THANK YOU!

Thank you so much for taking this journey with me! I truly hope you enjoyed "The Other Blue Sky"!
I would truly appreciate your feedback, even if it's just a few words. I do read each and every piece of criticism—good or bad, since it helps me grow as an author.
xoxo
Shari

If you haven't read "Last Words" yet, and you would like to hear Amelia and Charlie's story, make sure you pick up your copy!

#1 Bestselling Novel, Last Words, is where reality meets Fiction, and the lines in between are blurred by forbidden love.

Amelia - 1942:

The inside of my closet held the last bit of my freedom before I was torn from my home and shoved onto a dark train.

Our destination was even darker. "Women and children to the right. Men to the left," they shouted at us.

Everything was taken from me, leaving only the smoke filled air, piercing screams, and soul-burning cries.

I was slowly starved and weakened to the bone, but there was a man—a Nazi—who brought me extra food. He called himself a prisoner too, but he scared me, and I wondered if he was the enemy I should fear the most.

Emma - Current Day:

My grandmother hid her past in an old diary under her bed. The tattered, brown leather book sat there for years until she asked me to find it and read her unspoken words. Now, her stories and secrets are consuming every moment of my life.

She's dying ... and asking for a man no one in our family has ever heard of.

I never imagined a hand-written book could change my entire life, but it has. It opened my eyes to a new beginning, and I learned that love is not the unsaid word my grandmother has refused to speak. It's an action—it's longevity, taboo and sometimes forbidden. Do we fight for what's wrong, or do we spend our lives searching for what's right?

Last words were never spoken because love doesn't stop until a heart is no longer beating.

PROLOGUE

Since 1945, my story has remained hidden deep within the corners of my mind and blacked out as if with permanent marker, in hopes that no one else would ever know. I've been holding on to these silent memories for such a long time, but I'm becoming weak. I've always known that the truth might someday be stronger than my will to be silent, but I can't imagine what my secrets would do to those I love.

This may be cliché, but I'm going to start my story with a once upon a time...except my life hasn't been a fairytale—far from it. In fact, for a long time, I believed a happy ending meant death.

During my early years as a child, I had a perfect life. The sun shone golden rays across Bohemia's breathtaking sky and bore its warmth down on the silky, green-grass-covered soil. I lived in color—rich with vivid hues, and I danced through the mustard fields, twirling my dress as my hair blew like weeping willows in the breeze. My heart was protected, my life blessed with knowledge, and I was surrounded by love. There was a lightness in my mind and a feeling of completeness in my soul that made each day feel like a gift from above.

Then, a day came when the sun was taken away. The sky became dark with heavy clouds, and my world turned gray. Raindrops that once fell from the sky bled into the tears that burned down my cheeks.

I thought darkness was all I had left after losing everything I'd ever known and loved, but through a cloud of dust and despair, I found a glimmer of hope—a smile amongst the sunken cheeks and rotting corpses.

He should never have smiled at me, and I shouldn't have acknowledged him when he did, but once it started, there was no turning back. I never considered the possibility of how it would end until I felt the heartbreak of loneliness again. His smile was gone, the warm touches we shared through my cold shivers would never heat my body again, and the worst part was that all hope was lost.

It was all for nothing. It would have been easier to have never felt that kind of love because once I knew how good it could feel, I didn't think I'd ever feel that way again.

As the world caved in on itself, I allowed the pain and misery to pour from my eyes one last time before making a silent vow to never give another ounce of power to those who wanted to dominate the weak.

I traveled through the phases of bitter denial, revenge, hate, sorrow—and finally, the emptiness that would be a part of me forever.

When the sun returned and the grass grew back, those who had survived slowly allowed their wounds to heal, but there was a numbness inside all of us—protection from feeling the pain of the memories that would last a lifetime.

To forget and move on as if it never happened was the only way to survive. I tried to convince myself that I hadn't lived through the most demoralizing and destructive five years this world has ever seen.

I moved to America, leaving the enemy behind. I lived on, shielding myself from the memories. I lived up to society's moral standards and expectations by getting married and having children. I cooked, cleaned, and supported those I love. Then, over time, my past became a part of the earth like the bones and ashes in that far away land.

There is one exception, though, and it's the part of me I have only pretended to forget—my secret. In fact, some would consider what I did to be as wrong, and equally horrendous, as what the heartless ones did to my whole race.

In my heart, I will never consider that it was wrong, and I will stand by my actions and beliefs because the heart wants what the heart wants. Sometimes, even the toughest warriors who survive the odds and somehow escape the shadows of death, can still fall helpless and weak at the mercy of love.